ECONOMIC INEQUALITY AND MORALITY

D1602711

THE ETHIKON INSTITUTE

The Ethikon Institute, a nonprofit organization, examines the social implications of ethical pluralism. Its dialogue-publication projects are designed to explore a diversity of moral outlooks, secular and religious, and to clarify areas of consensus and divergence among them. By encouraging a systematic exchange of ideas, the institute aims to advance the prospects for agreement and to facilitate the peaceful accommodation of irreducible differences. The Ethikon Institute takes no position on issues that may divide its participants, serving not as an arbiter but as a neutral forum for the cooperative study of varied and sometimes opposing views.

Economic Inequality and Morality

DIVERSE ETHICAL PERSPECTIVES

EDITED BY

Richard Madsen
William M. Sullivan

BROOKINGS INSTITUTION PRESS
Washington, D.C.

Library of Congress Cataloging-in-Publication Data.
Names: Madsen, Richard, 1941– editor. | Sullivan, William M., editor.
Title: Economic inequality and morality : diverse ethical perspectives / edited by Richard Madsen, William M. Sullivan.
Description: Washington, D.C. : Brookings Institution Press, [2019] | Includes bibliographical references and index.
Identifiers: LCCN 2019012061 (print) | LCCN 2019019515 (ebook) | ISBN 9780815737209 (epub) | ISBN 9780815737193 (pbk.)
Subjects: LCSH: Income distribution—Moral and ethical aspects. | Distributive justice.
Classification: LCC HB523 (ebook) | LCC HB523 .E355 2019 (print) | DDC 174/.4—dc23
LC record available at https://lccn.loc.gov/2019012061

9 8 7 6 5 4 3 2 1

Typeset in Baskerville

Composition by Elliott Beard

Contents

Acknowledgments

The directors and president of the Ethikon Institute thank all who contributed to the development of this volume.

We are especially indebted to the Sidney Stern Memorial Trust for their financial support.

Special thanks are due to Richard Madsen and William M. Sullivan for taking on the challenging task of editing this book, to William A. Galston for chairing a dialogue conference for participants, to Will Kymlicka for contributing to the project's design, to Alan Mittleman and Christopher Tollefsen for editorial assistance, and to Carole Pateman, Lea Ann King, and Michael Dodds, O.P., for their much-valued participation as general discussants.

We note with sadness that one of our contributors, Joseph Boyle, did not live to see the project to fruition. His essay here is the last he completed in his long, distinguished, and prolific career.

ECONOMIC INEQUALITY AND MORALITY

Introduction

RICHARD MADSEN
WILLIAM M. SULLIVAN

Economic inequality has come to the fore of public awareness to such an extent that it now dominates political debate in much of the world. In many countries, including the United States, differences among various segments of the population in both income and wealth have grown dramatically. The United States, the world's largest and dominant economy, illustrates these larger trends in an extreme form. The United States has become the most unequal of all industrialized democracies. A deep "wealth gap" has opened between the wealthiest Americans—the now-infamous "1%," who have seen their incomes and wealth grow dramatically—and the rest of the population. Among the remaining "99%," things have not been nearly so good.

Only the upper fifth has seen a significant rise in income during the past three decades, and the top one percent has taken the lion's share of these gains. At the same time that the richest have seen vast growth in their "share of the pie," the poorest, a group that includes a full fifth of the population, or two out of every ten Americans, have seen their incomes decline. Meanwhile, the majority of the population, the groups in between the poorest twenty percent and the most affluent twenty percent, the "middle class," have not had a "raise" in their share of the nation's income for decades, although they now work longer hours than before.[1] Long celebrated as a land of opportunity, economic opportunity has stagnated for most Americans. When it comes to chances for economic advancement, the American economy has grown sclerotic. Social mobility, like growth in wealth, is now monopolized by the upper-income groups, not because of different levels of skill or education, but because almost all the growth of recent decades has gone to the already wealthiest.[2]

Besides the attrition of social mobility, the inequality gap has been accompanied by rising economic insecurity. This threatens the ability of individuals and families to meet expenses and plan for future needs, such as paying for their children's further education. Those concerns fostered the excessive debt that contributed to the economic collapse of 2008. For many, the increasingly harsh, competitive aspect of economic life has chilled their sense of sharing in the benefits of American life. The tightening competitive scramble for less-equal outcomes has helped divide and polarize electorates throughout the industrialized democracies. The rising anxiety has stoked distrust and resentment between groups, weakening the trust and cooperation on which democracy depends. This growing volatility has produced a "populist explosion" of anger that is destabilizing political life not only in the United States, but also across Europe.[3]

The negative effects of a high level of inequality are therefore not confined to the economic realm. They underlie the current disturbances in political life across the world. But such steep differences in economic inequality also have severe consequences for personal and social life. As all countries with a high degree of economic inequality, the United States is now experiencing a wide divide between the affluent minority and everyone else in regard to very basic aspects of human welfare. The affluent live longer, have better physical health, enjoy more stable family relationships, participate more politically and socially, and have better access to education than their less-affluent fellow citizens. This is true even when the population is ethnically homogeneous.[4] But these trends, which have intensified wherever inequality has increased, are both ominous for the vitality of democratic institutions and make the successful inclusion of immigrants in a shared prosperity more problematic.

The recent growth of economic inequality in industrialized countries has reversed a trend toward greater equality amid stable growth that marked the post–World War II era. However, beginning in the 1980s, inequality accelerated—the consequence or at least the accompaniment of a major shift in public policy that has placed greater reliance upon international finance and open markets to foster growth, facilitated by the curbing of government regulation. This shift greatly intensified after the collapse of the Soviet Union in 1991, inaugurating what is now called the era of "globalization," or sometimes the "neo-liberal" era. This period has been marked in the West by the continuation of the liberal order of constitutional government based on individual rights and the rule of law, but the rise of China shows that, for a rapidly developing country at least, authoritarian government may be as much or even more compatible with neo-liberalism than democracy. However, the greater reliance on less regulated and unguided market forces that operate across national borders and penetrate and constrain national political regimes has become increasingly controversial. While the United States and the United Kingdom have embraced these developments most enthusiastically, others have resisted them to various degrees. Partly as a result, the level and growth of inequality have been uneven across the developed world.[5]

For its celebrators, who generally view its most successful groups as valuable innovators, globalization, or neo-liberalism, represents the fulfillment of modern aspirations toward technological advance and individual freedom to shape one's own life. Especially important, in this view, has been the success of more open market economies in China and India in enabling millions of their population to finally escape grinding poverty.[6] At its imaginative core, neo-liberalism proclaims a vision of social progress through global markets, as enunciated at the annual meetings of the World Economic Forum in Davos, attended by leaders of finance, industry, and governments from around the world. For its critics, however, when compared to the more regulated, national form of capitalism that preceded it, this regime appears deficient, due to its strong tendency to sharply divide societies into winners and losers, a process driven by an "unceasing stream of new technologies, unfettered market competition and weak or fractured social institutions."[7] The costs of having made unfettered market competition the primary decision mechanism for social development, say the critics, have proven to greatly outweigh the benefits, leaving the societies that have experienced such globalization with few means of restoring a sense of national cohesion or of taking charge of their collective destiny.

By any standard, then, today's growth in economic inequality is a major historical trend affecting all parts of the world. Not surprisingly, reactions to these developments have been quite varied, both in the popular media and in scholarly analysis and debate. Few contemporary topics have stirred such strong opinion. Is inequality really a problem—and if it is, what kind of a problem is it? That is, how should we think about it, through what cultural and intellectual lenses should we view it? How can we make sense of it and decide from what perspective to judge the situation and formulate a response?

The premise of this book is that economic inequality, while clearly in need of analysis from the viewpoints of economics, sociology, and political science, is more than a scientific or technical problem. It is preeminently an ethical and moral issue. Addressing an earlier phase of world economic crisis before the Great Depression of the twentieth century, economist John Maynard Keynes presciently observed: "The fiercest contests and the most deeply felt divisions of opinion are likely to be waged in the coming years not round technical questions, where the arguments on either side are mainly economic, but over questions which, for want of better words, may be called psychological or, perhaps, moral."[8] Keynes argued that modern capitalism was a transitional social form driven by an internal moral contradiction. Together with modern technology, it had greatly expanded productive capacity and wealth, but it had done so by inverting traditional moral values, sanctifying once-scorned vices such as rapacity and greed. What the simple celebrators of acquisition overlooked, however, was the social and moral price this inversion of moral values exacted. In order to grasp the larger picture, Keynes insisted that the parameters of the economic viewpoint had to be expanded toward a wider moral horizon than sheer expediency.[9] Such is also the unanimous conviction of the contributors to this volume.

The Ethikon Approach

Part of the Ethikon series, this book is based on a dialogue between distinguished experts on liberalism, Marxism, feminism, natural law, Christianity, Judaism, Islam, Confucianism, and Buddhism. These are broad traditions of thought on how to understand and respond to moral problems, each developed within a particular community and passed down through generations while undergoing constant elaboration and reinterpretation by those who consider themselves members of that community. To give coherence to the dialogue and to the book, each author was asked to consider a common set of concerns from ethical standpoints regarding equality, property, natural resources, products, wealth, income, employment, and taxation.

Each tradition contains disagreements about these issues, but the parameters of such disagreements tend to differ across traditions. Each author was asked to present the range of disagreements within the tradition under consideration. Some of the authors had difficulties finding answers within their tradition to some of the common questions. This was because the questions best fit the modern philosophical traditions that have arisen within global modernity—liberalism, Marxism, and feminism. The fundamental ideas of justice developed in the religious traditions presented here arose out of reflection on relatively small scale, mostly agrarian economies. Yet globalized modernity seems to be generating problems that cannot fully be answered within modern secular philosophical traditions. The struggle to make earlier religious and moral traditions speak to the dilemmas of global modernity is extremely urgent, for we will need all of the moral resources bequeathed by our traditions if we are to address the controversies and discontentments engendered by rising modern inequalities.

After two days of very stimulating discussion at a workshop near Los Angeles, the authors revised their papers into the chapters of this book. Stephen Munzer then crafted a concluding chapter that systematically compares the arguments of each essay.

How to Read This Book—What to Expect

One way to read this book would simply be to compare how each author answers each of the common questions that structure each chapter. But the reader should also attend to the overall context in which these answers are given. A sense of this context is briefly discussed in the introductory section of each essay. Each ethical tradition draws on different assumptions about human nature and the relationship between the individual self and society; different forms of moral reasoning from basic assumptions to concrete circumstances; and different authoritative texts and different ways of interpreting them. None of the traditions supports absolute equality, but they differ in their ideas about what kinds and what degrees of inequality are legitimate or not and for what reasons—and if inequality is excessive, what can and should be done about it. In the following sections of this introduction, we set our ethical dialogue in the larger historical context of the making of the modern world.

The Unique Problematic of Global Modernity

Making moral sense of today's rising economic inequality requires taking a larger moral, rather than a purely technical, economic view. The steep rise in inequality is problematic for a number of reasons, as we have noted. But it is chiefly troubling because it contradicts a central moral premise of all modern societies: the idea that technological and economic advance is a good, because it enhances individual as well as collective well-being. This idea of progress stands at the core of the new civilization that arose in the Atlantic world in the wake of the European Enlightenment of the eighteenth century and expanded around the globe with the industrial revolution of the nineteenth and twentieth centuries that continues today. This civilization has measured progress by the material metrics of technological advance, economic growth, education, and improving population health. But the ultimate standard of progress has remained the degree to which these material advances have contributed, either in the present or in the expected future, to the enhancement of individual human lives.

Today's global society, linked by communications technology and economic interdependence, espouses individual and collective empowerment as paramount goals everywhere. So pervasive have the ideals of this civilization become that revolts and revolutions against Western imperialism have themselves largely been justified on the basis of these values, while authoritarian rule inevitably must base its legitimacy on its alleged movement toward material betterment and individual protection. The dominant articulation of these ideals remains the philosophy of liberalism, which traces its origins to the early modern era in Europe. This liberal philosophy has promoted and justified the market economy and representative government, the chief institutional innovations of the eighteenth- and nineteenth-century "age of revolutions," as means toward the overarching goal of universal rights to self-expression by autonomous individuals. It is the capacity of particular institutional arrangements to secure this moral and political aspiration that increasing economic inequality seriously calls into question today, in the societies previously most successful at achieving the goals of modernity.

To understand the significance of growing inequality within societies, it is important to recognize the historical uniqueness of the contemporary situation. Since it started in the eighteenth century, in Europe, the spread of this increasingly universal civilization of progress has been made possible by a simultaneous explosion of the human capacity to capture energy resources and to use the captured energy to improve control over the natural environment. This rapid and unprecedented increase in technological capacity—the industrial revolution based on the use of fossil fuels—has set in motion a transformation of the human situation in the world so fundamental that it can rightly be understood as a break in historical continuity.

The change can be graphically illustrated. Before the invention of the steam engine in late-eighteenth century Europe, the amount of energy available to human societies everywhere was limited to what could be obtained by a combination of human and animal muscles, supplemented by a limited energy yield from wind and water power. The steam engine changed all that, setting in motion an increase in the amount of energy available per capita that has continued to rise at unprecedented rates to levels without parallel in the past.

If the aggregate amount of energy that could be mobilized in Europe or Asia before the age of steam is given a value of about 38,000 kilocalories per capita, by 1970 that figure had risen to 230,000 kilocalories—seven times more in just two centuries. And the available energy resources keep rising steeply.[10]

While the modern technological and economic regime greatly expanded wealth and the ability to mobilize and deploy resources, it did not spread these advantages equally, either among societies or within them. So, as Western societies industrialized during the nineteenth century, they became much more unequal economically. But those societies also became far wealthier than those that remained less industrialized, creating a great global imbalance in wealth and power among societies. In earlier centuries, the various agrarian societies had also been highly unequal internally, but the gap among nations was smaller.

Per capita energy consumption in the core regions of West and East AD 1–2000

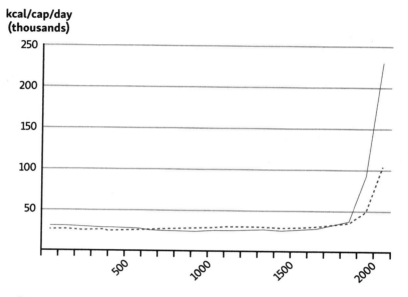

Source: Ian Morris, *Foragers, Farmers, and Fossils: How Human Values Evolve* (Princeton University Press, 2015).

More recently, as industrialization has spread around the world, this pattern of inequality in national wealth has reversed, so that the wealth gap between early industrializers and currently developing nations has shrunk substantially. However, inequality within societies has followed an opposite course. During the middle of the twentieth century, following depression and world wars, a "great compression" of wealth amid economic expansion significantly reduced inequality within societies. But in the present era, as economies have become more globally integrated, the economic divide within nations has grown, with destabilizing consequences, as noted earlier in the case of the United States.[11]

These are the material changes that have made modernity so different from all that has gone before in human history, with vast, still-unfolding reverberations through the moral sphere. Traditional ways of life, ingrained in most human cultures until the age of fossil-fuel economies, provided individuals with a sense of being embedded in a cosmos that was thought to represent divine or sacred values. This was true of pre-modern

Christendom in Europe as well as of Islam, Judaism, Hindu India, and the Confucian and Buddhist societies of South and East Asia. For these traditions, the ethical task is to exemplify in individual and social living the patterns of value held up by their classic texts and traditions as paradigmatic for human existence.

Over the past two centuries, to an accelerating degree, these traditional, agrarian-based social and moral orders have been undermined. The intrusion of the highly productive Western forms of capitalist economy, as well as industrial and military technologies, was accompanied by new, apparently more successful understandings exported by the modern West—above all, natural science. These new perspectives were thought to embody "progress." Their appearance weakened the credibility of the traditional paradigms. While the traditional paradigms did not suddenly disappear, the resulting clash between traditional moral understandings and modernity set in motion a variety of responses, first in the West and then throughout the world. Among these responses were new adaptations by adherents of the several great religious and moral traditions to the conditions of modernity, some of which provide the substance of chapters in this volume.

An Age of Innocence:
Europeans Discover Liberal Economics

Just as the transition to fossil-fuel technologies was getting underway, in the late eighteenth and early nineteenth centuries, European thinkers "discovered" the economy as a social sphere potentially independent of older forms of authority and regulation. As the cosmopolitan intellectuals of the Enlightenment outlined it, the economic realm followed its own laws of motion—an analogy to the laws of physical motion epitomized in the new mechanical sciences of nature. Individuals were the atoms of the new social physics. Driven by the "gravity" of self-interest, the "natural effort of every individual to better his condition," famously described by Adam Smith, could be harnessed by the market to make possible a stable, growth-oriented society. At the moral core of this cosmopolitan vision of peaceful commerce stood the concept of the free individual, able to enter into contracts with other self-interested individuals for the sake of mutual benefit. The resulting "progress of opulence" would benefit all who took part in the buying and selling of the market, even if not equally so.

This was a new and sunny vision of human possibility. It was based upon confidence in a kind of secularized providence. Markets worked because they followed laws of supply and demand that were embedded in a harmonious natural order. This also provided a new angle of vision on history in which markets, commerce, and economic laws drove a narrative of progress. Thinkers of the Enlightenment, such as David Hume, Adam Smith, Montesquieu, Voltaire, and Immanuel Kant extended and systematized John Locke's earlier sketch of human progress into a scheme of social development. Progress had meant moving from formerly nomadic, hunting-and-gathering ways of life into pastoral society, and then to settled cultivation. The climax of history came with the emergence of a new kind of state, guided by enlightened opinion, which protected a legal sphere of free commerce, the true civilizing agent and source of enlightened morality and manners. In this eighteenth-century view, markets served to order and balance individuals' natural instincts so as to produce the general good. It was the theory of liberal capitalism in its first innocence.

Loss of Innocence: Challenges to the Classical Liberal Vision

Spurred by the new energy regime and confidently broadcast in the new theories of progress, the global race was on. The winners would be those societies best able to reshape themselves and their people's lives to take advantage of the new technologies. The universal goal was to achieve wealth, population, and power equal to that enjoyed by the early adopters of a fossil fuel–supported way of life. This global competition, which remains the basic global force in our own time, has led to ever more rapid transformation of social reality everywhere, though at very uneven rates of change and degrees of competitive success. With these fast-rising waves of change have also come widespread uprooting of traditional ways of life and, often, the eclipse of traditional institutions and authorities. These forces eroded confidence in traditional paradigms of social and moral order while stimulating a search for new ways to understand historical events. The resulting intellectual developments came to shape the horizon within which moral discussions of today's global economy, and so the issues of economic inequality, are largely taking place.

In the nineteenth century, the harmonious models of civilization promoted by the Enlightenment faced competing views of how social evolution really worked. Following the traumatic experiences of the French Revolution and vast European wars, a spate of new theorists, ranging from Georg Hegel and Karl Marx to Auguste Comte and Herbert Spencer, proposed conflictual, even violent conceptions of historical advance. The significance of these intellectual currents is hard to overestimate.

Their viewpoints were adopted and promoted by the most successful groups within the advanced, fossil-fuel economies, but they were also employed by critics and enemies of those groups throughout the increasingly interconnected world. Taken together, they restructured the way educated people the world over came to see themselves, their past, and their future possibilities. "New" or "advanced" suddenly displaced "good" or "righteous" as epithets of commendation. A new scale of development grew into place as the taken-for-granted background of discussions of social and political matters. This scale was used to rank nations, peoples, ethnic and racial groups, as well as their religions and moral norms, along a continuum from "advanced" to "primitive" or "fossilized." As this conception became ever more hegemonic, first in European societies and then increasingly across Asia, Africa, and the Americas, it caused a still-reverberating cultural and intellectual crisis for all inherited moralities.

Yet, as the nineteenth century unfolded, all was clearly not well with the economic model that the Europeans had held up for universal emulation. One key underpinning of liberal philosophy—namely, the practical success of the unregulated global market and governments organized to protect it—was far from self-evident. In that first era of a globalizing, technology-based economy, even as production expanded and aggregate wealth grew, economic inequality was spiraling upward. Liberal confidence that properly channeled self-interest would benefit all by making societies more efficient and enlightened became a highly vulnerable target. This benign image of the free market would never again remain uncontested.

Karl Marx provided a historically very influential counter-image of the global market as a monstrous sorcerer's apprentice destined to be undone by its own insatiable needs. Driven by ever-tighter competition, the capitalist system would inevitably self-destruct as its agents pushed to lower their costs of production, immiserating their workers. They thereby would undermine the very demand on which their profits depended. Thus, as the system intensified its mobilization of human and natural resources on a global basis, it would eventually drive its workers to revolt. After the overthrow of capitalism, a planned economy run by and for the former proletariat would be able to direct the new productive capacities on a rational course toward general betterment. Marx's vision claimed a goal-directed logic of historical development that recast the moral ideals of the liberal Enlightenment, such as individual freedom and social equality, as the inevitable outcomes of world-historical struggle between classes.

Another, very different but also highly influential perspective on social development was promulgated by Herbert Spencer. Taking Charles Darwin's new scientific view of evolution as a model, Spencer viewed human history as an unguided process of random variation and natural selection of the best-adapted life-forms. In Spencer's view, markets were selective devices that promoted progress through competitive struggle, allowing the more efficient and "fit" to drive out the inefficient. Inequality among individuals, groups, and societies was therefore inevitable, because it was necessary for progress in the long run. Now, conceived as a Darwinian competition, the progress of technology and the capitalist, global economy—like the military struggles between nations and groups in the international arena—would inevitably produce winners and losers. But interfering with these natural processes in the name of older values, such as traditional justice or compassion, would only slow humanity's advance.

Powerful critiques like these, which stressed the social and historical determination of both ideas and human agents, challenged core liberal tenets. As individuals came to seem to be not so much autonomous rational actors as highly conditioned products of social processes, classical liberalism's basic premises were opened to new scrutiny and potential rejection. If markets were not necessarily harmonious natural formations—as the developing discipline of political economy had construed them—but social institutions whose rules embodied the interests of social classes or national communities, the earlier confidence in the natural providence of commerce and contract could be challenged.

Affirming Human Agency and Responsibility

Advocates of the liberal tradition have formulated several kinds of response to these challenges. To counter the problem of persistent inequality within societies organized according to liberal principles of voluntary contract and the rule of law, twentieth-century liberal governments began to improvise ways to bring social practices closer to liberal norms and ideals. Liberal governments began to intervene in the workings of the market to open up wider opportunity, as through publicly supported education; to redistribute highly unequal patterns of wealth and income through progressive taxation; and to provide greater security of personal and family life through public programs of health provision and social insurance. The thinkers in the liberal tradition also innovated intellectually, as in justifying active state-intervention in markets on the basis of creating more equality of opportunity.

More radically, liberals such as John Maynard Keynes challenged the reality of the self-regulating character of markets, that quasi-providential "invisible hand" idea inherited from the Enlightenment, and advocated the active shaping of market institutions by governments. Most radically of all, a new line of liberal thinking in the twentieth century accepted the premise that individuals were shaped and fulfilled by social relationships, so that protecting and enhancing forms of social membership came to be seen as inherent in promoting liberty and opportunity. This so-called social liberalism showed affinities with the ideas of social democracy that subordinated economic goals to the well-being of the members of a national community. These more activist forms of liberal thought clashed with the tradition's earlier, residually providential belief in self-regulating markets, setting up major contemporary conflicts in response to neo-liberal globalization. Therefore, liberal thinking entered the twenty-first century not as a single intellectual position but as a family of views that, while sharing a lineage and key values, differed profoundly in how they framed the issue of inequality.

These differences within the liberal tradition illustrate a more general, unresolved problem that conditions contemporary debates about economic inequality. If a historical necessity of some type is not driving toward an inevitable outcome, there is need for ways to think about and evaluate possible responses. That is, there is a need for ethics, the disciplined inquiry into what is good and right. But what viewpoint or viewpoints should guide such responses? Can Western liberalism provide the moral resources, conceptual and practical, to address the contemporary inequality challenge that application of its own principles have exacerbated, if not directly brought about? If these resources are not adequate to the challenge, then where to turn? Although the dominant theories of justice used by economic and political elites in Western democracies come from the liberal tradition, the public opinion of citizens of these countries is influenced directly or indirectly by other traditions, including Marxism, feminism, natural law, Christianity, Judaism, Islam, Confucianism, and Buddhism. And some of the latter religious traditions are predominant in countries seeking to challenge Western hegemony. Vast transformations in global communication and commerce over the past generation have not only helped bring about increasing inequalities but brought about new challenges to liberal governments, both from within and without. One manifestation is angry populist movements driven by a strong sense of economic injustice. Thus, there is an urgent need to attend to the diversity of ethical traditions.

The Organization of This Volume

The chapters that follow are intended to stimulate a critical dialogue among various ethical traditions. The greater problem in each case is how are these viewpoints to be made relevant to the problems raised by economic inequality? To meet this need, the chapters are organized to provide not only an overview of a particular tradition of thought but also specific responses to problems that today's economic inequality pose for all traditions. These problems concern public-policy issues that, while widely taken up, have grown out of the practice of liberal governments, often guided by the kinds of revised liberalism described in the last section.

The chapters can be thought of as divided between different ethical starting points. One set—liberalism, Marxism, and feminism—report on traditions that proceed from the moral premises of the liberal Enlightenment: the goods of human autonomy, dignity, and equality. The privileged place of liberalism in this discussion is due to its historical and normative place as the philosophical charter of modern political and economic life. However, along with the liberal tradition itself, these chapters also set out Marxism—a tradition that has radically criticized liberalism on its own premises—and feminism, another modern tradition rooted in liberal ideals but highly critical of liberalism's own application of those notions to matters of gender in the economic realm.

The second grouping of chapters includes traditions that proceed from persistent paradigmatic normative visions of social life that derive from premises other than the Western Enlightenment. These chapters report on the traditions of natural law, Christianity, Judaism, and Islam, as well as Buddhism and Confucianism. These chapters explicate how these inherited ethical traditions understand economic life, both traditionally and in response to the modern market economy, and then take up the same set of questions that the post-Enlightenment traditions also address.

For both groups of traditions, the operative question is the same, or at least analogous: how can this body of ethical thought be "applied" or "brought to bear" on the issues of contemporary inequality that this introduction has outlined?

In the first essay, William A. Galston shows how three different forms of liberalism have grown out of the tradition's central preoccupations—a commitment to "liberty" from arbitrary authority, which included all authority not based on the consent of the governed. Liberals believe that all individuals should have equal liberty, but acknowledge that differences in talent, character, and drive will leave some individuals better off than others. What to do about these disparities? Classical liberalism, which Galston illustrates in its modern form with the work of Robert Nozick, rejects any interference by government in the distribution of wealth and income. Distributive liberalism, illustrated by John Rawls, would opt for the more equal distribution of economic values necessary to sustain a system of social cooperation for mutual advantage. Social liberalism, as exemplified by Leonard Hobhouse, emphasizes the "economic preconditions of human flourishing, to which every individual is equally entitled."

As Andrew Levine then argues in his essay on the Marxist tradition, the distinctive theoretical positions of Marxism have led to a great variety of political economic movements, some bitterly opposed to each other. But classical Marxism would have difficulty answering Ethikon questions, because Marx "was not so much a moral theorist as a critic of morality, hostile not just to particular notions of justice and morality, but also to efforts at prioritizing those concerns." Nonetheless, Marxism-inspired revolutionaries in the twentieth century did make moral arguments about the need for social equality. Although Marxism-inspired regimes have collapsed, academic Marxists still carry on the concerns for social equality promised (and often betrayed) by those regimes. In practice, this academic Marxist theory of justice is like a "left-Rawlsianism."

Christine Di Stefano shows how modern feminism critiques a "variety of co-implicated injustices that affect women and girls, resulting in gender inequity." In seeking the goal of gender equity, feminism critically draws on a wide range of modern theories, including classical liberalism and Marxism. Gender inequity is defined in a broad sense that seeks "the empowerment of women . . . relative not only to men and patriarchal power but to other structures and mechanisms of power, domination, and oppression, including racism, homophobia and heterosexism, colonialism, and class stratification."

The next essays are about traditions that originated in pre-modern streams of thought but are trying to give relevant guidance to modern problems.

Joseph Boyle writes on the theory of natural law, a rich body of thought that achieved an especially influential synthesis in the philosophy of Thomas Aquinas (1224–1274). Although embraced by the Catholic Church, this tradition appeals to "right reason" rather than revelation, and has had influence far beyond Roman Catholicism. Natural law theory starts from a conception of basic human goods, which are dependent on cooperation within community. A flourishing community requires not only the provision of individual goods but the maintenance of a common good. The tradition can be applied to a wide range of societies and is indeterminate about the details of policies toward inequalities in the modern world. It offers a powerful basis for critique, however, of modern inequalities that would undermine the common good of communities and destroy the dignity of human persons.

D. Stephen Long takes on the "impossible task" of presenting a Christian perspective on economic inequality—impossible because the multiple versions of Christianity have adopted many different theories of economic justice. After summarizing the broad contours of this diversity, Long proceeds by adopting an approach that considers economics through "the practices of the church, its doctrines, liturgies, scriptures, and faithful exemplars, what I have called 'ecclesial ethics.'" Although such an ethics can and does accept inequality, at a minimum it would say that no one should live in poverty and that the pursuit of wealth should be subordinate to love of God and neighbor.

Joseph Isaac Lifshitz also notes that Jewish texts, especially the Talmud, contain many diverse opinions. "Thus, any contemporary claims about Jewish ethics and economic (or other) thought must be made with a sense of limits." However, behind the diversity is a principle of the "sanctity of property rights, as an expression of divine justice." Another principle, though, is charity, which can be seen as a "social-justice agenda for balancing class gaps." Ethical debate often centers on how to resolve these principles in application to modern interdependent societies.

Islamic thought, as Mohammad H. Fadel presents it, is also the product of numerous and diverse traditions based on juridical interpretations of the revealed sources of Islam—the Quran and the practice of the Prophet Muḥammad. Those sources contain strong denunciations of the vices associated with private property and wealth, but at the same time condemn theft of property and affirm the rights of ownership. Revelation thus posits "an alternative ethic of property based on generosity and solidarity." From such principles, Islamic thinkers in the twentieth century have tried to develop a particularly Islamic approach to economic justice that distinguishes it from market capitalism and socialism. "Instead of taking success as a sign of divine entitlement, a Muslim is supposed to reflect on the fortuitous nature of worldly success, and be spurred to acts of generosity that countermand the worse impulses of a market economy."

The Confucian tradition, as Stephen C. Angle shows, is based not on divine revelation but on a body of rational reflection passing through three periods of creative growth, all proceeding from principles enunciated by Confucius and his disciples from the fifth through second centuries BCE. A key concern is for social harmony, which is achieved through respect for proper hierarchical relationships, and moral cultivation to transcend the selfish impulses to profit at the expense of others. In most respects, Confucians "are not egalitarians, but neither will they countenance extreme inequality: their goal is a harmony that is good for each and all."

For Buddhism, as presented by Christopher S. Queen, "material wealth and poverty are regarded as utterly inconsequential in the quest for salvation." Wealth is a consequence of good karma and is morally good insofar as it is gained without greed or harm to others and offers an opportunity to gain merit by being generous, especially to the religious community.

"In light of these principles, modern notions of equality, human rights, and distributive justice, particularly as they relate to economic opportunity and prosperity, do not find direct parallels in early Buddhism." In the modern world, however, practitioners of various forms of "engaged Buddhism" in both Asia and the West have formulated strategies to combat the collective, systemic, and institutional causes of human suffering, including exploitive economic systems that cause gross inequality.

Finally, Stephen R. Munzer overviews the various traditions and discusses their relevance to critical contemporary policy debates. He outlines areas of moral agreement—notably agreement that poverty should be eliminated or at least reduced—but he finds considerable areas of disagreement—especially on the degree to which governments should redistribute wealth. He also finds "spaces that have been left empty"—in particular, "the chance to figure out what, if anything, is so attractive about economic equality."

Notes

1. Lane Kenworthy, *Social Democratic America* (New York, New York: Oxford University Press, 2014), 17–48. See also Jacob S. Hacker and Paul Pierson, *Winner-Take-All Politics: How Washington Made the Rich Richer—and Turned Its Back on the Middle Class* (New York, New York: Simon and Schuster, 2010), 11–40.

2. Hacker and Pierson, *Winner-Take-All*, 35–37.

3. John B. Judis, *The Populist Explosion: How the Great Recession Transformed American and European Politics* (New York, New York: Columbia Global Reports, 2016), 12–17 passim.

4. Richard Wilkinson and Kate Pickett, *The Spirit Level: Why Greater Equality Makes Societies Stronger* (New York, New York: Bloomsbury Press, 2010), esp. 3–30.

5. This variety of ways of reacting to the expansion of neo-liberal policies—with continental Europe and Japan less enthusiastic than the United States and United Kingdom—is itself a subject of research. Michael Mann has provided a large-scale overview of these divergent pathways in *The Sources of Social Power, Volume 4: Globalizations 1945–2011* (Cambridge, Great Britain: Cambridge University Press, 2013).

6. The argument for the overall positive effects of the neo-liberal regime was first spread widely by Thomas L. Friedman, *The Lexus and the Olive Tree: Understanding Globalization* (New York, New York: Farrar, Strauss, and Giroux, 1999).

7. John Gray, *False Dawn: The Delusions of Global Capitalism* (London, Great Britain: Granta Books, 1998). It is perhaps noteworthy that both Gray's and

Friedman's sharply opposing assessments appeared almost simultaneously at the close of the last century. For an overview of the longer historical context, see Mark Blyth, *Great Transformations: Economic Ideas and Institutional Change in the Twentieth Century* (Cambridge, Great Britain: Cambridge University Press, 2002).

8. John Maynard Keynes, *The End of Laissez-Faire* (London, Great Britain: Hogarth Press, 1927), 50.

9. Robert Skidelsky, *John Maynard Keynes: The Economist as Saviour, 1920–1937* (London, Great Britain: Macmillan Publishers, 1992), 233–238.

10. Ian Morris, *Foragers, Farmers, and Fossil Fuels: How Human Values Evolve* (Princeton, New Jersey: Princeton University Press, 2015), 95.

11. Ian Morris provides a synthetic overview of these processes, with attention to measures of economic inequality, in *Foragers, Farmers, and Fossil Fuels*, esp. 36ff and 101ff.

Liberalism

ECONOMIC JUSTICE IN THE LIBERAL TRADITION

WILLIAM A. GALSTON

Introduction

As scholars have often observed, the liberal tradition represents a centuries-long accretion of ideas and influences. Although it is possible to draw out some common threads, Ludwig Wittgenstein's famous metaphor of "family resemblance" may best describe the relations among the various pieces of this tradition. Alternatively, one may seek to connect them historically—just as in the Bible: A begets B, who begets C, and so on.

As its name suggests, liberalism embodies a commitment to liberty, variously construed. For Greeks and Romans, liberty inhered not only in "free men" as opposed to slaves, but also—and, in many respects, principally—in independent and self-determining political communities. For liberals, the emphasis from the start was on the individual.

The first iteration was liberty as liberation from what came to be viewed as arbitrary authority. Governments restricted the liberty of individuals to act as they chose; so did mediating institutions such as guilds and corporations; and so did organized religious authorities. As a liberation movement, accordingly, liberals pushed for new arrangements, such as representation, to rein in the abuses of public power; they sought to create zones in which a range of religious commitments could be freely exercised and in which areas of individual conduct were removed from religious and governmental interference; and they worked to dismantle laws and institutions that restricted individuals' ability to make contracts and conduct commercial activities.

The practical struggle for liberation from arbitrary power spawned new principles. Because public power was often defended as natural or even God-given, liberal theorists attacked the "divine right" of kings and analogies between political and paternal authority. In their place, momentously, liberals advanced conceptions of public institutions as human contrivances drawing their power and justification from consent. The traditional holders of public power appealed to long-established hierarchical class relations and to inequalities among human beings; liberals countered by asserting fundamental human equality. "When Adam delved and Eve span," went one popular ditty, "who was then the gentleman?" Liberty meant *equal* liberty.

In many respects, however, human beings are unequal, and these inequalities can play a legitimate role. For early liberals, there was no problem if differences of talent, character, and drive left some better off than others. So understood, liberalism has an intrinsic affinity with meritocracy, but not with hereditary aristocracy.

And finally, traditional power-holders believed that established religions and publicly enforced morality were essential to the pace and good order of society; liberals dissented in the name of religious toleration and the capacity of ordinary human beings to make their own decisions. Government, they argued, should be competent within its appropriate sphere, but that sphere should be strictly limited.

From its inception in the seventeenth century, liberalism understood as liberation—"classical liberalism," for short—slowly transformed Great Britain, suffused political debate throughout Europe, and shaped the culture and political institutions of the nascent American Republic. During the nineteenth century, however, issues that classical liberalism had left unaddressed came to the fore. Two were of particular importance. As technology sparked new modes of production and industrial organization, economic inequality surged, as did asymmetries of power between capital and labor. In this context, freedom of contract often led to troubling human and social consequences, and liberal thinkers began asking whether the prevailing conception of limited government was adequate to these new circumstances. What could the meritocratic principle of "careers open to talents" mean if the opportunity to develop these talents was available to some but not others? Over time, these doubts led to a new understanding, which I shall call distributive liberalism, in which policies and institutions sought to contain market-based inequalities of income, wealth, and opportunity.

A second hiatus concerned the consequences of societies shaped by egalitarian principles and market relations. John Stuart Mill was neither the first (Alexis de Tocqueville preceded him) nor the last to worry about the leveling tendencies of individual choices understood as preferences or "tastes" exempt from moral evaluation. The arch-utilitarian Jeremy Bentham famously argued that pushpin was as good as poetry. Mill could not agree; some preferences, he argued, are more elevated and ennobling than others. Happiness may be the ultimate human good, or "utility," but it is not the same thing as pleasure, whence Mill's dictum, "Better to be Socrates dissatisfied than a fool satisfied."[1] True utility, Mill insisted, is grounded in the "permanent interests of man as a progressive being,"[2] and he agreed with Wilhelm von Humboldt in identifying these interests with the "highest and most harmonious development of [an individual's] powers to a complete and consistent whole." The encounter of nineteenth-century English liberal thinkers with German sociologists and philosophers produced what I call social liberalism, which judged economic and social relations by their propensity not only to improve material conditions but also to elevate human character.

There was, third, a fundamental disagreement about the nature of human society. Classical and distributive liberalism regarded society as the product of voluntary agreement, understood as either a series of incremental steps or an all-at-once social contract. Both conceived of society as a system of cooperation for mutual advantage, with advantage understood as security, prosperity, and the rule of settled law rather than arbitrary decree. By contrast, social liberals regarded social life as part of what makes us human. While we choose freely among institutions and policies, we do so within an unchosen framework of social membership. In seeking economic justice, therefore, social liberals coordinate the individual and social dimensions of human existence, understood as equally fundamental and mutually irreducible.

In the body of this chapter, I will refract the topic questions through the three strands of liberalism just sketched—classical, distributive, and social. To state the obvious, these are Weberian ideal types, with many specific thinkers crossing conceptual categories. To make my task manageable, I have selected exemplary thinkers as the principal representatives of each variant—John Locke, Robert Nozick, and Friedrich Hayek for classical liberalism, John Rawls for distributive liberalism, and Leonard Hobhouse for social liberalism.

Equality

None of the three ideal-typical versions of liberalism requires strict equality of holdings or contributions. Classical liberalism endorses a conception of formal equality: all individuals are equal in moral worth, and none should be excluded from a chance to compete for valued possessions and positions. As we will see, classical liberalism does accept some equality-based limits on "primitive acquisition." In addition, some classical liberals embrace an egalitarian principle of need: no one should go without what Hayek calls a "uniform minimum" of essentials such as food, shelter, and health care.[3] If some individuals cannot earn enough to provide these essentials for themselves, society should step in to fill the gap. Anything beyond that represents the imposition of an arbitrary theoretical pattern on the working of a free society.

Nozick generalizes this point. He asks why any conception of equality beyond the equal moral standing of all individuals should constitute the default setting in our understanding of justice, and he insists that "liberty upsets patterns"—all patterns. If liberals are committed first and foremost to equal liberty, they must reject redistribution based on any state-administered conception of appropriate shares of what we value. If individual liberty is to be our polestar, then only one principle of justice is possible: "From each as they choose, to each as they are chosen."[4] No slavery, no forced labor, no state-assigned occupations; but also no forced contributions designed to transfer goods, tangible or intangible, from some to others.

Distributive liberalism adopts a similar point of departure—a conception of individuals as free and equal—but arrives at a different destination. Rawls asks what an aggregation of such individuals, understood as citizens adopting a basic framework of justice for their political community, would agree to if they do not know what social and economic positions each will end up occupying. Suppose you have bad luck; how far do you want to fall? Suppose your worst enemies were to determine your lot in life; what principles would you want to constrain them? In such circumstances, he argues, we would opt for an equal distribution of economic values—unless an unequal distribution would be to everyone's advantage, including those at the bottom.[5]

Why is this question the right way of approaching the issue of equality? Rawls's answer: society is a system of cooperation for mutual advantage, and no one would willingly participate in such a system without receiving the greatest possible compensation. The issue is not envy of those who have more, but rather maximizing one's own reward for engaging in the cooperative activities needed to produce what we value as individuals.

Social liberalism focuses on the economic preconditions of human flourishing, to which every individual is equally entitled. In advanced economies, Hobhouse contends, "Every citizen should have the full means of earning by socially useful labour so much material support as experience proves to be the necessary basis of a healthy, civilized existence."[6] And he takes a broad view of what constitutes socially useful labor. For example, mothers of young children are performing a "service to the community" by raising healthy and happy children. If some mothers decide that they can best perform that service by staying home full-time, the support they receive from the public treasury should be regarded not as charity but rather as "payment for a civic service."[7] Underlying Hobhouse's view of work worthy of remuneration is a conception of a harmonious society to whose well-being different forms of activity can contribute.

Property

The classical liberal understanding of property begins with the premise of self-ownership. "Every man has a property in his own person," Locke says, and nobody has any right to it except himself.[8] His own person includes not only his body, but also his activities, including his labor, so forced labor is an unjust expropriation.

Self-ownership does not mean that we can do whatever we choose with our physical existence and capacities. For example, Locke insists, we cannot enslave ourselves voluntarily; nor can we place ourselves under the "absolute, arbitrary power" of another.[9] Some aspects of property—life and liberty—are inalienable: they can be neither taken away nor traded away.

Classical liberals disagree about the extent of self-ownership, however. Some take the position that our property in our own bodies is near absolute, so laws banning organ sales and prostitution are per se illegitimate. Others say that such transactions, however voluntary they may be, have social consequences that legislation may rightly take into account.[10]

Differences of merit, virtue, and age may justify certain economic and social inequalities, Locke says, but they do not legitimize placing some individuals under the arbitrary power of others, to be disposed of as those others see fit. We own ourselves, and do so equally, but we cannot own other human beings, including our children. To be sure, parents have a kind of authority over their young children, to which the children did not consent (a fact that becomes a matter of increasingly vociferous protest as children mature). But the bonds of parental authority are "temporary," according to Locke: "Age and reason . . . loosen them til at length they drop quite off, leaving a man at his own free disposal."[11] Our children are ours, but not in the way the house we own is ours.

In Locke's theory of property, human endeavor is the source both of ownership and of value. Through acts of appropriation from the "commons," we make something ours. By mixing our labor with what nature provides, we make it conform to our needs and desires. And labor is the source of nearly everything that makes nature valuable to human beings. A parcel of untilled land that will barely sustain one person can be cultivated so as to support one hundred or even one thousand. Labor abolishes scarcity.

Locke's theory presupposes a pre-civil condition generally known as the "state of nature." In these circumstances, legitimate appropriation is limited in two ways. While we may take, and make ours, what we can use, we may not take more than that, only to waste it through spoilage. When we do so, we have wrongly appropriated what could belong to—and serve the needs of—other individuals. Second, we may take for ourselves only to the extent that we leave what Locke terms "enough, and as good" for others. When we use water from a river to quench our thirst, we leave the same opportunity for those who come after us. By contrast, diverting the river into a lake on a parcel of land we have enclosed could violate Locke's proviso.

When a transition occurs from the state of nature to civil society, these constraints on primitive acquisition are eased. The invention of money makes possible the accumulation of property in a form that does not spoil, and the superior productivity of the civil economy legitimizes the accumulation of land and other aspects of nature beyond what a literal application of the enough-and-as-good principle would permit. As Locke puts it, a person who encloses ten acres and makes it produce what one hundred acres of uncultivated land would provide "may truly be said, to give ninety acres to mankind." Industrious men are benefactors, not thieves, even when their holdings dwarf those of others. So as long as economic arrangements in civil society leave everyone better off than they would be in the absence of society, acquisition is essentially unlimited. And they are; as Locke puts it, the king of a large and fruitful territory in the state of nature "feeds, lodges, and is clad worse than a day labourer in England."[12] Whatever its merits, this argument left the factory workers of the nineteenth century unmoved, with fateful consequences.[13]

While classical liberalism sees the acquisition and ownership of property as grounded in a natural right, distributive and social liberalism see it as a societal creation that can be shaped to meet the requirements of both justice and efficiency. Rawls views his theory of justice as indifferent, at least in principle, between socialism and what he terms, following J. E. Meade, a "property-owning democracy."[14] The limits on property holdings are of a piece with the limits on all other socially valued goods and are subject to the same mechanisms of adjustment and redistribution (more on this later).

One thing is clear: Rawls rejects the principle of proportionality for stocks as well as flows of social values—that is, for holdings as well as for income. "To each according to his contribution" fails as a distributive principle, because background circumstances shape both the ability of individuals to make a contribution and the remuneration that different kinds of contributions will receive, and these circumstances are not exempt from normative scrutiny. Nor will "to each according to his talents (or virtue)" do as a principle of distributive justice, because background circumstances shape individuals' ability to develop socially valued talents and traits of character. "To each according to his need (among other things)" comes closer. But definitional difficulties intrude: need for what, exactly? Someone with enormous native musical ability may need expensive instruments and instruction to develop and exercise this talent. In a just distributive scheme, should the claims of those with expensive needs predominate? Rawls sidesteps all these difficulties by arguing that the principles of justice people select in fair circumstances create the framework of "legitimate expectations," within which all principles of proportionality can be assessed.[15]

The fundamental problem of economic policy, says Hobhouse, is "not to destroy property, but to restore the social conception of property to its right place under circumstances suitable to modern needs."[16] For social liberals, property is societal in two senses. First, it is the organized force of society that protects the rights of property owners against thieves and predators. If the titan of industry who flatters himself a "self-made man" digs a bit deeper, he will find that society not only safeguards his possessions but is an "indispensable partner" in their creation. And second, there is a social element in both production and value. An individualism that ignores this social influence will deplete national resources, deprive the community of its just share of the fruits of industry, and produce a "one-sided and inequitable distribution of wealth."[17]

Hobhouse rejects the proposition that the political community as a whole has a right to dispose of no more than it can persuade its citizens, especially those of high income and wealth, to surrender through taxation. The depletion of public resources is "a symptom of profound economic disorganization." May it not be, he asks, "that in a reasoned scheme of economic ethics we should have to allow a true right of property in the member of the community as such which would take the form of a certain minimum claim on the public resources?" It is because property is in part a creature of society that the community may claim a share of the holdings of its members as a matter of right and may dispose of this share to discharge its responsibilities—to secure the conditions in which the mind and character of each individual can develop and in which all who are able can secure through their own efforts the resources needed to provide for themselves and their families.[18]

To achieve these objectives, social liberalism does not specify a minimum property holding to which each individual is entitled as a matter of right. Justice requires, rather, an adequate stream of income earned through work when possible and supplemented by the state when necessary. To mobilize the resources needed to provide this guarantee, the state may rely heavily on sources of private income and wealth whose social utility is hard to discern.

Hobhouse focuses on wealth gained through speculation and also through inheritance. If someone buys shares at 110 and sells them at 125, he asks, in what way has he "earned" his profit or contributed to the process of production? In principle, there is nothing to prevent the state from imposing what he terms a "special tax," now called the capital gains tax, on income derived from this source. (We should rethink this policy only if experience shows that it has the effect over time of reducing investment and production.) Nor is it wrong, again in principle, to impose high taxes on inherited wealth. There is no reason to believe that such a tax would reduce the incentives of those who acquire it, and much evidence to suggest that inherited wealth does reduce these incentives.

Along with ensuring the ability of individuals to support themselves and their families at a level that provides opportunities for self-development, the point of remuneration is to draw forth the greatest contribution that individuals can make to the economy and society of which they are members. Below a certain rate of return, holders of wealth will hesitate to invest. Below a certain salary level, highly trained individuals will be reluctant to contribute their skills.

Hobhouse is certain, however, that the compensation individuals at the top of large enterprises typically obtain far exceeds what would be needed to evoke their best effort. In his view, no compensation of more than 5,000 British pounds (£1,771,000 or about $2.5 million today) can be justified on this basis. This is why he argues that it would be legitimate even to impose what he calls a "super-tax" on large incomes and property from whatever source, in effect creating a cap on individual holdings.[19]

Another argument leads social liberals to a similar conclusion. Beyond a certain point, concentrated property holdings give a small minority disproportionate and arbitrary power over others. This kind of property, Hobhouse argues, ceases to serve either as compensation or as incentive for its possessor and becomes "an instrument whereby the owner can command the labour of others on terms which he is in general able to dictate."[20] Given this asymmetry of power, the result of this transaction between owners of property and those who have only their work-effort to contribute is unlikely to yield wages that meet minimum social needs for workers and their families. Social liberals argue that the community may use collective resources to close the gap. It may also require employers to pay more than workers can achieve through contractual arrangement. And finally, it may seek to break up concentrations of power, especially when the law has contributed to them by creating conditions in which monopolies can form.

Natural Resources

Much of what I summarized under the heading of property can do double duty for natural resources. For classical liberalism, nature in its original state is conceptualized as unowned rather than collectively owned. (This was the crux of Locke's critique of Sir Robert Filmer's theory of property.)[21] Because natural resources are originally unowned, individuals may appropriate and take ownership of them, subject to the non-waste and enough-and-as-good provisos. The latter restriction applies with special force to essential natural resources, such as water, for which satisfactory substitutes are often nonexistent.

In the real world, as Locke well knew, political authorities often take possession—through conquest or diplomacy—of natural resources in vast quantities. When this happens, these resources pass directly from a condition in which they are presumptively owner-less to one of collective ownership by the community headed by the appropriating authorities. The authorities may then decide whether to retain ownership for public purposes, such as parks and "nature preserves," or to make these resources available for distribution to individuals through gift or sale. In the nineteenth century, to encourage the settlement of Western territories, the U.S. government decided to make vast tracts of publicly owned land available for individual purchase. Nonetheless, the government continues to own and control large amounts of land—indeed, the majority of the acreage in several Western states—a status that evokes intense and continuing protest.

Ownership is not mere physical possession of a resource, of course. Lawyers describe it as a "bundle of rights" that public policy can limit and disaggregate. For example, patents provide a kind of time-limited ownership to inventors and researchers. But not everything can be patented. For example, the U.S. Supreme Court has long held that "Laws of nature, natural phenomena, and abstract ideas are not patentable." This exclusion is in part pragmatic: patenting what the court has called the "basic tools of scientific and technological work" would contradict the fundamental purpose of the patent system—to promote innovation, not restrict it. But suffusing the legal and philosophical discussion of this issue is the sentiment that in the same way that human beings can own animals but not other human beings, some aspects of the natural world are excluded by their nature from the realm of legitimate ownership. In 2013, the Supreme Court decided that the discovery of the genetic marker for high risk of developing breast and ovarian cancer could not be patented by the company that had made the discovery. In Lockean language: simply discovering something that exists naturally is not the same as mixing one's labor with it, and granting someone exclusive title to a discovery for an extended period may not pass the enough-and-as-good test.[22]

Even from the standpoint of classical liberalism, and a fortiori for distributive and social liberalism, some public purposes override otherwise secure ownership rights. That is why the U.S. Constitution authorizes governments to take private property for public use, provided that its private owners receive just compensation. It should come as no surprise that the scope of "public use" and the parameters of "just compensation" have remained matters of dispute down to the present day. But the principle is clear: while government may take private property, government may not simply expropriate it.

For all forms of liberalism, the case for public ownership of natural resources is especially strong when the resource is essential for life and commerce and when substitutes for it do not exist. It is on this basis that numerous states control their water supplies and develop complex schemes for allocating it. When these schemes award long-term water rights for specific uses such as agriculture, farmers come to regard these rights as their inviolable property. But in times of crisis, governments may have no choice but to exercise their authority to meet urgent needs, whatever the disruption of long-settled expectations.

In principle, both distributive and social liberalism can restrict holdings of natural resources for a wider range of reasons than classical liberalism permits. Distributive liberals have no difficulty concluding that in an agricultural economy, land—the basis of income and wealth—should be divided equally unless all would benefit from an unequal division. And as Hobhouse notes, social liberals can institute public ownership of arable land to recreate the basis for small independent family farming that the concentration of large tracts in the hands of a small class of landed aristocrats had destroyed.[23] It is a harder question whether distributive liberals may declare certain kinds of ownership illegal in order to achieve controversial public purposes such as the protection of endangered species. Rawls argues that public subsidies for the arts cannot be justified on the grounds that culture is intrinsically valuable, and it is notoriously difficult to devise a compelling instrumental justification for these subsidies.[24] While some endangered species may pass this test (if they are medically useful, for example), most will not. Hindus may protect cattle on the grounds that they are sacred; distributive liberals may not.

Products

As we have seen, classical liberalism sees a distinct link between labor and ownership, at least in the state of nature. "As much land as a man tills, plants, improves, cultivates, and can use the product of, so much is his property."[25] By mixing their labor with natural resources, individuals both take possession of those resources and add value to them, with labor contributing the lion's share to the value of what they produce. During and after the transition to social and political life, however, human beings consent to decouple labor from ownership of its products, and to allow possession in excess of what individuals can use. It is the invention of money, Locke argues, that makes the difference, because "gold and silver . . . may be hoarded up without injury to anyone, these metals not spoiling or decaying in the hands of the possessor."[26] The transition from the natural to the civil state leaves unchanged each individual's exclusive ownership of his labor-power, which may be neither forcibly appropriated nor permanently alienated but only exchanged for compensation through voluntary agreement.

Because distributive liberalism does not take the doctrine of natural rights as its point of departure, it does not see an intrinsic link between work and ownership. In a modern economy, moreover, virtually everything is the product of many hands, and it is impossible to assess the relative contribution of each one. "To each according to his contribution" yields indeterminate results, and "to each according to his marginal product" subjects individuals to contingencies that are irrelevant from a moral point of view. The only option is to regard the fruits of productive enterprise as a common pool to be distributed according to principles unrelated to the process of production.

Speaking for classical liberalism, Nozick protests that Rawls's approach amounts to treating the fruits of human labor as "manna from heaven" rather than as a joint production the terms of which are negotiated among the producers.[27] Rawls's principle, says Nozick, is the moral equivalent of asking students in a class to distribute among themselves a total of grades without knowing whether they are good, mediocre, or poor students. If the total is fixed, they would agree ex ante to an equal distribution; if variable, they may well choose to maximize the lowest grade. If this strikes us as counter-intuitive and unfair, Nozick concludes, then so should the difference principle.[28] To this Rawls would reply that even setting aside the difficulty of determining actual contributions to a joint product, it is often the case that not all individuals have a fair chance to make a contribution. Unequal access to education and training may compel individuals to sell their labor cheaply; sustained unemployment will prevent them from selling it at all. Allowing wages to serve as a proxy for contribution simply begs the question.[29]

Social liberals join distributive liberals in regarding virtually all products in modern economies as jointly produced. And those who share in the production go well beyond those directly involved in the process of production. Every business owner relies on order enforced by the state, on infrastructure and educational systems for which he does not pay, and on past generations of accomplishment and invention. Against this backdrop, how is ownership or just distribution to be inferred from the market value of products or from direct participation in their production? Instead, says Hobhouse, compensation should reflect two key components: what all individuals need to provide decent and progressive lives for themselves and their dependents; and what is needed to provide sufficient incentives for those who perform each social and economic function to do so at a level of high effectiveness, sustained over time.[30]

Wealth

The liberal tradition does not offer a precise definition of what it means to be "wealthy." In Victorian and Edwardian England, this status was informally defined as being able to live off the income from one's holdings without dipping into principal.

For distributive liberalism, holdings are morally justified if and only if they maximize the economic and social standing of the least advantaged members of society. (Large concentrations of wealth are unlikely to meet this test.) For social liberalism, the test is different—the compatibility of holdings with a harmonious society in which every individual receives an adequate and reliable stream of income and in which social institutions have the resources they need to carry out their essential functions.

Classical liberalism leans against limits on wealth. The guiding principle is that if individual holdings are legitimate, then any outcome of voluntary exchanges among these individuals is itself legitimate and exempt from criticism on grounds of injustice. To this end, Nozick offers his famous Wilt Chamberlain example (readers too young to remember Chamberlain may substitute LeBron James or any other top-flight sports figure). Suppose Chamberlain negotiates a contract with the owners of his team to the effect that 5 percent of the proceeds from every ticket sale will go directly to him. As fans enter, they deposit the star's share in a lockbox. It will not take long for Chamberlain to become immensely wealthy. Who has just cause for complaint, Nozick asks? The owners, fans, and the player have all consented to the transaction, and no one outside the circle of consent has been injured.[31]

Similarly, classical liberals see no basis for blocking intergenerational transfers of wealth or imposing special taxes on estates—assuming, again, that the assets represent legitimate holdings. (Government may seize what children inherit from parents who gained their wealth from criminal enterprises.) Social liberals regard inherited wealth as exempt from taxation or even confiscation only to the extent that they contribute to the economy. So not only may social liberals choose to recoup through taxation what the law determines to be society's contributions to individual estates, but also they may impose taxes as they choose, if they can do it "without diminishing the available supply of capital and without losing any service of value."[32]

For their part, distributive liberals will apply to intergenerational transfers the same principles they use to determine economic justice generally. As Rawls puts it, distributive institutions will impose inheritance and gift taxes and restrict rights of bequest so as "gradually and continually to correct the distribution of wealth and to prevent concentrations of power detrimental to the fair value of political liberty and fair equality of opportunity."[33] For distributive liberalism, then, otherwise legitimate concentrations of wealth may be broken up if they restrict the opportunities of the non-wealthy to participate in political and economic affairs on terms that principles of justice deem fair.

As far as I know, classical and distributive liberals do not single out legal sources of income and wealth for special opprobrium. By contrast, social liberals take into account the contribution of different activities to the overall well-being of society. Noting that "speculation" is an important source of private wealth in modern economies, Hobhouse pointedly asks whether it is also a source of "social wealth" and whether it produces anything for society. From his standpoint, speculative investments bear the burden of proof: if they cannot show that they contribute to society, they may be singled out for taxation, the limits of which (if any) he does not specify.[34]

Income and Employment

Concerning these topics, I have already said much of what is possible under other headings. A few additional remarks will clarify the remaining details.

Classical liberals do not accept the moral imperative of reducing the gap between minimum and maximum incomes. Distributive liberals focus on maximizing the minimum, which may or may not be consistent with reducing the gap. Social liberals are willing to specify both a floor (based on physical and developmental needs) and a ceiling beyond which incomes cannot plausibly be linked to social functions.

It is not clear that classical liberals are of one mind on the issue of a basic income to which everyone is entitled. It might be possible to infer such an entitlement from the enough-and-as-good proviso, but I can find no evidence that Nozick explicitly does so. Other classical liberals are willing to accept what is now known as a Universal Basic Income (UBI), especially if it replaces a jumble of welfare and means-tested programs, whose moral and economic effects they regard as perverse.[35] For his part, Hayek endorses a socially guaranteed basic income for "all instances of proved need," with the proviso that "nothing which is not paid for by personal contribution is given without such proof." He acknowledges that the provision of a social minimum involves some redistribution of income, but he distinguishes between this and a more ambitious redistributive scheme that seeks to align incomes in accordance with some overall pattern.[36]

Liberals of all stripes regard differences of compensation for identical work within the same firm as evidence of unjustified discrimination. This is distinguished from equal pay for "comparable" work, which requires some external metric to guide judgments about comparability. If maids are paid less than janitors, is this a *per se* violation of the principle of formal equality?

Liberals also unite in viewing income earned through work as preferable to income that is socially provided. The question is what to do when wages fall short of the defined basic minimum, which may be defined in individual or family terms, depending on prevailing social practices. Most distributive liberals see no bar to requiring employers to pay a legally defined minimum wage. Most classical liberals object, in part because they regard any minimum wage as a violation of freedom of contract, and in part because they believe it will reduce employment opportunities for young and disadvantaged workers. In place of a minimum wage, they often urge a socially provided wage supplement to close the gap between market earnings and the social minimum. In the United States, this supplement, known as the Earned Income Tax Credit, has come to represent one of the government's largest redistributive programs, in part because many distributive liberals have come to accept it as a less contentious means to the goal they favor.

As we have seen, social liberals endorse the same principle and approach. To reiterate: in advanced economies, says Hobhouse, every citizen should have "full means of earning by social useful labour so much material support as experience proves to be the necessary basis of a healthy, civilized existence." If wages do not yield enough to meet this standard, each worker is held to have "a claim not as of charity, but as of right on the national resources to make good the deficiency."[37] And in his view, socially useful labor includes work in the family that typically goes without wages or market compensation.

Taxation

Few topics evoke greater differences among the various types of liberalism. Classical liberals view taxation with suspicion and seek to minimize it. Hayek mounts a vigorous critique of the arguments underlying progressive taxation. To finance the limited state activities he regards as legitimate, he accepts only a "proportional" tax (now called the flat tax), which taxes the incomes of the rich and poor at the same rate.[38] Some go farther: taxation of earnings from labor, Nozick notoriously argues, is "on a par with forced labor," even in the name of serving the needy.[39] Taken literally, this proposition would make it impossible for society to meet such needs beyond what individuals are willing to contribute through charity, an implication from which Nozick does not flinch.[40]

At the other end of the spectrum, social liberals see the types and overall levels of legitimate taxation as determined empirically—by the extent of social needs and by the requisites of a productive economy. When these factors collide with individual claims, however deeply felt, social considerations must win out.

Distributive liberals occupy a middle position. As we have seen, Rawls has no difficulty justifying redistributive taxes on gifts and bequests. More broadly, he endorses a system of taxation sufficient to raise the revenues that justice requires—to "provide for the public goods and make the transfer payments necessary to satisfy the difference principle."[41] He regards the kinds of taxes used to meet these goals as questions of political judgment outside the scope of a theory of justice. For example, justice does not require a progressive income tax. Indeed, Rawls suggests that a flat tax on consumption rather than income might be best, all things considered, at least in well-ordered societies. If a single-rate consumption tax interferes less with economic incentives and is more conducive to productivity, it may make it possible to satisfy the difference principle at a higher level than could otherwise be attained. (There may, however, be a compelling argument for progressive taxation in imperfectly just real-world conditions.)[42]

A concluding note: Nozick argues that liberty upsets patterns. And so it does. Maintaining any given pattern over time will require ongoing interference in the aggregate consequences of individual choices. Rawls replies, in effect, So what? The first virtue of social institutions is justice, not liberty. In fact, actions that violate principles of justice have no intrinsic worth, so the costs of preventing such actions are measured in pragmatic rather than moral terms. It seems appropriate that deep differences among variants of contemporary liberalism turn out to depend on the meaning of liberty and its status relative to competing considerations.

Notes

1. John Stuart Mill, *Utilitarianism* (Mineola, New York: Dover, 2007), 8.

2. Mill quotes this passage from von Humboldt in *On Liberty*, republished in John Stuart Mill, *Three Essays* (Oxford, Great Britain: Oxford University Press, 1975), 71.

3. F. A. Hayek, *The Constitution of Liberty* (Chicago, Illinois: University of Chicago, 1960), 257–258, 303.

4. Robert Nozick, *Anarchy, State, and Utopia* (New York, New York: Basic Books, 1974), 160.

5. John Rawls, *A Theory of Justice*, revised edition (Cambridge, Massachusetts: Harvard University Press, 1999), 54.

6. Leonard Trelawny Hobhouse, *Liberalism* (Oxford, Great Britain: Oxford University Press, 1911), 68–71.

7. Hobhouse, *Liberalism*, 77.

8. John Locke, *Two Treatises of Government*, Peter Laslett, ed. (Cambridge, Great Britain: Cambridge University Press, 1994), 287.

9. Locke, *Two Treatises*, 284.

10. For a useful discussion, see N. Scott Arnold, *Imposing Values: An Essay on Liberalism and Regulation* (New York, New York: Oxford University Press, 2009), 105–106.

11. Locke, *Two Treatises*, 304.

12. The selection of the appropriate baseline of comparison is a much-disputed matter. Nozick argues that a medical researcher who invents a life-saving drug, patents it, and then refuses to sell it except on his terms (however exorbitant they may be) has not made anyone worse off than if he had never made his discovery (*Anarchy, State, and Utopia*, 181). Perhaps not; but is that all that can be said about this case? Doesn't the patent make it impossible for someone else to make and sell this discovery? If the knowledge of nature is a commons analogous to nature itself, isn't removing a parcel of knowledge from the knowledge-commons subject to analogous constraints?

13. For the preceding three paragraphs, see generally "Of Property" in Locke, *Two Treatises*, 285–302.

14. Rawls, *Theory of Justice*, 242.

15. Rawls, *Theory of Justice*, 273–77.

16. Hobhouse, *Liberalism*, 81.

17. Hobhouse, *Liberalism*, 81–82.

18. Hobhouse, *Liberalism*, 68.

19. Hobhouse, *Liberalism*, 86.

20. Hobhouse, *Liberalism*, 80.

21. Locke, *Two Treatises*, 156–171 *passim*.

22. Association for Molecular Pathology *v.* Myriad Genetics, Inc., 569 U.S. 576 (2013).

23. Hobhouse, *Liberalism*, 75.

24. Rawls, *Theory of Justice*, 289.

25. Locke, *Two Treatises*, 290.

26. Locke, *Two Treatises*, 302.

27. Nozick, *Anarchy, State, and Utopia*, 198.

28. Nozick, *Anarchy, State, and Utopia*, 199–201.

29. For the moral reasoning behind Rawls's position, see *A Theory of Justice*, 86–89.

30. Hobhouse, *Liberalism*, 82.

31. Nozick, *Anarchy, State, and Utopia*, 161–163.

32. Hobhouse, *Liberalism*, 85.

33. Rawls, *Theory of Justice*, 245.

34. Hobhouse, *Liberalism*, 84.

35. For a discussion, see Christine Emba, "Universal Basic Income," *Washington Post*, September 28, 2015. She cites the views of Milton Friedman and Charles Murray, among others.

36. Hayek, *Constitution of Liberty*, 301, 303.

37. Hobhouse, *Liberalism*, 79.

38. Hayek, *Constitution of Liberty*, 314–318.

39. Nozick, *Anarchy, State, and Utopia*, 169–170.

40. Nozick, *Anarchy, State, and Utopia*, 265–268.

41. Rawls, *Theory of Justice*, 246.

42. Rawls, *Theory of Justice*, 246–247.

Marxism

INEQUALITY AND MORALITY

ANDREW LEVINE

Introduction

Marxism can refer to the thought of Karl Marx (1818–1883) or to any of the political currents that identified with his views over the past century and a half; the connections between the two are seldom straightforward.

Marx advanced distinctive theoretical positions concerning the structure and direction of human history, the nature and role of class divisions and class struggles, "the laws of motion" of capitalist societies, and relations between economic structures and what he called "legal and political superstructures" and forms of consciousness. These theories, and others related to them, though freestanding, hang together closely enough to comprise a distinctive "worldview."

Thanks to the diffusion of Marx's writings and his leading role in the International Working Men's Association—the First International (1864–1876)—there were Marxists in Western Europe from the 1860s on. By the time of the founding of the Second International in 1889, Marxism had blossomed into a full-fledged ideology, capable of guiding theory and practice. It was a leading force in the German Social Democratic Party.

Second International Marxism was a casualty of World War I and the Bolshevik revolution. The Second International that survives to this day, though historically contiguous with the original, is comprised of center-left political parties, none of which any longer self-identify as Marxist. After the Russian revolution, the Soviet Union became the focal point around which Marxist political parties and movements oriented themselves.

From the 1920s on, Communist parties, born out of the Third International (established in Moscow in 1919 and officially dissolved in 1943), constituted something like a universal church, organized nation-by-nation but controlled from the center. There were dissenters, of course: old-style orthodox Marxists, independent "Western Marxists," and, after Leon Trotsky was forced into exile in 1928, Trotskyists as well.

Following through on the church analogy, it would be fair to say that Communists were like Catholics, while Trotskyists were like Protestants. Notwithstanding the founding of a Fourth (Trotskyist) International in the 1930s, they were prone to sectarian divisions over ideological differences that seem abstruse to outsiders but that insiders deemed momentous.

After the Sino-Soviet split of the late 1950s and early 1960s, dissident Marxists in Western countries found another way to oppose official Communism, while still continuing to identify with the Bolshevik revolution: they became Maoists. The Chinese neither discouraged nor encouraged this phenomenon. Because so little was known in the West about revolutionary China, Western Maoism was based in part on illusions about the revolutionary heroism and purity of Chinese Communism. Other Asian Marxisms had a similar appeal, though on a smaller scale.

Joseph Stalin died in 1953. Three years later, the Soviet government, under the leadership of Nikita Khrushchev, set a "de-Stalinization" process in motion. From that point on, the nearly hegemonic influence of official Communism began to wane. However, Marxism remained a pole of attraction, laying the groundwork for a Marxist renaissance in many parts of the world in the late 1960s and early 1970s. This turned out to be less of a new beginning than a last gasp. As the 1970s wore on, and neo-liberal economic policies took hold, radical political currents, Marxist and otherwise, suffered debilitating, ultimately devastating, "crises." By the end of the 1980s, they had nearly all gone extinct.

The Soviet Union itself imploded in 1991, seventy-four years after its founding. Before long, what remained of Communism, and of Marxisms that defined themselves in relation to Communism, effectively withered away, though some of their institutional expressions linger.

Remnants of Asian Marxism survive in remote quarters of that continent; progressive movements in Central and South America, and, to a lesser extent, Africa, remain connected, in attenuated ways, to the Marxist tradition. However, there is no denying that, as a descriptive term designating political ideologies joined together by historical connections and family resemblances, *Marxism* has become a dead letter.

The varieties of Western Marxism that emerged in the 1920s and that became influential in academic precincts decades later survived longer. But they were too unlike one another, and too dissociated from real-world politics, to coalesce into a new Marxist paradigm. The great Western Marxists—among others, Georg Lukács, Karl Korsch, Jean-Paul Sartre, Maurice Merleau-Ponty, Louis Althusser, and leading figures of the Frankfurt School—are nowadays known as much for their contributions to the general culture as for their Marxism. To this day, there are also Marxist academics in economics, sociology, philosophy, and history departments. In this case, too, the more successful ones are seldom known for their contributions to Marxist theory. Many of the less well-known ones battle on in difficult and professionally precarious situations.

The reasons many Marxist academics identify with the Marxist tradition are not just theoretical: they are political, too. This is less common, however, among self-described Marxists who work in fields like cultural studies and literary theory, which address issues remote from Marx's own concerns. Many of them are, for all practical purposes, apolitical; accountable only to the standards and norms, such as they are, of their respective disciplines. They, too, may think of themselves as political beings, but their conceptions of politics, including identity politics (the only kind they explicitly address), typically veer off toward the arcane.

In light of Marx's own thinking and the history of Marxist theory and practice, it would be fair to say that the very idea of a purely academic Marxism is untenable on its face, no matter how illuminating work done under that description may be. Scholars, working on Marx and Marxism, do not become Marxists themselves for that reason alone. However, to address Ethikon's questions from the standpoint of the Marxist tradition, the work of some academic Marxists is relevant; it is, arguably, even indispensable.

One reason why is that Marx and orthodox Marxists would have more of a problem with the Ethikon questions than most academic Marxists do—because Marx, like Nietzsche (though for different reasons), was not so much a moral theorist as a critic of morality, hostile not just to particular notions of justice and morality, but also to efforts at prioritizing those concerns. Orthodox Marxists followed Marx's lead; they would therefore have trouble with the Ethikon questions, too. Connections between Marxism and egalitarianism are complicated as well. Marx and Marxists after him were egalitarians of a sort, but not in ways that distinguish them from others to whom that description applies. On the other hand, some of the very best academic Marxists, or former Marxists, are egalitarians above all.

Indeed, academics who engaged Marx's work in recent years from within a broadly analytic perspective have been concerned primarily with the kinds of questions Ethikon is asking. Because their work has always been accountable mainly to the standards of their respective academic disciplines, not to political constituencies, their efforts were only tenuously Marxist. But the standards they observed were rigorous and conducive to fruitful theoretical work. Their achievements help clarify what, if anything, a distinctively Marxist ethical tradition might be.

Marx and the orthodox Marxists who followed him disparaged socialists, who appealed to notions of justice and morality in order to make a case for socialism, communism's first stage; they called them "utopian socialists." By way of contrast, they called themselves "scientific socialists." In retrospect, the orthodox case against utopian socialism can seem wrongheaded or disingenuous, or both. Clarifying this problem was Topic A for analytically trained philosophers working on Marx several decades ago.

I could report on the debates around these issues and, by offering opinions and arguments, intervene into them. But I cannot uncontroversially report on what the Marxist tradition has to say about most of the questions Ethikon is asking—not so much because the positions self-identified Marxists have taken are all over the map, but because Marx and most Marxists, and therefore the mainstream Marxist tradition, deemed those questions wrongheaded.

What they believed instead was that history advanced according to a developmental logic that, barring exogenous interferences, made communism historically inevitable, and moral questions generally superfluous.

This was never just an article of faith. Marxists were committed, for rationally compelling reasons, to theoretical positions according to which history admits of real epochal divisions in much the way that, say, matter—the stuff of which everything in nature is made—is comprised of discrete elements. History, in Marx's view, is comprised of discrete "modes of production," or economic structures, each of which have their own characteristic notions of justice and morality.

If they are right, there can be no defensible trans-historical account of what justice and morality require, and particular accounts could only be compelling from within the forms of consciousness appropriate to the modes of production they help to sustain. Therefore, for Marxists, intent on moving history along—ultimately, to (small-c) communism—there is no philosophical reason to care about those standards at all. Some form of taxation, say, might be just or unjust within capitalism (in general, or in one or another of its forms or stages), and it might be politically efficacious to point this out. But for anyone engaged in doing capitalism in, how well or poorly that form of taxation measures up according to capitalist standards is of no deeper importance.

I would therefore suggest that, for Marx and Marxism, the most useful way to address the questions Ethikon poses is to set them into a larger framework, more in line with the religious traditions Ethikon is also investigating. To that end, we need to look at Marxism as one ideology among others within the larger socialist tradition, and indeed within the tradition of the political Left in general. This would include at least some strains of liberal theory and practice.

From time immemorial, there were inklings of socialism in many of the world's cultures and ethical traditions. Liberalism, in the modern sense, predates the French Revolution and therefore the emergence of a political Left. But "classical German philosophy" was onto something when its leading exponents—Marx among them—saw the emergence of a new consciousness arising out of the political and social transformations that the French Revolution set in motion. Marxism is of a piece with that world-historical development, notwithstanding the fact that Marx, and orthodox Marxists after him, were intent on distinguishing their own theory and practice from those of other socialists and, more plainly still, from liberal political movements.

With Marxist orthodoxy in decline, scientific socialism seems to have drifted into utopian socialist territory. The old lines of demarcation are therefore less salient than they used to be. This not entirely salutary development has made it more feasible than it would have been, say, twenty or thirty years ago to address some of the questions Ethikon poses from a point of view that is not too wildly out of line with recent, if not quite "contemporary," standpoints.

"Analytical Marxists" (I among them) sought, at first, to reconstruct and defend versions of scientific socialism or, failing that, to defend Marx's theory of history against any of a number of objections leveled against it. This all took place at a time when the work of John Rawls was coming to exercise an almost hegemonic influence over moral and political philosophy in the English-speaking world (and beyond). Rawls was a liberal egalitarian; the book for which he is best known, *A Theory of Justice*, was a theory of liberal egalitarian justice, not of justice *sub specie aeternitatis*. Its influence was such that, from the time it was published in 1971, it dominated nearly all discussions of the topics it addressed. Because analytical Marxists were ensconced in milieus where this was happening, high on the list of topics they engaged were the ones that Rawls investigated. And because they subjected orthodox positions to relentless, albeit friendly, criticism, many of those positions fell into disfavor—sometimes for rationally compelling reasons, sometimes because that is the way the spirit of the times tended. And so, finding themselves no longer able to defend positions that Marx and Marxists held, except by transforming them in ways pioneered within the academic mainstream, analytical Marxists effectively morphed into Rawlsian liberals, distinguished only by their interest in topics associated with Marx and the Marxism of the Second and Third Internationals.

One way of answering Ethikon's questions would therefore be from a left Rawlsian perspective. There may be no other way at this point—not because Rawls's views are the only ones worth taking seriously, but because there is a paucity of rival *marxisant* purchases on justice and equality available. This, therefore, is what I will do. However, by alluding, when appropriate, to the bona fide Marxist tradition of years past, I will do my best to resist the temptation to answer those questions in ways that liberal egalitarians with no interest at all in Marx would.

Nevertheless, these "stubborn facts," as Marx's collaborator Friedrich Engels would call them, remain: that there is no useful way to address the Ethikon questions from within a scientific socialist perspective, and that, insofar as Marx and orthodox Marxists were utopian socialists despite themselves, they have little, if anything, to add to liberal egalitarian views.

There are two introductory questions posed by Ethikon that I will conclude by addressing. A third such question, pertaining to the "major elements of the tradition's worldview" that "shape its ideas on economic justice," has already been addressed.

There is no distinctively Marxist purchase on either question, though from a Rawlsian vantage point, the answers are straightforward.

First, Rawlsian justice is about the distribution of "primary goods," means for realizing any of a range of "reasonable" objectives. These include not only income and wealth but also basic rights and liberties, "powers and offices," and, depending on which of Rawls's several formulations is taken on board, such things as "the bases of self-respect," leisure, and health.

Second, liberal justice, in Rawls's view, is about patterns, not processes. The most influential defender of the rival view, in the period in question, was Robert Nozick. Ironically, toward the end, some of scientific socialism's most incisive former defenders latched onto the idea that aspects of Nozick's, expressly non-Rawlsian, account of justice—his notion of self-ownership especially—were powerful in their own right, and important for defenders of Marx's account of exploitation to take seriously. I disagree, but there is no need to press that point here, because there is plainly nothing in Nozick's neo-Lockean theory of justice that resonates, even in the attenuated way that Rawls's theory of justice does, with Marx's work or the work of mainstream Marxists.

Equality

Liberal egalitarian justice acknowledges a presumption for an equal distribution of whatever the relevant distribuand is; for Rawls, that would be primary goods. However, this presumption can be, and typically is, overridden. In Rawls's view, it should be overridden to improve the distributive share (of primary goods) of the least well-off, and so on up the line, in accord with the so-called difference principle. For utilitarians, it should be overridden to improve total or average utility. These are not the only possibilities. None of the contenders have anything to do with Marxism, however, except insofar as Marxism is a species of liberal egalitarianism.

Egalitarians call for an equal distribution of one or another distribuand. Insofar as they consider equal distribution of that distribuand a defeasible objective, as they almost always do, their egalitarian commitments need not put them at odds with proponents of liberal egalitarian justice. The difference is academic—in both the literal and derogatory senses of the term. Liberal egalitarian philosophers, like Rawls, *defend* particular conceptions of just distribution; philosophers investigating egalitarianism are interested in ascertaining what egalitarians *qua* egalitarians want. From a practical point of view, the difference hardly matters; from a theoretical point of view, the issues are orthogonal to one another.

In the 1990s, there was a lively debate in Anglophone philosophical circles on what the correct egalitarian distribuand should be. The principal contenders fell into two main categories: welfare and resources. Primary goods are a kind of resource. In time, the "conversation" trailed off inconclusively, nearly all lines of argument having been exhausted. En route to that end, however, the welfarist/resourcist division largely broke down. Also, capabilities entered into the discussion, and the emphasis shifted from equal distribution per se to the equal distribution of opportunities for the acquisition and possession of one or another distribuand.

Regardless of the philosophical interest inherent in that comparatively long-running debate, the practical implications were nil. The way to advance any properly egalitarian vision is to distribute income and wealth less unequally than capitalist markets do.

Lapsed analytical Marxists figured prominently in the discussions that raged over these questions, but Marx and Marxism did not figure in them at all. This was not an oversight. Marxist concerns may or may not lead to liberal egalitarian or other egalitarian destinations, but if Marxism means what it has meant for a century and a half, the Marxist position on debates surrounding justice and equality, and other utopian socialist ideals, is, so to speak, *je m'en foutiste*.

This is not to say that Marxism and egalitarianism are at odds; not by any means. As socialists, Marx and Marxists opposed private ownership of some (or all) of a society's (major or not so major) means of production. And they opposed inherited wealth. They therefore opposed the most important sources of unequal wealth in capitalist societies.

In full-fledged socialist societies, where all (or nearly all) productive assets are socially owned, there would be little, if any, egalitarian reason to redistribute anything. Some people would work longer or harder than others, and some might save more. Even so, the resulting distribution would be very nearly flat. However, if, for any reason, the need arose, Marxists would have no principled reason to object to familiar redistributive measures.

Less radical socialists are less intent on doing away with the mechanisms that generate inequality under capitalism. Therefore, for them, redistributive taxation, in conjunction with massive social spending, is indispensable for realizing egalitarian, or less inegalitarian, outcomes. Ironically, though, these less radical socialists are actually more egalitarian, at least in an aspirational sense, than Marxists. Marx and Engels, and Marxists after them, never expressly defended strictly equal distributions of income or wealth, at least not as a matter of principle. The canonical text that bears most directly on this issue, *The Critique of the Gotha Program* (1875), expressly defends unequal wage rates under socialism, conceived there as a form of society suitable for the transition from capitalism to communism.

Under socialism, so understood, wages should be proportional to workers' productive contributions. Presumably, these contributions would be measured in ways that accord with analytical principles set forth in Marx's economic writings, though exactly how is unclear. The only productive factor Marx and Marxists expressly acknowledge is labor power, which they regard, for analytical purposes, as undifferentiated or homogeneous. However useful this notion may be in general, it is not helpful for ascertaining how much particular workers, or categories of workers, actually contribute—because there is no good way to take into account labor intensity (as distinct from labor time) and differential skills. Expressly non- or even anti-Marxist analytical categories developed toward the end of the nineteenth century, during the so-called marginalist revolution, serve this purpose better. For marginalists, though, labor power is not the only pertinent productive factor; what capitalists do (supply capital, organize production processes, incur risks, and so on)—and, insofar as there is a difference, what managers do—would also have to be taken into account.

The important point for the present purpose is just that Marx and his co-thinkers endorsed unequal pay—in the kinds of post-capitalist societies they deemed achievable in their time and place. It would therefore be fair to say that, if pushed, they would also have endorsed differential wage rates under capitalism. This accords with Rawls's account of justice; for Rawls, the only reason why inequalities in the distribution of income and wealth enhance the position of the least well-off is that they function as incentives, spurring on productive contributions that increase the total amount of income and wealth that there is to distribute.

Many socialists would agree; certainly social democrats would. It should be noted, however, not only that more radical positions are conceivable, but also that support for them doesn't always correlate with opposition to private property. "Equal pay for work," as distinct from "equal pay for equal work," was, for a while in the 1970s, expressly promoted by non-Marxist social democrats in Sweden and elsewhere. It has never been proposed, so far as I know, by socialists who identify with the Marxist tradition.

The Critique of the Gotha Program was also where Marx proclaimed that, under communism, distributions would go "from each according to ability, to each according to need." As a distributional principle, this, too, does not mandate equal distributions. But it is not really a distributional principle at all. It is more nearly a prediction about how burdens and benefits (or, on more refined analyses, the several distribuands that figure in various theories of justice) would be distributed in a world in which what David Hume (and Rawls) called "the conditions of justice"—scarcity and basic self-interest—are generally overcome. (Small-c) communism would be a society *beyond* justice, in which benefits and burdens would be distributed in much the ways that they presently are in (some) families—in accord with a general or collective interest that is not reducible to the individual interests of the family's members.

Property

Except perhaps in (exceedingly rare) moments of revolutionary upheaval, Marxists (people in political parties or movements that identify with Marx and Marxism and unaffiliated "fellow travelers") in capitalist societies, like most socialists and many non-socialist leftists, tend to favor low ceilings, high floors, and few gaps in income and wealth distribution. Marxists are also generally on board with efforts to achieve income and wealth equality, or diminish inequality, through normal (legal, parliamentary) means. They also tend to support unions and other civil society organizations that advance these objectives.

However, these are default positions; exceptions could be, and often were, made. If, for example, it would be good for workers, or helpful for enhancing working-class capacities, to strike broad alliances with non-socialist, non-egalitarian, pro-capitalist political parties and movements, Marxists could get on board even with that. The general point is that what matters, in the end, is movement toward a socialist, and ultimately (small-c) communist future; therefore, means matter, but only insofar as they bear on that objective.

This is not to say that anything goes, that the end justifies the means, according to the usual understanding of that expression. Revolutionary Marxists sometimes veered close to that understanding, dismissing moral constraints as counter-revolutionary blather. The amoralism implicit in Marxist accounts of relations between economic structures and forms of consciousness could be, and sometimes were, invoked in defense of casting moral constraints aside. But it would be fair to say that, when this happened, Marxist doctrine was not a major factor. Far more important were modes of thinking and acting that revolutionaries, radical ones especially, find difficult to resist.

In practice, Marxists in socialist societies (the formerly existing ones) were second to none in implementing egalitarian distributions. Though able in theory to countenance inequalities for instrumental reasons, the societies they concocted were as egalitarian as any on earth. Even so, workers received unequal compensation, mainly for incentive reasons. Also, state and party officials did better than the most well-paid workers—not so much because socialist societies were corrupt (they were, of course, but not inordinately so), but because, as in capitalist societies, it was taken for granted that individuals whose responsibilities exceed those of ordinary citizens should be compensated accordingly. In any case, the gap between workers and management, especially top management, in capitalist societies vastly exceeds the gap in (formerly) socialist countries. The American case is especially egregious.

If by property we mean rights to control and benefit from resources, then state and party officials in (formerly existing) socialist countries benefited from unequal property rights, too. Ordinary citizens could have personal holdings gained from savings or, in some cases, earned through minor (small-scale) enterprise. But notwithstanding the defining principle of socialist societies, that productive resources be collectively owned, persons high up in the ranks of the *nomenklatura* did have property rights of a sort in all kinds of enterprises. However, in Weberian terms, their holdings were prebendal, not patrimonial; they existed at the pleasure of state and party officials and were revocable and therefore always insecure. Also, they could not be inherited—except indirectly, in the ways that "social capital" is transferred from generation to generation in capitalist societies.

Beyond holdings of personal items, there would be no real property relations in (small-c) communist societies that could raise questions about ceilings, floors, and gaps. Again, think of families, happy ones, in societies like ours. Family members own their own toothbrushes and clothes but, though some may control its use more than others, the refrigerator belongs to them all. This is how it would be, writ large, in (small-c) communist societies. It would be fair to assume, though, that because citizens' (comrades') circumstances would be more alike than is normally the case in families, that outcomes would generally be flat—with ceilings low, floor high, and gaps few and far between.

Most Left currents, even some liberal ones, were, from time to time, *revolutionary*. This was the case with Marxism more than most, though not to the extent that many self-identified Marxists like to think. Still, as noted, it is fair to say that Marxism falls not only in the socialist tradition, but also in the tradition of revolutionary sects and movements; that Marxists are, or were, *revolutionary* socialists.

The kind of revolution they envisioned would not be undertaken directly in order to advance equality or diminish inequality. That outcome would be a (nearly) inevitable by-product of efforts to transform underlying property relations. Even so, one way to answer the "how is this to be done?" question would be to say: by revolution. A better way would be to change the question. It would be better to ask how to transform property relations in ways that would reduce inequality.

One answer could be: do it through the ordinary workings of the political system. But, in the face of ruling-class resistance, this will rarely be a feasible option. For this reason—and because, ultimately, the aim is not just to change "the economic base," but also the superstructural institutions and forms of consciousness that depend upon it—the most effective, and often the only, way to get from here to there is by "expropriating the expropriators"; in other words, by social revolution.

Natural Resources

There are Marxist theories of many things that Marx himself, and his closest followers, never expressly discussed, but the questions posed under this heading are not among them.

For one thing, Marx and his most "orthodox" followers were creatures of a moment in history in which hardly anyone, including liberals, paid much attention to issues pertaining to the ownership and distribution of natural resources, as distinct from resources generally. For another, insofar as there are Marxist views about how resources of all kinds should be owned, they pertain to (small-c) communism and to socialism, its earliest phase. Because Marx and Marxists were intent on not providing "recipes for the cook shops of the future," but instead on waiting for socialist and then communist men and women to find their own ways democratically, through collective deliberation and by undertaking experiments in living, such Marxist views as there may be were never elaborated or developed.

This much is clear, however: under socialism, natural resources would be owned (and therefore controlled) by the state; this would end under communism, because the state would by then have "withered away," "the governance of men," as Engels called it, giving way to "the administration of things." Exactly what that means, however, is far from clear.

For Marxists, as for most socialists, nearly everything that could be owned privately, including natural resources, would be owned collectively—though, again, it is not clear what this would involve, once the state is out of the picture. Presumably, exceptions would be made for small "personal" holdings, but even this is not clear. Inasmuch as there is nothing special about nature, or at least nothing that would lead to special ethical requirements, it would be fair to say that whatever the situation might be with respect to ceilings and floors for personal property generally, it would apply to plots of land as well as to tables and toothbrushes.

There could be Marxist, or Marxist-inflected, discussions of, for example, versions of liberalism like John Locke's, in which notions of natural-resource ownership play a role; and there are, of course, ample, sometimes scrupulously insightful, accounts of property relations and, therefore, of natural-resource ownership, in non-socialist (or communist) societies. Normative discussions are another matter, however. Marxists have nothing distinctively Marxist to say about normative questions, or nothing to say at all—not just because Marx and Marxists took no interest in these matters, but also because they had principled objections to doing so.

There is, therefore, no good way to tease out Marxist answers to stand in for the ones that the tradition doesn't provide. This is another consequence of the fact that, unlike liberalism and unlike traditions grounded in the several world religions, Marxism is not, and never has been, a full-fledged "comprehensive doctrine" in the Rawlsian sense; its worldview is too narrowly focused for that, and its distinctive theories don't bear on many of the issues Ethikon is asking about.

There is not much to say, either, about Marxist views on natural resources that can be gleaned from reflecting on the vicissitudes of self-identified Marxist political projects. The environmental policies of the Soviet Union and its Eastern European allies, and of China, were dreadful, and it would not be unfair to ascribe some of the blame for this to Marxist views about the importance of developing "productive forces." But, then, all theories of development, including anti-Marxist ones, were similarly tolerant of environmental depredations. On the other hand, Marxists in the West were, on the whole, as environmentally conscious as anyone else. But because Marxism started to fade from the political scene around the time that environmental concerns were beginning to register in the dominant (liberal) political culture, nothing much came of it.

Nowadays, there is a large and growing environmentalist literature that is more or less explicitly anti-capitalist, and that is at least partly shaped by historical ties and conceptual affinities with longstanding Marxist political currents. But for much the same reason that a report on Jewish views would go astray were it to focus on positions taken by militants in the Workmen's Circle (*der Arbeiter Ring*), or a report on Christian positions based on the thinking of (atheistic or agnostic) Unitarians or socially conscious Quakers would be misleading, the linkages are too attenuated, and often too idiosyncratic, to warrant inclusion in a report on Marxist views.

Products

What holds for natural resources holds as well for products, "things that people make or cause to be." But there are important differences, because while Marx and Marxists had little, if anything, to say about natural resources, they had a great deal to say about "use values"—socially useful objects of labor. Use values and exchange values (that regulate the exchange of use values) play crucial roles in what was perhaps the central theoretical project of Marx's life from the 1850s on: developing a critique of "classical political economy," the economic doctrines and theories of late-eighteenth- and early-to-mid-nineteenth-century political economists. "Critique" here means criticism, but also, as in "classical German philosophy," an account of the conditions for its possibility.

The classical economists tried to explain economic growth, what Adam Smith called "the wealth of nations," in private-property regimes coordinated through market arrangements. Marx took issue with their several accounts of profit, the share of national wealth going to capitalists, the owners of means of production—as distinct from wages, the share going to workers, and rents, the share going to owners of land and other non-reproducible assets. It was in this context that he developed the theories of surplus value and exploitation, for which Marxist economics is mainly known.

Thanks to the work of Marxist economists and others from the late 1950s on, we know that there is no compelling theoretical reason for focusing, as Marx did, on the exploitation of labor. On Marx's account, the "surplus value" workers produce, the value in excess of what is needed to reproduce their "labor power," is appropriated by capitalists, the owners of the means of production with which workers labor. It can be shown, according to the most exacting contemporary standards, that Marx's account is sound. However, it can also be shown that the reasons for continuing to uphold the canonical formulations are political, not theoretical—because it is possible, with equal cogency, to view economic growth as a consequence of the "exploitation" of any productive factor. The reasons for focusing on labor, then, are driven by political concerns: Marxists focus on the exploitation of labor because they are on the side of the working class. Strictly speaking, this is not a "value judgment" in the positivist sense; it is an implication of a view of history according to which an empowered working class is the bearer of post-capitalist social relations.

As remarked, scientific socialists eschew value judgments altogether. But, in practice, they really don't, at least not in a consistent way. Why, for example, would Marx have spoken of "exploitation," if he did not intend to suggest that there is something normatively objectionable about the situation the word denotes? Analytically inclined philosophers and economists working on Marx pondered questions such as these decades ago; so, too, less conspicuously, did some leading Western Marxists from the 1920s on. The problem is not intractable, but the issue is not easily dismissed.

I would note, finally, that there is at least a superficial similarity between popular understandings of exploitation in the Marxist sense and the kinds of intuitions about self-ownership and labor's role in establishing property rights that neo-Lockean liberals—libertarians of the Nozick type—weave into justifications for (virtually) unlimited private property rights (in external things, not in other persons' bodies or powers). In the neo-Lockean view, it is wrong when the state "takes" property that individuals have justly acquired, even if it does so for morally defensible reasons. In the popular Marxist view, a similar harm is done when workers are exploited (taken unfair advantage of) by capitalists appropriating the surplus value they produce. Consistent scientific socialists would say, of course, that there is no (normative) harm done in this case. But when the issue is the appropriation of surplus value, even orthodox Marxists were usually inclined to lighten up a little on the scientific socialist side. Ralph Waldo Emerson got it right when he pointed out that "a foolish consistency is the hobgoblin of little minds."

Wealth and Income

How rich must someone be to count as wealthy? There is no Marxist position on that; there are only the usual norms and understandings, confused and contradictory as they may be, that Marxists and non-Marxists share.

For a scientific socialist, there is and can be no trans-historical moral justification for privately held wealth; there are only justifications specific to prevailing modes of production. But because Marxists are socialists and therefore members in good standing of an egalitarian political culture, they would nevertheless tend to think ill of the rich, and to be suspicious of "philanthropists," especially the kind who donate to institutions that help reproduce existing social relations. On the other hand, no Marxist, especially in these dark times, would gainsay philanthropic efforts aimed at enhancing the capacities of workers and others to create Left alternatives within capitalism or, better still, to overthrow capitalism itself.

Marxists *qua* Marxists have no theory-driven views about how wealth is used. Insofar as individual Marxists have opinions about these matters, they would generally be of a piece with those that prevail in the larger society. However, the larger society is not of one mind. Even in circles that celebrate the rich and famous, opinions about wealth acquired through "nonproductive financial transactions" and inheritance vary. It would be fair to expect most Marxists, along with most socialists and egalitarian liberals, to regard the idle and/or unproductive rich with contempt. But there is nothing inherent in Marxist theory or in a broadly Marxist worldview that is not shared with other strands of thought that undergirds these sentiments.

If there were, Marxists would be obliged to oppose unconditional basic-income grants—because they go to everyone, regardless of what they do. This is what distinguishes them from other forms of state-funded and state-administered financial support to individuals; it is what makes a basic-income system an alternative to the welfare state. Unless the conditions for receiving grants are extremely permissive, conditional basic-income grants would just be a kind of welfare entitlement. The theory behind unconditional basic-income grants—above all, the idea that revenue-yielding natural resources should be owned in common—had defenders among early-socialist and proto-socialist thinkers in the eighteenth and nineteenth centuries. But the idea itself is fairly recent. And while it has been championed by a few theorists associated with the Marxist tradition, it has never been actively embraced within that tradition. There are at least two reasons why: for one, by the time the idea came to fruition, hardly anyone still unabashedly identified with Marxism; for another, Marxist political movements have always been wedded to the idea that the way to get from here (capitalism) to there (communism) is through socialism. That commitment need not conflict with proposals to establish basic-income grants, though, in practice, it pulls in another direction.

In principle, socialist societies could provide unconditional basic income instead of or in conjunction with other forms of non-market income transfers, including those associated with the welfare state. But one of the principal reasons for supporting basic-income grants is that, being unconditional, they would not give rise to many of the problems that welfare-state provision does; they would not be subject to bureaucratic snafus, they would not stigmatize recipients, and they would not impose views about how individuals ought to live.

Welfare-state institutions were concocted to mitigate the savage inequalities capitalist markets inevitably generate—not just by relieving poverty, but also, mainly, by providing insurance against life's inevitable and accidental vicissitudes. Robust welfare-state institutions can give capitalism a human face. Socialist societies rely on them, too—not so much to humanize the system (socialist systems need less humanization), but simply to socialize life's burdens and distribute its blessings in a fairer and more equitable way. In this sense, socialist societies have welfare states, too.

Could (small-c) communists dispense with socialism, communism's first phase? Marx and Marxists thought not. But then they weren't thinking about unconditional basic-income grants large enough to free persons from the clutches of the cash nexus, leaving them free not to undertake remunerative employment, should they so choose. With everyone assured of large enough grants, people could cooperate with one another or not, based on their preferences for consumption and leisure, not on the need to maintain a minimally decent standard of life. Basic-income grants could open up a capitalist road to (small-c) communism. The problem, though, would be to find the money to pay for it all.

Grants large enough to move humankind to a (small-c) communist future would, of course, have high floors. Low ceilings are another matter. There is no word in the political lexicon that describes capitalist roads to communism. *Socialist* won't do, and neither, of course, would *Marxist*. But "basic-income communists," let's call them, and socialists, including Marxists, are cut from the same cloth; they share the same values and envision the same historical objectives. The difference is that basic-income communists would have no reason to prohibit individuals from engaging in capitalist acts—unless, of course, their doing so would block or derail the larger emancipatory project to which they, along with Marxists and other socialists, have dedicated themselves. Individuals could choose to be as entrepreneurial and even mercenary as they please, just as they could choose to be as idle as they please. There is, therefore, no way to say how high or low the ceiling would be; it would depend on the consequences of what genuinely free individuals would choose to do in the circumstances they confront.

Doctrinaire (small-d) democrats might object, because democratic collective choice would play no role in determining the ceiling's height. Doctrinaire egalitarians might object, too, because the size of the gap between the floor and the ceiling, being dependent on individuals' choices, could result in outcomes in which income and wealth are unequally distributed. But this might not much matter to many egalitarians, because, with the floor as high as feasible, egalitarian (or quasi-egalitarian) ideals that privilege sufficiency over strict equality would be easily realized, and it might then seem that demands for yet more equality would be merely gratuitous.

Employment

The prescriptive views of Marx and Marxists with respect to wage levels pertain to socialism ("to each according to productive contribution") and to communism ("to each according to need"); with regard to wage levels in capitalist economies, they had nothing to say. Neither did they have anything prescriptive to say about other issues that bear on employment. Why would they? Even if, contrary to what they thought about themselves, they implicitly did endorse trans-historical ethical standards, the last thing that they would have wanted to do was to help policy-makers smooth over capitalism's rough edges.

On the other hand, as (descriptive) political economists, they had a great deal to say—based on the critique of political economy that Marx undertook. As proponents of a labor theory of value, they deemed the value of labor—or, rather, of "labor power"—equal to the value of the goods and services necessary to reproduce it. They then went on to describe and account for the many ways that the price labor fetches—i.e., actual wages—deviates from labor power's value.

Of course, Marx and the Marxists sided with workers engaged in struggles for higher wages and shorter hours; and, in his masterwork, *Das Capital*, Marx chronicled those efforts in ways that complement the economic analyses he provided. Marxists saw themselves as integral, indeed leading, parts of the broader labor movement that industrialization had brought into being and that capitalist development simultaneously encouraged and constrained.

However, they were also creatures of their time and place. In an era in which prevailing norms dictated a sexual division of labor, in which male heads of households were providers, while women worked without additional compensation at home, workers struggled for family wages; therefore, Marxists did, too.

In the twenty-first century, executive salaries and bonuses and other forms of compensation, in the United States especially, are obscenely out of line with workers' incomes. Also, women earn less than men, and factors such as race and age affect compensation levels and conditions of employment. Marxists deplore these injustices; but, again, not for distinctively Marxist reasons. Higher pay based on seniority or educational levels is another story; this is something workers have long fought for, and that all but the most ardent egalitarians—those who would flatten all wage differences ("equal pay for work," not just equal work)—find unobjectionable.

Marxists also have nothing distinctive to say about compensation for work performed outside labor markets in capitalist societies—for the work that homemakers do, for example. Where there are family wages, and stable families, the issue would seldom arise; this was the situation, for the most part, throughout the hundred years or so that Marxist political movements flourished.

Socialists of many stripes, Marxist and otherwise, have long called for the involvement of workers in economic decision-making—for self-management, workers' control, and so on. (Small-d) democratic Marxists tend to support such efforts. However, not all Marxists are (small-d) democrats. Indeed, in the days when the Soviet Union and later China were points of reference for nearly all Marxist political parties and movements, the prevailing attitude was more *dirigiste* than democratic. There is a case to be made to the effect that Marxists ought to be (small-d) democrats, that there are elements of Marxist theory that point in this direction. But there are too many counter-examples to assert this unequivocally.

Taxation

As socialists, Marxists would rather fund the state and/or institutions involved in "the administration of things" at the source, rather than by income taxes. But where this isn't feasible, or when it is otherwise undesirable, they have no principled objection to obtaining revenues through taxation, as political authorities have been doing from time immemorial. Similarly, while Marxists would prefer to cut off inequality at its sources

—in market transactions and gifting—they would not object to using the tax system to redistribute income and wealth in egalitarian ways. Whether and to what extent Marxists would actually want to do so depends on practical, not moral, considerations.

In capitalist societies, the Left favors government-organized redistributive measures of many kinds, including redistributive taxation. As part of the broader Left, Marxist political parties could usually be counted on to go along, and therefore to favor progressive over flat rate or regressive tax schedules.

Were there ongoing efforts to make tax assessments proportional to an individual's or institution's utilization of socially provided goods and services, Marxists and other socialists would likely object on the grounds that doing so would diminish social solidarities. In principle, though, other considerations could be more persuasive—when, for example, there is no other feasible way to provide necessary public goods.

Nobody likes to be taxed, but taxation is a necessary evil—without it, governments would be unable to do anything at all. Debates over taxes are, therefore, about how much and what kinds of taxes there should be. There are no distinctively Marxist positions on these matters, except perhaps in cases in which the tax system can help to foster social solidarities— for example, by raising funds for educating children, regardless of whose children they are. Then Marxists, along with other socialists and egalitarian liberals, would have a reason to think of taxation as a positive good.

Conclusion

Insofar as Marxists are scientific socialists, they are amoralists. They do believe, of course, that Marxist theory helps explain how inequalities of various kinds are generated and sustained. But the accounts it provides are, in positivist terms, descriptive, not normative. However, inasmuch as they cannot help falling, at least to some extent, into the utopian socialist camp, the positions they endorse and the attitudes they evince are hardly unique. They are of a piece with those of non-Marxist socialists and others in the broader Left.

The questions Ethikon has posed pertain, for the most part, to ongoing debates within the broad ambit of liberal theory and practice. Self-identified Marxists take, or have taken, positions that cluster around the

Leftmost poles in those debates, but for reasons that have more to do with history and politics than doctrinal commitments.

And while some individuals who have identified with Marx and Marxism have contributed substantially to ongoing discussions about inequality and morality, as those notions bear on Ethikon's questions, it is fair to say that, strictly speaking, there really is no distinctively Marxist purchase on these issues at all.

Feminism

FEMINIST PERSPECTIVES ON ECONOMIC JUSTICE

CHRISTINE DI STEFANO

Introduction

Considered as a tradition with a worldview, feminism may be regarded broadly as a critical contestation directed against a variety of co-implicated injustices that affect women and girls, resulting in gender inequity. Gender inequity is displayed in numerous measures of power, social standing, and material well-being, including political representation, leadership and participation in major social institutions, educational attainment, income, wealth, bodily integrity and safety, health (physical and mental), and cultural representations. Feminism is guided by shared commitments to normative equality and dignity, political inclusion, practical freedom and material (as well as spiritual) well-being for women, as well as recognition for their standing as valued (rather than second-class) members of their societies. Economic inequality is a contemporary fact of life for women worldwide, and a core component of gender inequity. Thus, economic justice figures as a prominent issue for contemporary feminism.

As Carole Pateman has argued, the critical contestation of "men's government of women" is a core aspect of feminism.[1] I have suggested

that feminism is also characterized by a commitment to the empowerment of women, and relative not only to men and patriarchal power but
to other structures and mechanisms of power, domination, and oppression, including racism, homophobia and heterosexism, colonialism, and
class stratification.[2] Other major elements of the tradition's worldview include contributions from (or affinities with) classical liberalism, Marxism,
social feminism, democratic theory, critical theory, and, more recently,
care ethics. Classical liberalism supplies feminism with a number of core
concepts, including individualism, normative equality, the right of free
contract, and the importance of freedom. Marxism draws attention to the
significance (and plight) of labor, divisions of labor, and exploitation, especially within the context of capitalism. Social feminism, with affinities to
republican theory, engages with women as (under-acknowledged, yet vital)
contributors to the relational network of civil society. Democratic theory,
with its emphasis on participation in politics and representation in institutions, not only encouraged women to agitate for the right to vote, but also
helped feminists bring attention to autocratic patriarchal decision-making
within the institution of the family. Critical theory, with an avowed genea-
logical connection to Hegel as well as Marx, encourages attention to issues
of "recognition" as well as "distribution." And care ethics, a distinctively
feminist contribution to the literature on morality, proposes to situate relationships of caring for and being cared for at the heart of ethical inquiry.

The normative goal of feminism is gender equity. However, different
historical and regional contexts, as well as differences among the life circumstances of contemporaneous women living in the same societies, have
made it challenging and very often counter-productive for feminists to
come up with uniform recommendations that will address the needs of
differently situated women. As a result, contemporary feminist investiga-
tions and interventions have increasingly focused on contexts. The concept
of "intersectionality" draws attention to the fact that women (as well as
men and those who refuse to be defined by binary gender categories) are
embedded in and constituted by multiple axes of power, including race,
ethnicity, sexuality, ability, nation, and religion, along with gender.[3]

In comparison to the other traditions discussed in this volume, feminism is younger, less embedded in an established canonical tradition, and
mostly secular in orientation. The historical emergence of feminism, like
that of Marxism, is closely bound up with key developments in the mid-

nineteenth century, especially industrial capitalism and democratic revolutions.[4] But feminism has no single intellectual founder like Karl Marx or core canonical text like the Old Testament. And while some feminists have emerged from religious traditions, feminism on its own does not supply a theological worldview. Because most traditions of thought have not devoted sustained attention to women's welfare and well-being, feminists have been forced to "think outside of the box." As a result, they are inclined to borrow from diverse traditions, to create hybrid theories, and to be inventive.

Among the traditions discussed in this volume, feminism has been shaped to a significant extent by liberal and Marxist influences. For many decades, feminists who were dissatisfied with liberalism (and especially critical of capitalism) borrowed from Marxism.[5] More recently, care ethics has emerged as an alternative or supplement to the liberal ethic of justice. The contrast between these two ethical discourses is well-stated by Virginia Held:

> An ethic of justice focuses on questions of fairness, equality, individual rights, abstract principles, and the consistent application of them. An ethic of care focuses on attentiveness, trust, responsiveness to need, narrative nuance, and cultivating caring relations. Whereas an ethic of justice seeks a fair solution between competing individual interests and rights, an ethic of care sees the interests of carers and cared-for as importantly intertwined rather than as simply competing. Whereas justice protects equality and freedom, care fosters social bonds and cooperation.[6]

Care ethics has become increasingly influential in feminist discourse on matters of economic inequality. Whether or not care ethics should supplant the liberal ethic of justice or supplement it remains an open question.

This chapter will begin with a brief discussion of the sexual division of labor and women's disproportionate responsibility for the care of dependents as well as those who imagine themselves to be independent. Proceeding to a discussion of specific topics proposed by the editors—equality, property, natural resources, products, wealth and income, employment, taxation—we will explore some of the distinctive feminist contributions to these.

For the most part, I will refrain from using labels, with two exceptions. Care ethics and the capabilities approach offer *systematic* and *distinctive* theoretical approaches to feminist engagements with economic inequality. Furthermore, each of these approaches has been developed by feminists and with feminist purposes (among others) in mind. Readers may also be interested to know that two of the authors frequently cited in this chapter, Nancy Fraser and Iris Marion Young, claim sympathetic alliance with the project of socialism. In their case, however, that alliance does not exhaust or completely account for their distinctive theoretical contributions. The same could be said for Susan Moller Okin, who worked within the political-theoretical frame of liberalism and pushed it much farther than many thought it could go. Martha Nussbaum, who has played a key role in developing the capabilities approach, proclaims her affinity with liberalism and also quotes the young Marx in several of her books. Labeling her a liberal feminist does not do much to advance appreciation for, as well as criticism of, her work. Thus, labels are to be avoided, unless they are actually helpful.

Finally, I would note that this chapter offers a *selective* account of feminist perspectives on economic inequality. On the one hand, feminist thought is not always or exclusively concerned with economic issues. Thus, many other aspects of feminism will not be discussed in this chapter. On the other hand, economic justice has figured as a key concern for many feminists, and especially as a result of the emergence and consolidation of capitalist economies. The historical record offers rich documentation of women's critical and proactive engagement with the economic and social dislocations of industrial capitalism, particularly as these impacted women and children. During the early twentieth century, Marxist women activists in Europe and Russia, as well as Progressive-era social feminists in the United States, devoted considerable attention to improving the economic prospects for women in their societies. Today, in the context of globalization and neoliberalism, women and feminists in nearly all regions of the world are grappling with their implications. A single chapter in an edited volume cannot do justice to the historical record or contemporary panorama of feminist engagement with economic inequality. Thus, I hope that readers will treat this chapter as an invitation to delve more deeply into the topic.

Feminism, more than any other tradition of thought, has brought the sexual division of labor to public and critical scrutiny. Iris Marion Young provides a very useful explanation of what she calls "a structural account of the sexual division of labor":

It is a theoretical framework that asks whether there are tasks and occupations usually performed by members of one sex or the other, and/or whether the social norms and cultural products of the society tend to represent certain tasks or occupations as more appropriately performed by members of one sex or the other. For any society, both today and in the past, the answer is usually yes, but there is nevertheless considerable variation among them in *which* occupations are sex-associated, the ideologies often legitimating these associations, how many tasks are sex-typed, and what implications this sexual division of labor has for the distribution of resources among persons, their relative status, and the constraints and opportunities that condition their lives.[7]

With respect to the vast majority of societies that delegate a disproportionate amount of responsibility for the care of vulnerable and dependent members of households to women, feminists locate this phenomenon within the sexual division of labor. Contemporary feminists argue that the gendered nature of care work is deeply implicated in women's economic inequality.[8]

What was previously thought to be "private" rather "public," unconnected to matters of economic concern and political deliberation, is now understood to be a cornerstone of the problem of economic inequality for many women. Furthermore, women's propensity for caring labor, along with their responsibility for it—what had been variously rendered as the result of personal and private choice, along with natural inclination and divine mandate—was recast by feminist analysis as the outcome of a combination of powerful and suspect factors, including patriarchal power, gender socialization, and limited opportunities in the labor market.

Women's disproportionate responsibility for care work is not only implicated in the fact that women become economically vulnerable as a result; it is also operative in the strange semantics of how labor is valued in the formal economy. "Feminized" labor, which connotes types of labor associated with the household (such as childcare, care for the infirm and elderly, house-cleaning services) is notoriously undervalued and poorly paid. Furthermore, when particular occupations have a significant proportion of female employees (regardless of the tasks performed), they also run the risk of becoming "feminized" (translation: paid less than they would be if they were not feminized) as a result of guilt-by-association-with-women. Another consequence of the sexual division of labor is that women with disproportionate household responsibilities for children, other dependents, and housework will find it difficult to keep up with the demands of full-time paid employment. The "disproportion" of their responsibilities has to do with the facts that their men tend not to step up to the plate and their societies are unwilling to fund public services that would take up some collective responsibility for the provision of care to dependents.[9] Many of these dynamics are now implicated in global patterns of labor supply chains, where immigrant women from poor countries are hired as nannies, maids, and sex workers in rich countries, and frequently without the rights and protections that are formally extended to labor.[10]

While feminist views on economic justice are certainly concerned with the distribution of resources and costs, they encompass other concerns as well. Feminist economics has worked to amplify conventional economic understandings of "resources" and "costs" by drawing attention to the existence of understudied informal and care economies, and by situating economic interactions in relation to the broader field of social and political dynamics and relationships.[11] Feminist inquiry has also taken issue with strictly distributive accounts of economic justice. For example, Iris Marion Young has argued that distributive accounts of justice deflect attention from the causes of mal-distribution and do not account for the full spectrum of injustice and inequity;[12] Nancy Fraser has distinguished a "politics of recognition" from a "politics of redistribution";[13] and Martha Nussbaum has proposed the capabilities approach as a preferred way of addressing what people need for a "decent quality of life."[14] In order to achieve a threshold level of human capabilities, she argues that some people may need "more" than others. Thus, unequal distributions of resources may be justified; and it is capabilities (what people are able to be and do) rather than what they have that gets to the heart of questions about economic justice.

At the risk of over-simplification, I would argue that the feminist tradition is more committed to gender-just outcomes than to presumably neutral or fair processes or procedures. Indeed, feminists are not especially sanguine about the "free" market.[15] At the same time, however, feminists have linked women's underrepresentation in political, economic, and social decision-making to economic outcomes that disadvantage women. Thus, the feminist tradition is inclined to endorse democratic decision-making at all levels of society, including household, community, regional, national, and international arenas, as well as places of employment.[16]

Equality

Equality between women and men figures prominently as a desideratum for feminism, and the distributive notion of equally shared costs and benefits is a key component of this conception. In particular, the feminist tradition of liberal democratic feminism has advocated for equal rights and opportunities for women.[17] But this tells only part of the story. While various forms of discrimination—in the domains of law, politics, education, and employment—clearly contribute to gender inequities, removing these hurdles may not be sufficient to achieve gender equity. Furthermore, discriminatory and unfair distributions of costs and benefits may accumulate over extensive periods of time, with deep-seated and far-reaching consequences for beneficiaries as well as losers. Thus, the feminist quest for equality has also directed attention to specific vulnerabilities incurred by women and girls, especially as these are shaped by sexual divisions of labor, legacies of colonialism, racism, dynamics of economic development, and processes of globalization. Such vulnerabilities are better addressed by calls for proportional, rather than strict, equality. Affirmative action policies would be an example.[18]

Most feminists regard the welfare state as a key component of economic justice for women. In particular, feminists have drawn critical attention to the inequitable distribution of costs and benefits in societies that rely on unpaid caring work within households (performed mostly by women) to shore up the economic productivity of labor, reproduce the next generation, and fill in for the deficiencies of societies that are not willing to take collective responsibility for the care of dependents. Although various efforts have been made to calculate the economic value of this unpaid labor—according to some estimates, "the total value of unpaid care and domestic work is equivalent to about a third to a half of most countries' GDP"[19]—the probability of coming up with a strict summary of costs and benefits is low to nil. Thus, while the ideal of equal distribution of costs and benefits inspires the feminist criticism of economic inequality, strict equality will not always be a requirement of feminist justice.

Feminist engagements with the modern welfare state—created to ameliorate economic vulnerabilities resulting from capitalism—have grappled with several outstanding questions: Should the resources of the welfare state be directed toward supporting the unpaid caring labor of women within households? Or should they be used to encourage women to enter the labor force?[20] Feminist scrutiny of the welfare state has also revealed problematic constructions of dependency as a feminized aberration from the masculine norm of independence, dubious and harmful distinctions between the deserving and undeserving poor, and collusion with patriarchal norms of citizenship.[21] Nevertheless, many feminists regard the demise of the welfare state as cause for concern.

Feminist concerns about the unequal social distribution of costs and benefits have also emerged in response to structural adjustment policies and austerity measures designed to drive down the amount of debt incurred by governments. Feminists have observed that these policies impact women in disproportional ways, by silently assuming that women will step in to make up for social-service deficits.[22]

In the domain of paid employment, strict equality is sometimes (but not always) easier to assert as a requirement of economic justice. "Equal pay for equal work" is now a legally and culturally enshrined principle of economic justice in many economies, although not always honored in practice. Nevertheless, gendered income-gaps persist, largely as a result of the fact that men and women do not participate in the same types of occupations. Feminized sectors of the labor market tend to be remunerated at lower rates. "Comparable worth" campaigns attempted to address the limitations of "equal pay for equal work," with mixed results.[23]

How, in general, should one determine which costs and benefits are ethically appropriate candidates for which type of equality? In general, feminists would say that legal and political rights should be regarded as candidates for equal distribution, whereas needs-based claims should aim for proportional equality, based on the notion of what is due to specific individuals and members of groups.[24] When justice calls for proportional equality, various factors and criteria may help to determine the fairness of those proportions, including need and social welfare.

From a feminist perspective, aptitude and productivity are suspect and imperfect criteria for determining the fairness of proportions. Ascribed talents (such as nimble fingers) have been used to typecast particular groups of women as ideal employees for tedious, boring, and low-paid work. Furthermore, negative aptitude has conventionally been invoked to explain why girls and women do not pursue studies in STEM-related fields or political careers. Feminists are suspicious of claims made about women's special aptitudes, and for good reason. Not only do these claims undermine norms of individual merit and worth, but they relegate women to a group with predetermined aptitudes that are rarely subject to serious etiological investigation. Furthermore, the feminine "aptitude" for care has been invoked to diminish its market value. When "care" is viewed as something that women are naturally fit to do, then market factors such as training and education are discounted in the evaluation of the market value of that labor. "Productivity" is suspect because it relies on market measures of social contribution. How should the "productivity" of an adult daughter caring for an aging parent with Alzheimer's be measured? Is "productivity" the appropriate measure of value in this case?[25]

While feminists are concerned about the discounting of unpaid caregivers' contributions to the economy and social welfare and would like to see these contributions acknowledged, they are also unwilling to harness entitlements to benefits exclusively to market measures of productivity and social contribution. On the one hand, feminists argue that care should not be regarded as a commodity. On the other, they maintain that all persons are entitled to having their basic needs for care met, regardless of their contributions to society.

The capabilities approach offers an appealing path for feminist efforts to pursue economic justice. By treating capabilities as fundamental entitlements and aiming for equality of capabilities among persons, this approach pursues the normative goal of equality via affirmative support for the development of capabilities. Equality is understood to reside not in "the space of resources" but rather in "the space of capabilities."[26] Accordingly, quality of life is assessed with respect to "what people are actually able to do and to be" rather than to the resources that they have. Of course, resources are important for the development of capabilities, but their comparative distribution does not suffice for an account and assessment of justice.

Property

Property has been—and continues to be—an issue of key importance and some controversy for feminists. Marxist legacies and socialist influences have cast suspicion on private property as a universal entitlement, viewing it instead as an invitation to exploitation and inequality. Within the frame of this critique, the distinction between personal property for use and modest income and private property that is used for the generation of wealth (in particular, capital) is important to keep in mind. Nevertheless, liberal influences in contemporary Western feminism have predominated, although feminists are not reluctant to explore socialized alternatives to certain types of private property, such as privately owned and administered health-care services. Feminists endorse the notion that women should have property rights on an equal basis with male members of their societies; they are also aware of the fact that equal rights to property do not necessarily translate into egalitarian patterns of property ownership. For example, in the United States, a major producer of agricultural goods, where women enjoy equal rights to property, they make up just 9 percent of agricultural landowners.[27]

Historically, women's rights to property have been fragile, especially for married women.[28] They remain so today, particularly in agrarian economies. Even in the absence of legal discrimination, female owners may not exercise actual control over their properties, and they may be pressured to cede their inheritance rights to male relatives. Bina Agarwal has argued that in rural economies, independent rights to ownership and control of arable land are key to narrowing "the gender gap in economic well-being, social status and empowerment."[29] What makes them key has everything to do with the fact that women are disadvantaged relative to men.[30]

It is interesting to note that Martha Nussbaum includes "being able to hold property (both land and movable goods), and having property rights on an equal basis with others" on her list of the central human capabilities.[31] For Nussbaum, property is associated with the material aspect of control over one's environment, which also includes the right to seek employment. While some feminists (including this one) might quarrel with Nussbaum's assumption that property rights in land should be universal, most would agree that specific property rights regimes should not discriminate against women. What Agarwal's analysis suggests is not that women everywhere should have command over property in land, but that they should have it when land is a vital resource for subsistence and economic development, and when its control is monopolized by men. An alternative scenario for land, which would be compatible with feminist aspirations as well as the capabilities approach, would be treating land as a common resource that should be used and shared equitably among prospective claimants, for some combination of private and public benefits. In contexts where land has become a scarce resource relative to population, being able to hold property in land may function as a license to exclude and exploit, or it might contribute to the creation of increasingly smaller parcels that are less productive or less conducive to the goal of privacy for resident-owners. In these cases, alternatives to individual ownership rights, such as group rights, should be explored and considered.

Feminism has not had much to say specifically about ceilings, floors, and ethically permissible gaps for property holdings, nor should we expect it to speak with one voice on these issues. Nor has it had much to contribute to the question of how morally required reductions in property holdings ought to be done. While Marxist feminists have not been shy about contesting the presumptive right to property, most other feminists have advanced agendas that, if taken seriously, would entail lowered ceilings and heightened floors. As a modest minimum contribution to these questions, feminists have suggested that democratic debate and decision-making should be key components of these decisional processes.

There is at least one type of property that has come up for vigorous debate among feminists, and that is the right to property in one's body. Feminists have been divided on the issue of prostitution, as well as surrogate mothering. While the right to property in one's body undergirds the liberal right to contract, it is also invoked to support the controversial claim that sexual and reproductive services for hire are legitimate. While many feminists support the decriminalization of prostitution (at least for sex workers, if not for their customers), others argue that sexual service should not be treated as a commodity.[32] In a similar vein, surrogate mothering, which involves contracting with a woman to carry a fetus to term for the benefit of an infertile couple, has generated a significant amount of heated conversation among feminists. The right to property in one's body (celebrated by founding liberal thinkers such as John Locke, and taken to be emblematic of a basic equality among contracting parties in the labor market), has been criticized by Marx as well as feminists by drawing attention to the background conditions of power relations. As Marx argued, "free" labor is free of all encumbrances: the free laborer has nothing to bring to market but his or her labor power. The worker must find an employer, or s/he will starve. In an analogous manner, some feminists draw attention to the conditions of unfreedom that attend women's decisions to provide sexual or reproductive services for payment. By contrast, other feminists have decided to hitch their wagon to the liberal notion of property in one's person. According to this logic, women have as much of a right to property in their person as do men. Capital's commodification of labor may be unfortunate, but to the extent that this logic rules, women should be as free as men to capitalize on their resources.

This de-sentimentalization of laboring activities, in the spirit of commodification, was also pursued by the feminist Wages for Housework campaign in the 1970s, which has been recently revisited by Kathi Weeks.[33] As she astutely observes, it would be a mistake to interpret this campaign— waged by Marxist feminists—as a serious bid for getting housewives on the state's payroll. Rather, the promise of commodification had far more to do with the openings that it created for women to refuse to do housework, to put some distance between themselves and the presumption that this kind of labor was natural.

Natural Resources

For many feminists, the just distribution of natural resources should be attuned to context-specific environments, practices, and needs. For example, women in rural South Asia depend on forests for subsistence, whereas women in the global North do not. In contexts where men enjoy ownership rights to natural resources, feminists would assert the same for women; or they might argue against the presumption of individual ownership rights to particular natural resources for all persons. In both cases, the logic would have to do with basic issues of fairness and equality.

Just distribution and ownership of natural resources such as arable land may also take group or communal as well as individual forms. For example, with the "feminization" of agriculture (as a result of male migration to urban employment centers), proposals for Public Land Banks address the needs of small-scale women farmers who do better with group-based access to land, credit, production inputs (such as fertilizer and seed), technology, and markets.[34]

In some cases, feminists would argue that the just distribution of natural resources is determined by residency. According to this logic, villages should be able to control natural resources within adjacent forests, and indigenous communities should have clear access and use rights to the natural resources on their reserved lands and adjacent waterways. In these cases, feminists would insist that the women of these residential groups should be involved in collective decision-making and represented in allocations of property and use rights.[35]

In parts of the world undergoing "development," and also as an aspect of globalization, the commodification of natural resources that were previously understood to be part of the commons, and in some cases controlled by women, has been contested by women activists. For example, Vandana Shiva has opposed corporate patents on seeds and indigenous Indian plants, coining the term "biopiracy" for the patenting of life.[36] In this example, certain natural resources are not justly amenable to private ownership. Shiva is also concerned about how local seed-saving activities and the indigenous knowledge with which they are bound up, typically engaged in and enjoyed by women, are being appropriated by corporations.

The "resource curse," as it affects resource-exporting countries, is also ripe for feminist assessment. As Scott Wisor argues, women are specifically and adversely affected by three classes of harm associated with natural-resource exports: civil conflict, authoritarian governments, and economic mismanagement (which includes lack of economic diversification).[37] Wisor proposes "making gender central to the assessment of justice by considering whether and to what extent the benefits and burdens of existing (and possible alternative candidate) resource regimes are distributed among men and women."[38]

A strand of feminism known as eco-feminism is especially germane to the topic of natural resources, although it should be noted that eco-feminism is controversial within feminist circles. The controversy centers on the perception that some eco-feminists claim that women enjoy a privileged relationship to nature, either as the result of their embeddedness in natural functions and processes (such as pregnancy), or as a result of their "naturalization" within narratives of humanism that privilege man's distance from, and domination of nature—and thus dehumanize women. While this criticism is sometimes warranted, it does not do justice to the full panoply of eco-feminist thought. Eco-feminism situates feminist theory and practice with respect to environmental and ecological concerns. Eco-feminists frequently criticize the instrumental assumption that nature should be viewed as an exploitable resource; they also draw attention to issues of sustainability. From eco-feminist perspectives, issues of distribution by no means exhaust the implications for justice of the human relationship to nature.[39] Eco-feminists are especially committed to thinking about non-dominative relations between humans and nature, and to undermining the presumptive divide between the two. In a related vein, it is interesting to note that Martha Nussbaum includes "being able to live with concern for and in relation to animals, plants, and the world of nature" as one of the ten central human capabilities.[40] Echoing the focus on relationships that has been elaborated most fully in feminist care ethics, eco-feminism and the capabilities approach urge us to think about nature as something other than brute matter.

While feminism on its own cannot offer a set of clear guidelines about the distribution of natural resources, their private ownership, and their fair apportionment, because so much depends on context, and because feminists draw on different traditions, feminist settlements on these questions will center on issues having to do with the balance of power and benefits between men and women, as well as women's specific needs.

Products

For feminism, norms for the just distribution of products do not differ substantially from norms applicable to other resources. Such norms include "fairness" in the sense of equitable access and distribution, "need," and "human flourishing." Let's begin with fairness. If men in the United States were permitted to purchase firearms, and women were not, feminists would see this as a problem, regardless of their views on gun control. In a related vein, when economic-development agencies make various products, such as tools and fertilizers, available to male farmers but not to female farmers, feminists see this as a problem. In an especially compelling real-world example, in economies where food is a scarce resource, when men (and sometimes boys) get the first crack at eating the household meal, in advance of women and girls (not an uncommon practice), they typically consume more than their fair share, leaving women and girls nutritionally deprived. Fairness directs our attention to inequitable patterns of distribution and access. The injustice of these inequitable patterns is amplified, however, when need is brought into the picture. Thus, women's need for firearms in the first example is debatable, except as a counterweight to their possession by men. In the second example, if development agencies have decided that farmers need their assistance, women farmers are as entitled to having their needs met as their male counterparts. The third example draws our attention to an especially urgent need, particularly in the context of scarcity. Human beings depend on food for their basic health and survival.

"Need" draws our attention to the specificity of human requirements for survival and well-being. These requirements may be universal or specific, and more or less urgent. For example, pregnant women have enhanced nutritional requirements, single parents (mostly women) with children need social support (including access to food and shelter, as well as child-care services), and people with physical disabilities need to be able to access the distributional networks of products (such as food markets) with the assistance of other products (such as wheelchairs). A notable specific need for women during their reproductive years is access to birth-control products, because they bear a disproportionate burden of labor and vulnerability for pregnancy and childbirth, as well as long-term responsibility for the care of their offspring. (Men also need access to birth control, but feminists would argue that this need is less urgent for them. Feminists would also applaud efforts to make birth-control products available to men.) A recent class-action lawsuit in the United States contests the sales tax leveled by several states on menstrual pads and tampons, arguing that these products are necessities for menstruating girls and women. In a related move, some school districts have decided to make these products available for free in schools with poor and low-income student populations. Follow-up research indicates that the absentee rate for female students in these schools has declined.[41]

"Flourishing" directs our attention to the notion of lives well-lived in the fullness of human capability and potentiality. Assuming that all human beings, including women, have equal rights to flourish (and not merely to survive), feminism draws our attention to the inequitable distribution of products that impacts women's prospects for realizing their potential. These include equal access to informational resources, such as books, newspapers, and the Internet (which presupposes literacy skills), as well as access to the products of culture and the arts. In conjunction with access to the products that are needed for survival and meeting specific-need requirements, the promise of access to information and culture has to do with inspiring women to regard themselves as dignified beings who are entitled to multidimensional, decent lives. The African American feminist Audre Lorde captured this sentiment very well when she asserted that "poetry is not a luxury."[42] For feminists, products that feed the spirit and enrich the sensibilities are no less important than products that sustain the body.

With the exception of luxury products, and bearing in mind that "luxury" is both context-specific as well as open to contestation, feminists would argue that everyone is justly entitled to products that serve human needs for survival and a "decent" (also context-specific) standard of living. Feminists drawing on the insights of the central human capabilities approach would argue that the distribution of products should aim for equalizing the capabilities, and this may mean that some people are entitled to different types as well as quantities of products. Feminists would also argue that enhanced modes and levels of human flourishing should be on the agenda of every society. When the amounts of products to which people have a just claim contribute to inequality in the meeting of basic human needs, the achievement of a "decent" standard of living, and levels of flourishing, feminists would support redistributive policies, the design and implementation of which should be pursued democratically.

Wealth and Income

Feminists have drawn critical attention to wealth and income disparities between men and women, as well as to women's disproportionate burden of poverty. They are committed to reducing and eliminating these disparities, and to proposing policies and practices that address the problem of poverty. Paying specific attention to poverty is important, because reducing gender disparities does not necessarily mean that women are doing better. In some cases, diminishing disparities are the result of a decline in the economic fortunes of men. Thus, equality on its own does not suffice as a measure of economic well-being for women.

While feminists are generally committed to the redistribution of wealth as a means of improving women's and children's life-chances, they do not speak with one voice on the extent of such redistribution. While some are committed to economic equalization as the desired result of redistribution, others tend to focus on the equalization of opportunities.

On its own, feminism has not contributed distinctive answers to specific questions about wealth, such as how much need-exceeding surplus qualifies an owner as "wealthy," or whether possession of wealth requires moral justification. Feminists who are interested in these questions typically draw on the resources of other traditions. In response to the argument that a philanthropic agenda provides adequate justification for the accumulation of wealth, feminists would be sensitive to the fact that philanthropic agenda-setting is dominated by wealthy men. While feminists might well be divided on the question of whether philanthropy justifies wealth, they would agree that male-dominated agenda-setting is a problem. Thus, in some of the wealthier countries, some feminists have devoted attention and resources to educating women of means about philanthropic endeavors, in an effort to get more women involved in the allocation of philanthropic resources.

Many feminists would argue that some defined portion of privately held wealth should be used for the benefit of those who are less well-off, and they would likely argue for a hierarchy of purposes, beginning with basic needs for food, shelter, medical care, and physical safety. Feminists would include maternal and reproductive health care and services, as well as rape-prevention programs, on the list of basic needs. Another set of purposes would involve various supports for the forms of care that are vital to the well-being of humans and their societies. Feminists of the care persuasion would draw attention to the needs of vulnerable dependents such as children, the elderly, the infirm and disabled, as well as the needs of their caretakers.[43] Education would closely follow the basic needs as an essential need, and feminists would be especially interested in the education of women and girls as a means of improving their prospects for employment, political participation, and autonomy. Feminists could also draw on the human capabilities list in order to argue that some portion of privately held wealth should be used for capability-building projects.

While feminism has not weighed in with one voice on the question of whether the savvy exploitation of non-productive financial transactions is a morally licit means for the acquisition of wealth, feminists would be quick to observe that this skill is disproportionately exercised by men, and that the financial rewards are disproportionately enjoyed by men. Feminists would also observe that these financial transactions and actors (who are democratically unaccountable to those who are affected by their actions) frequently harm specific populations and economies. In light of the evidence, feminists have two options before them. One is to equalize the playing field by encouraging women to develop their skills for this wealth-creating activity. The other option is to delegitimize this activity as a morally illicit means for the acquisition of wealth, or to insist on democratic mechanisms of oversight and accountability.

With respect to inheritance and similar types of transfer, feminists are faced with a comparable set of choices. In cultures where inheritance and similar types of transfer, especially among family members, are customary practices, feminists focus on ensuring that women enjoy the same rights as men, and that they have the means of enforcing these rights. Whether or not inheritance and similar types of transfer constitute ethically appropriate ways to dispose of and acquire wealth is a separate question. Feminists who are committed to socially egalitarian outcomes for all members of society will be more likely to criticize inheritance and similar types of transfer; they may support inheritance taxes, designed to lower the overall value of intergenerational wealth that is distributed to beneficiaries. Feminists who are committed to equalizing the power balance between men and women within the same class will focus instead on ensuring that women enjoy the same rights of inheritance as their brothers and husbands.

With respect to income, feminist attention to the idea of a basic guaranteed income has been gaining traction over the past two decades.[44] This is due, in part, to the demise of the welfare state, along with feminist concerns about how declining welfare entitlements for women are bound up with disciplinary regimes that mandate employment (typically elusive and low-paid) as a requirement for means-tested benefits. In addition, feminists have long been concerned with negative and frequently racialized stereotypes of welfare recipients—the single mother, in particular—as well as others who find themselves in situations of dependency. Feminists of the care persuasion have argued effectively that dependency should be figured as normal, rather than abnormal, condition; and that cultural celebrations of the independent citizen are implicated in the disingenuous denial of dependency as a fact of life. This denial is also operative in the invisibility and low estimation of the value of care work for dependents, which is disproportionately provided by women.

Thus, feminists are sympathetic to the claim that everyone has an unconditional claim in justice to a basic level of income. For example, Carole Pateman argues that "the logic of democracy: that citizenship is unconditional and that respect is owed because an individual is a citizen" (as expressed in universal suffrage) should be extended to the terrain of the living standards of citizens. "If the vote is essential for participation in collective self-government, then a decent standard of life is essential for individual self-government and participation in social life more generally."[45]

While feminists have not specified a maximum or ceiling beyond which individual income should not rise, they are not averse to using progressive income taxes as a means of redistributive leveling. Significant gaps between maximum and minimum levels of income are morally questionable for feminists for several reasons and under particular circumstances. For example, when the minimum levels of income are too low to support a decent standard of living, this is a problem, regardless of the breadth of the gap. In circumstances where the minimum levels of income are sufficient to ensure a decent standard of life (defined by Carole Pateman as "a standard sufficient to provide them with a meaningful degree of choice about how they live their lives and the ability to participate in social, cultural, economic, and political life to the extent they wish"),[46] income gaps may still be morally questionable, especially for democracies, if they contribute to power asymmetries. Feminists would be especially concerned in cases where these income-related power asymmetries map onto gender.

Employment

Employment has been a central concern for feminists, particularly in economies where the cash-nexus prevails. In those economies, when women are refused employment opportunities, or when their employment opportunities are sex-typed and low-paid, women are deprived of the means to lead independent lives. They become "dependents" of income-earners or, as a last resort, of the state.[47] When employment opportunities are insufficient to meet demand, and the welfare state has been dismantled, women become increasingly vulnerable to extreme poverty.[48] This accounts for growing feminist interest in the guaranteed basic income. At the same time, however, some feminists worry that it might encourage more women than men to opt out of labor-force participation and devote their energies to their households, thus preserving a sexual division of labor in the household that leaves employed men (presumably also beneficiaries of a guaranteed basic income) with more earned income than their female counterparts.

Feminists are inclined to argue that workers' compensation should be supported by a floor of some sort. This could take the form of a minimum or living wage, as well as a basic guaranteed income. Although feminists have been critical of the growing income gap within domestic economies and internationally, they have had less to say specifically about caps on individual earned income. An easier route to "capping" individual earned income would be via progressive tax policies.

Although there might be some room for dispute about whether the amounts of a just wage should be individual-based or family-based, most feminists today would argue that just wages should be paid to individuals. This is a significant departure from popular support for the family wage during the industrial era of capitalism, which assumed a household composed of male breadwinner, dependent housewife, and dependent children. As many feminists have observed, increasing rates of labor-force participation by women, declines in the stability of marriage, and other changes in the gender order have seriously undermined the family-wage ideal.[49] A family-based wage today raises issues of practicality and fairness for employers and employees, as well as unintended consequences for prospective employees. Would such a wage be paid universally to all employees, assuming that everyone is responsible for the support of dependents? If so, would this unfairly reward single employees with no dependents? In couples with two employed adults, would only one of them be entitled to the family wage? If so, how should this be decided? Furthermore, some feminists would be concerned that a family-based wage would privilege hetero-normative families to the exclusion of non-traditional households.[50] But the most important reason for feminists to support an individual-based wage has to do with the fact that—historically and worldwide—feminism has championed the notion that women should be regarded as individuals in their own right. Being regarded as individuals in their own right entails women's ability to earn just wages and salaries for their work, and maintain decision-making control over how that income will be spent.

While feminists are sensitive to the fact that employees have different needs, handicaps, and challenges, they would not be inclined to endorse the idea of differential compensation for the same productivity. It was precisely this kind of logic that justified paying women less than men in the same occupations, because women were presumably being supported by a male breadwinner, or looking forward to this in the future. Equal pay for equal or comparable work is a key principle for feminists. This statement of principle should not be taken to mean that "productivity" is simple to calculate or that methods of calculating it should not be periodically revisited.

Women make significant unpaid contributions to economies and societies. Feminists are divided on the question of whether or not this work should be compensated. The dilemma takes the following form: To the extent that much of this unpaid work is feminized within the structure of a sexual division of labor in households, compensating the people who perform this work (mostly women) preserves gender. But failing to recognize the value of this unpaid work perpetuates gendered patterns of economic inequality in the care economy, and may also contribute to its undervaluation in the formal economy.

Susan Moller Okin grappled with this dilemma and offered the following suggestion for dyadic households where one of the partners is employed and the other provides domestic services: *"equal legal entitlement* to all earnings coming into the household. The clearest and simplest way of doing this would be to have employers make out wage checks equally divided between the earner and the partner who provides all or most of his or her unpaid domestic services."[51] Okin's recommendations were a feminist intervention into the family wage, which she reluctantly recognized for partners (mostly women) who choose to provide unpaid domestic services. But her preferred path was a combination of equally shared domestic work by both partners, women's participation in the labor force, and social provision of domestic services in the formal economy and at places of employment. For Okin, it was individual access to and control over income, rather than employment per se, that was key to women's empowerment.

Ten years later, Eva Feder Kittay proposed "a payment for dependency work, which can be used to compensate a mother for her time caring for her child, or allow her to use the money to pay for daycare."[52] Kittay included other dependency workers in her call for universal compensation for dependency work, such as adults caring for their ailing parents. And she went on to specify that "the level of reciprocation, furthermore, must allow the dependency worker not only merely to survive, but to have the resources to care properly for the dependent as well as herself. This means considering what else a dependency worker requires: health coverage . . .; certain in-kind services or goods or monetary equivalent; and housing."[53]

Like Okin, Kittay argues that those who make unpaid contributions through work, not employment, should be compensated. But the terrain has shifted significantly, from domestic work in "the family" to "dependency work" in society.

It's important to note that not all feminists subscribe to the view that employment is the key to freedom for women in all circumstances. Feminist work on "the feminization of labor" in the "global assembly line" draws our attention to low pay, substandard and dangerous working conditions, and lack of job security and benefits, among many problems.[54] Feminists have also been critical of welfare-state reform policies that force women to find employment (typically menial and low-paid) in exchange for paltry welfare benefits. Recent feminist reflection about the pathologies of societies with strong and inflexible work ethics, and during a time in which full employment for all is receding as a realistic goal, encourages critical and creative forays into the notion of "getting a life" that is not primarily defined or dictated by "getting a job."[55]

Feminists are inclined to endorse what the American philosopher John Dewey called "democracy as a way of life."[56] Thus, they would support the idea that workers should have a role in the economic decision-making of entities that employ them. In addition to shared concerns with their "fellow" employees, feminists would bring gender-specific considerations to bear on workplace deliberations and decisions. For example: what might employers do to better attract and retain female employees? Should employers provide on-site child-care facilities? Should lounges be provided for employees who are breastfeeding? Would flextime arrangements make it easier for parents to coordinate their work schedules? Does the employer have a well-conceived and well-publicized policy on sexual harassment? Feminists might also draw attention to the suppliers of various products that are used at their place of employment. For example: where did these textiles come from? Who made them and what are their conditions of employment? By using this particular supplier, are we supporting unethical labor practices that harm women and children (and men)? Should we try to persuade this supplier to treat his workforce with more care? Should we be willing to pay higher prices for these goods, which might result in a lowered profit margin for our company?[57]

Taxation

Feminists tend—implicitly and explicitly—to support progressive taxation systems in order to redistribute costs and benefits in ways that will reduce economic inequality, as well as to offset necessary costs of necessary social institutions and their necessary services. In particular, feminists have proposed that taxes should be used to remunerate women (and men) for their unpaid labor on behalf of household and family members, to provide affordable and quality services such as childcare and elder care, to ensure that when people become vulnerable and dependent on the care of others they will receive the assistance that they need, and to provide a supportive floor for those who do not make enough income to be self-supportive. Feminists would also argue that many of these costs are necessary, that they are associated with necessary social institutions (such as families), and that the feminized labor of care is essential to the well-being of human beings, their communities, and societies.

Although feminists have often been forced to adopt pragmatic means and modest or "realistic" goals in their efforts to make societies more hospitable to women and girls, this does not mean that the moral standing of redistributional taxation is affected by its political feasibility. If political feasibility were a criterion of the moral standing of political demands, feminism would never have gotten off the ground. We should remember that national suffrage for women in the United States was politically unfeasible for many decades before passage of the Nineteenth Amendment in 1920, granting women the right to vote.

Should tax assessments be proportioned to a taxpayer's utilization of socially provided goods? In considering this question, feminists would urge us to pay attention to the kinds of goods involved, particularly social goods. Consider the case of an individual who does not intend to have any children. Should that individual be exempt from the portion of her property taxes that supports public education? Feminists (along with others) would be inclined to say that all taxpayers should contribute to the public school system, regardless of whether or not they utilize that good. The education of children is a social, not a private good, because societies depend on younger generations to become productive members and help support the older generations as they retire and require care. Feminists would argue that taxes may both properly exceed and fall below their utilization levels. Negative income taxes, endorsed by some feminists (along with others), offer a good example of the latter. On the other hand, feminists would not in principle be averse to taxes that are selectively imposed on those who utilize discretionary goods, such as luxury cars.

From a feminist perspective, the rationale for taxation is not limited to reimbursement for resources delivered by the state. Social interdependence, solidarity with those others with whom we share relationships, and care for and about the common good also furnish a compelling rationale for taxation. In recent years, feminists have also explored the global aspects of the responsibilities incurred by this rationale.[58]

Final Thoughts

Economic inequality is a key moral concern for feminists, because women are predictably and disproportionately disadvantaged by economic transactions and dynamics that extend from the domain of the household to the terrain of the global economy. In recent years, feminists have increasingly turned their attention to the transnational arena.[59] Feminist appreciation for interdependency as a key component of the human condition suggests that the effective pursuit of global economic justice will require a significant feminist presence.

Notes

1. Carole Pateman, "Feminism and the Varieties of Ethical Pluralism," in Richard Madsen and Tracy B. Strong, eds., *The Many and the One: Religious and Secular Perspectives on Ethical Pluralism in the Modern World* (Princeton, New Jersey: Princeton University Press, 2003), 301.

2. Christine Di Stefano, "Feminist Attitudes Toward Ethical Pluralism," in *The Many and the One*, 271–273.

3. See Brittney Cooper, "Intersectionality," in Lisa Disch and Mary Hawkesworth, eds., *The Oxford Handbook of Feminist Theory* (New York, New York: Oxford University Press, 2016), 385–406; and Ange-Marie Hancock, *Intersectionality: An Intellectual History* (Oxford, Great Britain: Oxford University Press, 2016).

4. See Estelle B. Freedman, *No Turning Back: The History of Feminism and the Future of Women* (New York, New York: Ballantine Books, 2002).

5. See Christine Di Stefano, "Liberalism and Its Feminist Critics," *Newsletter on Feminism and Philosophy*, American Philosophical Association, 88 (Spring 1989), 35–38; and "Marxist Feminism," in Michael Gibbons, ed., *Encyclopedia of Political Thought* (Hoboken, New Jersey: John Wiley & Sons, 2015).

6. Virginia Held, *The Ethics of Care: Personal, Political, and Global* (Oxford and New York: Oxford University Press, 2006), 15.

7. Iris Marion Young, "Lived Body vs. Gender," in *On Female Body Experience: "Throwing Like a Girl" and Other Essays* (New York, New York: Oxford University Press, 2005), 12–26, 23.

8. See Suzanne Bergeron, "Formal, Informal, and Care Economies," in *The Oxford Handbook of Feminist Theory*, 179–206; and Susan Himmelweit and Ania Plomien, "Feminist Perspectives on Care: Theory, Practice and Policy," in Mary Evans et al., eds., *The Sage Handbook of Feminist Theory* (London, Great Britain: Sage Publications, 2014), 446–464.

9. See Nancy Folbre, *Who Pays for the Kids? Gender and the Structures of Constraint* (New York, New York: Routledge, 1994).

10. See Drucilla K. Barker and Edith Kuiper, "Gender, Class and Location in the Global Economy," in *The Sage Handbook*, 500–513; Barbara Ehrenreich and Arlie Russell Hochschild, eds., *Global Woman: Nannies, Maids, and Sex Workers in the New Economy* (New York, New York: Henry Holt and Company, 2002).

11. See Maria S. Floro, "Integrating Gender in Economic Analysis," in *The Sage Handbook*, 413–430.

12. Iris Marion Young, *Justice and the Politics of Difference* (Princeton, New Jersey: Princeton University Press, 1990), especially chapter 1, "Displacing the Distributive Paradigm."

13. Nancy Fraser, "From Redistribution to Recognition? Dilemmas of Justice in a 'Postsocialist' Age," in *Justice Interruptus: Critical Reflections on the "Postsocialist" Condition* (New York, New York: Routledge, 1997), 11–39.

14. Martha C. Nussbaum, *Creating Capabilities: The Human Development Approach* (Cambridge, Massachusetts: Harvard University Press, 2011), 46.

15. See Marianne H. Marchand and Rocio del Carmen Osorno Velazques, "Markets/Marketization," in *The Oxford Handbook of Feminist Theory*, 428–453.

16. See Nancy Fraser, *Scales of Justice: Reimagining Political Space in a Globalizing World* (New York, New York: Columbia University Press, 2009); Joan C. Tronto, *Caring Democracy: Markets, Equality, and Justice* (New York, New York: New York University Press, 2013); and Iris Marion Young, *Inclusion and Democracy* (New York, New York: Oxford University Press, 2000).

17. See Anne Phillips, ed., *Feminism and Equality* (New York, New York: New York University Press, 1987).

18. See Iris Marion Young, "Affirmative Action and the Myth of Merit," in *Justice and the Politics of Difference*.

19. Susan Himmelweit and Ania Plomien in *The Sage Handbook*, 452.

20. See Nancy J. Hirschmann and Ulrike Liebert, eds., *Women and Welfare: Theory and Practice in the United States and Europe* (New Brunswick, New Jersey: Rutgers University Press, 2001).

21. See Eva Feder Kittay and Ellen K. Feder, eds., *The Subject of Care: Feminist Perspectives on Dependency* (Lanham, Maryland: Rowman and Littlefield, 2002); Carole Pateman, "The Patriarchal Welfare State," in Joan B. Landes, ed., *Feminism, the Public and the Private* (Oxford, Great Britain: Oxford University Press, 1998), 241–274.

22. See Elisabeth Klatzer and Christa Schlager, "Feminist Perspectives on Macroeconomics: Reconfiguration of Power Structures and Erosion of Gender Equality through the New Economic Governance Regime in the European Union," in *The Sage Handbook*, 483–499.

23. See Michael W. McCann, *Rights at Work: Pay Equity Reform and the Politics of Legal Mobilization* (Chicago, Illinois: University of Chicago Press, 1994).

24. See Nancy Fraser, "Women, Welfare, and the Politics of Need Interpretation," and "Struggle Over Needs: Outline of a Socialist-Feminist Critical Theory of Late Capitalist Political Culture," in *Unruly Practices: Power, Discourse and Gender in Contemporary Social Theory* (Minneapolis: University of Minnesota Press, 1989); Julie Anne White, *Democracy, Justice, and the Welfare State* (University Park, Pennsylvania: The Pennsylvania State University Press, 2000); and Iris Marion Young, "Insurgency and the Welfare Capitalist Society," in *Justice and the Politics of Difference.*

25. For criticism of market modes of valuation, especially when they exercise hegemonic influence, see Virginia Held, *The Ethics of Care*, and Joan C. Tronto, *Caring Democracy.*

26. Martha C. Nussbaum, "Capabilities as Fundamental Entitlements: Sen and Social Justice," *Feminist Economics*, vol. 9, nos. 2–3, 2003, 33–59, 56.

27. See Joni Seager, *The Penguin Atlas of Women in the World*, 4th ed. (New York, New York: Penguin, 2009), 86–87.

28. For an especially good overview of the historical importance of marital regimes and inheritance regimes, as well as legislative limits on married women's property rights, see Carmen Diana Deere and Cheryl R. Doss, "The Gender Asset Gap: What Do We Know and Why Does It Matter?" *Feminist Economics* 12:12, 2006, 1–50.

29. Bina Agarwal, "Gender and Command Over Property: A Critical Gap in Economic Analysis and Policy in South Asia," *World Development*, vol. 22, no. 10, 1994, 1455–1478, 1455.

30. See Bina Agarwal, "'Bargaining' and Gender Relations Within and Beyond the Household," *Feminist Economics*, vol. 3, no. 1, 1997, 1–51.

31. Nussbaum, "Capabilities as Fundamental Entitlements," 42.

32. See Martha Nussbaum, "'Whether From Reason or Prejudice': Taking Money for Bodily Services," *Journal of Legal Studies*, vol. XXVII (January 1998),

693–724; and Carole Pateman, "What's Wrong with Prostitution?," *Women's Studies Quarterly*, vol. 27, no. 1/2 (Spring–Summer 1999), 53–64.

33. Kathi Weeks, *The Problem with Work: Feminism, Marxism, Antiwork Politics, and Postwork Imaginaries* (Durham, North Carolina: Duke University Press, 2011).

34. See Bina Agarwal, "Food Security, Productivity, and Gender Inequality," *The Oxford Handbook of Food, Politics, and Society*, Ronald J. Herring, ed., (Oxford, Great Britain: Oxford University Press, 2014), Oxford Handbooks Online (www.oxfordhandbooks.com).

35. See Bina Agarwal, "Gender and Forest Conservation: The Impact of Women's Participation in Community Forest Governance," *Ecological Economics* 68, 2009, 2785–2799.

36. Vandana Shiva, *Biopiracy: The Plunder of Nature and Knowledge* (Cambridge, Massachusetts: South End Press, 1997).

37. See Scott Wisor, "Gender Injustice and the Resource Curse: Feminist Assessment and Reform," in Alison M. Jaggar, ed., *Gender and Global Justice* (Malden, Massachusetts: Polity Press, 2014), 168–188.

38. Wisor, "Gender Injustice," 181.

39. See Lori Gruen and Carol J. Adams, eds., *Ecofeminism: Feminist Intersections with Other Animals and the Earth* (New York, New York: Bloomsbury Press, 2014); and Vandana Shiva, *Ecofeminism* (London, Great Britain: ZED Books, 1993).

40. Martha C. Nussbaum, *Creating Capabilities: The Human Development Approach* (Cambridge, Massachusetts: Harvard University Press, 2011), 34.

41. See Iris Marion Young, "Menstrual Meditations," in *On Female Body Experience* (New York, New York: Oxford University Press, 2005), 97–122.

42. Audre Lorde, "Poetry Is Not a Luxury," in *Sister Outsider: Essays and Speeches by Audre Lorde* (Berkeley, California: Crossing Press, 1984). In this essay, Lorde means not only the reading of poetry but also the writing of it.

43. See Eva Feder Kittay, *Love's Labor: Essays on Women, Equality, and Dependency* (New York, New York, and London, Great Britain: Routledge, 1999).

44. For additional information on basic guaranteed income, see Matthew C. Murray and Carole Pateman, eds., *Basic Income Worldwide: Horizons of Reform* (London, Great Britain: Palgrave Macmillan, 2012).

45. Carole Pateman, "Another Way Forward: Welfare, Social Reproduction, and a Basic Income," in Terrell Carver and Samuel A. Chambers, eds., *Carole Pateman: Democracy, Feminism, Welfare* (London, Great Britain: Routledge, 2011), 194.

46. Pateman, "Another Way Forward," 195.

47. See Nancy Fraser and Linda Gordon, "A Genealogy of 'Dependency': Tracing a Keyword of the U.S. Welfare State," in Fraser, *Justice Interruptus*.

48. See Kathryn J. Edin and H. Luke Shaefer, *$2.00 a Day: Living on Almost Nothing in America* (Boston, Massachusetts: Houghton Mifflin Harcourt, 2015).

49. See Nancy Fraser, "After the Family Wage: A Postindustrial Thought Experiment," in Fraser, *Justice Interruptus*, 41–66.

50. For a thoughtful critique of "the Family as defined through the institution of marriage," see Iris Marion Young, "Reflections on Families in the Age of Murphy Brown: On Gender, Justice, and Sexuality," in Christine Di Stefano and Nancy J. Hirschmann, eds., *Revisioning the Political: Feminist Reconstructions of Traditional Concepts in Western Political Theory* (Boulder, Colorado: Westview Press, 1996), 251–270.

51. Susan Moller Okin, *Justice, Gender, and the Family* (New York, New York: Basic Books, 1989), 180–181.

52. Kittay, *Love's Labor*, 142–143.

53. Kittay, *Love's Labor*, 143.

54. See Christine M. Koggel, "Globalization and Women's Paid Work: Expanding Freedom?" *Feminist Economics*, vol. 9, nos. 2–3, 2003, 163–183; and Mary Beth Mills, "Gendered Divisions of Labor," in *The Oxford Handbook of Feminist Theory*, 283–303.

55. See Weeks, *The Problem with Work*.

56. John Dewey, "Democracy and Educational Administration," *School and Society* 45 (April 3, 1937), 457–467.

57. For examples of feminist efforts to address moral responsibility for injustice at the international and global levels, see Onora O'Neill, "Justice, Gender and International Boundaries," *British Journal of Political Science*, vol. 20, no. 4 (October 1990), 439–459; Iris Marion Young, *Global Challenges: War, Self-Determination, and Responsibility for Justice* (Malden, Massachusetts: Polity Press, 2007), especially chapter 9, "Responsibility, Social Connection, and Global Labor Justice," 159–186.

58. See Gillian Brock, "Reforming Our Taxation Arrangements to Promote Global Gender Justice," in Alison M. Jaggar, ed., *Gender and Global Justice* (Malden, Massachusetts: Polity Press, 2014), 145–166.

59. See Alison M. Jaggar, "Transnational Cycles of Gendered Vulnerability: A Prologue to a Theory of Global Gender Justice," in Alison M. Jaggar, ed., *Gender and Global Justice* (Malden, Massachusetts: Polity Press, 2014), 18–39.

Natural Law

A NATURAL LAW PERSPECTIVE
ON ECONOMIC EQUALITY

JOSEPH BOYLE

Natural-law theory brings to the topic of economic justice two fundamental convictions: first, that humans have bonds of social unity and cooperation bearing on the most basic human concerns, widely recognizable as interests for all who share in human nature. Second, at the specifically ethical level, that prominent among the moral principles widely available to human intelligence is the exclusion of arbitrary preferences among persons—the principle of fairness often expressed in the Golden Rule.

The application of these convictions to the questions posed for this volume is carried out in the sections below. Most of the common questions are addressed roughly in the order presented. However, these sections are organized in accordance with the salience of topics within natural-law analyses. This salience often differs from that found in current discussions of economic equality, and so leads to some variations in the order of topics. This distinction in salience of diverse topics also affects the way some of the common questions are addressed. Some answers must remain general and suggestive, since the tradition itself is indeterminate, especially in cases it regards as details, or as legitimate policy matters, or as not settled by moral principle. Some questions require considerable construction from natural-law materials.

Before explaining the details of the natural-law conception of economic justice, it is necessary to provide a basic account of what natural law and the millennia of reflection upon it mean in terms that are commensurate with those of contemporary ethical and political discourse. This encompassing tradition of moral inquiry has numerous strands of debt, not least to Stoic philosophy and to a multitude of analyses adapted from Plato and Aristotle; it also shares many themes common to the Jewish, Christian, and Islamic religious traditions, by which it has been enriched and which it, in turn, has enriched, most notably in medieval and reformation Western European Christian theology and practice. This embarrassment of riches calls for clarification, which is the subject of section I. It introduces both the basic notions of natural law and the sources I will use, and the natural-law conception of justice.

Introduction

Natural Law: Idea and Sources

The law referred to in the expression "natural law" is a prescription, not a regularity. It is a prescription held to be "natural" in several senses. First, it is naturally available to human beings: basic moral knowledge is available to all who are capable of rational reflection, including that required for criticizing received customs, moral codes, and group and individual biases. The natural knowledge of such moral principle is widely available to humans because of the close connection between human nature and fundamental moral principles.

Explaining this connection has divided natural-law theorists over the centuries. On this issue and more generally I will rely on the classic work of Saint Thomas Aquinas (1224–1274), which contains both a full treatment of natural law and its relationship to other elements of moral life,. such as the virtues, including justice. Thomas's account of human nature and moral principle begins with basic human interests, basic human goods. Thomas situates moral principles in relation to this human good, particularly as that good presents itself in practical reflection about what to do.

The basic human good one seeks to realize in a given human action is pursued because one judges its realization by one's action to be desirable and so worth doing ("to be done and pursued"). Empowerments—such as property, wealth, and other instrumental goods—are also desirable, but derivatively so: they are desirable insofar as they contribute to realizing basic human goods or other things people take to be such. Instantiating basic goods can be instrumental but is not necessarily so; the goods ground the desirability of the goals that either instantiate basic human goods or contribute toward that. They ground desirability because they are the elements that comprise the full being of humans. In short, the value theory underlying natural-law theories inspired by Thomas is perfectionist and cognitivist. The goods are objects of practical knowledge; they correspond to the basic dimensions of the human person that can be protected, secured, and promoted by human action. Thomas's list of these basic goods—clearly indebted to Cicero's list of un-derived natural human interests—includes life, the union of man and woman, knowledge, community with others, and religion (*ST* [*Summa Theologiae*]1–2, q. 94, a. 2).[1]

The list suggests the essentially interpersonal character of several of the goods and the practical dependence on social cooperation for the pursuit of the others. The union of man and woman and social life, including friendship, are essentially interpersonal. Thus, when a person pursues these goods, the perfection he or she seeks is not individualistic but fulfillment precisely as a member of a community—for example, as a spouse, a team member, or friend. One cannot pursue goods thus defined without reference to the other parties involved. Sometimes the concern for the other party fails to be as it should be, to the detriment of the good, even without specifically moral assessment, as when one prefers personal benefit to the benefit of the group. This indicates that the concern for others in these interpersonal goods is neither an extrinsic moral side constraint nor merely a consideration instrumental to one's own interests otherwise specified.

Other goods, such as life, knowledge, and religion, do not contain in their very conception as goods reference to other persons. But life is both threatened and protected in the business of living with family members, neighbors, and others; and knowledge presupposes language, conversation, and cooperation, as does most religious activity. The human good, therefore, is inherently social. When individuals join with others in deliberating and choosing together to pursue some good, that good is common to their action. Often such goods are basic, as in marriage or in the collaboration on a research project. The expression "common good" in natural-law discourse refers to the good of any community thus established. The expression's unqualified use tends to be in respect to the common good of a political society, the defining responsibility of which is to organize a community by adopting law, just coordination of the interactions of the members of the community, and ensuring security.

The idea of common goods has a presupposition that is important for the theory of justice. The basic human goods are the objects of practical intelligence. That is to say, the goods are not desires or other motivations, nor are they instinctual judgments about some experienced or imagined event sufficient to trigger desire or aversion. They are intellectual judgments that some imaginable state of affairs is a member of a class of states of affairs, namely, one defined by features the possession of which constitutes some goal as good, as to be done. The content expressed by these features is connected to the particular agent and that agent's motivations through the agent's recognition that an action he or she can perform will bring about a state of affairs realizing that good. The good the agent seeks in action is, upon reflection, one he or she knows other human beings, alone or as community members, can also enjoy.

Natural Law and Justice

The theory of justice plainly requires more than a theory of the good; it also supposes an account of specifically moral principles. Natural-law theories are as cognitivist about moral principles as they are about the theory of the good. A shorthand formula common among natural-law theorists is that morality is the requirement of acting in accord with reason, or "right reason," or "rectified reason" (see *ST*, 1-2, 94, 4). However, given the account of practical reason that emerges from the idea of the basic human goods, it is not obvious what further practical task reason might have besides its delivering judgments about basic goods and how to realize them.

One natural-law answer to this begins by focusing on situations in which choice among options is called for. In such cases, the practical rationality involved in knowing basic human goods is not sufficient to settle what one will do, since within the alternatives calling for choice there often are several human goods or incommensurable aspects of goods in view, and all of them promise some genuine fulfillment but not all can be done. This situation raises the question of how the choice of one of the options of this kind is to be motivated. There clearly are factors motivating the preference of one alternative over another that are not simply the rational appeal of the goods at stake—for example, that this alternative is easier, pleasanter, less fearful, beneficial to those I identify with. Plainly, in choices having this sort of motivation, moral direction is called for. Isolating such non-rational factors and excluding their inappropriate influence on one's decision gives sense to the idea of right reason, or rectifying reason, that is, a rational consideration excluding any skewing of an assessment of one's options by motivational factors not integrated with practical reason.[2] In short, the basic principle of morality requires that agents be attentive to factors that can lead them to choose an option that, while sufficiently con-nected to one or more basic human goods to be a real option, are not integrated with a rational allegiance to the demands of goods, but instead skewed by non-rational considerations. There are a variety of such factors that can be exposed by reflecting on the various ways sensory motivations can lead to formulating practical judgments about what to do that are not reasonable.[3]

One such factor is that people "naturally," but not inevitably, favor themselves and those near and dear over others when options arise in which benefits and burdens fall differentially on these distinct groups. Sometimes there are good reasons for favoring oneself or those near and dear, but often there is only the bias of self-preference, which, if articulated, would challenge conscience, and if excluded from one's decision-making would lead to rejecting the self-favoring option.

Exposing and rejecting motivations that favor, without rational basis, oneself and those near and dear over outsiders is carried out by the various techniques of the Golden Rule, whether they be putting oneself in anoth-er's position, or taking an impartial or impersonal point of view, or uni-versalizing one's maxims.[4] Thomas does not use the expression "Golden Rule," but quotes two versions and notes in several places its position within the self-evident principles of morality (*ST* 1-2, q. 94, a. 4; q. 99, a. 1, ad. 3; cf q. 100, a. 3, ad. 2). Since partiality among persons is so deeply implicated in questions about fair distribution of such economic benefits as wealth, property, and income, considerations based on the kind of re-flection expressed in the Golden Rule are bound to be center-stage in any natural-law account of economic justice. Along with the common goods of the communities, which give human sense to their members' exchanges, distributions of goods, and of the costs of securing them, these considerations of fairness are fundamental.

Natural-law theory includes a developed account of the virtue of justice and its various applications to human interactions. Many of these do not concern transactions that are focally economic, for example, justice as it bears on the life and bodily integrity of others, on persons' good name, and on the conduct of legal proceedings. Moreover, I am not aware that "economic justice" is a category singled out in natural-law theorizing. Nevertheless, natural law has an express treatment of several topics central to economic justice, notably, the use of non-human things for human benefit, including their possession, and commercial transactions and taxes. I will focus on these areas.

Equality

According to the natural law, human beings have an essential equality insofar as they are human beings. The fact noted in this claim is that, in spite of the many and obvious differences among human individuals, all are members of this rational kind. The practical significance of this equality is adumbrated in the fact that the basic goods pursued by any human being or group are, and are seen to be, goods any other human being can pursue, and with whom any of us might cooperate in pursuing. Human beings outside a rationally cooperating community are not like the other things humans must deal with, since they have the potential to join the common rational action. One can, of course, treat outsiders as simple items to be used or otherwise to be dealt with. But any fair consideration of those outside one's circle of preferred people will exclude such treatment. Relationships with other humans are with beings like oneself in a practically essential respect; they share our capacity to participate and share with us in human goods, and so are beings to whom there can be a debt, something owed. In short, natural law supposes that this basic form of equality extends the moral reasons for the rights we demand for ourselves and for those we care about to the members of the human community just as such.[5] The equality invoked here does not settle what those moral reasons are; it extends them. The conception of equality of moral status among human beings is, plainly, controversial; and that controversy cannot be joined here.[6]

Within natural-law thinking, the equality of common membership in the human species and the possibilities for community that involves are taken to be necessary for justice to exist, and are likewise taken to be necessary for the obedience/authority relations so essential for social life to obtain. Equal human status provides a basis for a distinctive conception of what is involved in dealing with others: there is something to consider besides one's own interest—something that is the other's own, something that is due the other.

This way of understanding rational creatures as equal leads to the idea that important rights are natural to human beings as such, immunities such as the right not to be killed or enslaved, and the immunity from being denied benefits on grounds unconnected with either the activity generating the benefits or a fair distribution of the benefits themselves. Thus, for example, while ability is a fair consideration for hiring, race and religion usually violate human equality; and while contribution to a project is a fair consideration in distributing the benefits of the project, personal connection to the authority in charge is not normally such a consideration, and using it violates the human equality of others.

That said, assessing fair distributions requires further reflection besides the presupposed equality of human beings just as human. This formal equality of moral status ordinarily is not immediately in play, but presupposed, when questions of economic justice arise. The distribution of benefits and burdens within a community of cooperating people does require a fair consideration of the interests of all the parties. But that demand generally does not settle what constitutes a fair consideration.

Still, fair consideration implies a further reference to equality. This is suggested by Thomas's definition of justice: "the idea of justice consists in giving the other what he or she is owed as a matter of equality" (*ST* 2-2, q. 80, a. 1; q. 57, a.1; q. 58, a. 11). It becomes clear that Thomas does not mean this to imply strict equality of outcomes in cooperation or of equal well-being, as necessary or sufficient for determining what is due a person: "Now each man's own is that which is due to him according to equality of proportion" (*ST* 2-2, q. 58, a. 11). John Finnis suggests that "equilibrium" and "balance" capture the relevant idea of equality.[7]

In summary, there is a form of equality—closely related to formal equality, "treat similar cases similarly," etc.—that is invoked in the proposition that human beings as rational creatures have equal moral status. That form of equality is invoked when some natural rights, particularly rights not to be harmed, abused, or refused benefits or opportunities, are denied to some people on the supposition that their human status is somehow lower than that of others. In the context of economic justice, human equality is used to identify the other beings toward whom individuals and communities owe something. But this equality does not settle the balance, proportion, or equilibrium needed to assess what a person is due in matters of distributing the benefits and burdens of social cooperation.

As far as I know, natural law includes no closed list of factors whose balancing will determine the equality or equilibrium that defines the fairness or equality involved in distributing economic and related burdens and benefits. Contribution to the private or public initiatives involving burdens and benefits certainly generates a claim, as do some of the features of contributing, such as its extent, complexity, arduousness, or riskiness. Other forms of merit might be significant but often are irrelevant. Some distributions by private persons and government officials are for the sake of providing benefits to those in need. Here considerations related to need, to the capacity of the provider to help, and to any special moral bonds between those needing and giving help are relevant, and other factors generally are not. This does not imply that in some cases the proportion, balance, or equilibrium of factors relevant for assessing what is someone's due will wind up being a strictly equal division—as when a borrowed item must be returned in at least as good a condition as lent, or when the balance of factors indicates that an asset be divided equally among those with a claim on it.

To sum up this section: the natural-law approach to issues of economic justice is not egalitarian. The equality or proportion required for justice only incidentally leads to an equal distribution, since that equality is a function of a variety of context-based factors. Natural law condemns any rejection of a distribution on irrelevant grounds as violating equal human dignity.

That provides a limited, but stringent, form of equality of opportunity. More robust equality of opportunity is morally required in societies where the resources allow it.

Property, Natural Resources, and Products

The Natural Law Justification of Private Ownership

The natural-law justification of property is the basis for addressing the limits of legitimate property holding, including the low-end requirement that all should have some property. Natural law supposes that the goods of the earth—what Thomas calls "exterior things"—are naturally and reasonably used by humans for human benefit. The idea that using things is natural for human beings is literally and descriptively true: humans are animals and anything we do, however mental or spiritual, includes material events. Human actions alter the world; some of them appropriate bits of it as in eating or making things. Given the connection between human action and the physical world, the pursuit of basic human goods presupposes that humans make use of the physical environment. As a result, making use of the physical environment, having dominion over it and possession of it, is practically reasonable. There is no pursuit of good without it.[8]

Thomas's own focus in defending the natural character of using things is somewhat different: to show that their human possession and use is compatible with God's dominion over the universe and its parts. He does not explicitly address any possible independent claims of animals or other exterior things against human possession, but clearly supposes (citing Aristotle's *Politics*) that they exist for the sake of human benefit (*ST*, 2-2, q. 66, a. 1). Presumably, the binary character of the idea of equal dignity of humans as rational creatures (as created in the image and likeness of God) excludes animals from the moral status required for holding rights.

Exterior things include everything in the world that can be used by human beings for human benefit outside the persons and actions of human beings. Thus, real estate such as land; domestic animals; artifacts such as buildings, clothing, and tools; and the fruits of cultivation and natural resources are among the goods in question. Wealth as measured by money also falls among them, insofar as it is an empowerment for accessing other exterior things. What defines this class of realities is that its members are items of use for human benefit, not the extent to which they have been improved to that end.

The possession and use of exterior things that is shown both natural to humans and a rational necessity for pursuit of human goods is not the possession of any particular item by any particular person or group, but possession of external things by human beings. The underlying thoughts do not specify who has possession of what, and do not exclude any person from possessing some external things.

The further specification of possession into particular items owned by particular persons is not settled by these basic natural-law considerations. That specification is achieved by reasonable conventions required for the responsible and peaceful use of exterior things in the actual condition of humankind. The rationale for and the exact sense of dividing external things into items "proper to" or "owned by" someone provides the general basis for such conventions, and so also for criticizing any of their more particular determinations.

Thomas argues that without a division of goods into items over which some persons have authority and discretion there would arise, given the motivations of most people in the ("fallen") world as it is, a set of very nasty effects (*ST* 2-2, q. 66, a. 2):

> Moreover, this [for a human being to possess property] is neces-
> sary to human life for three reasons. First because every man is
> more careful to procure what is for himself alone than that which is
> common to many or to all, since each one would shirk the labor and
> leave to another that which concerns the community as happens
> when there is a great number of servants. Secondly, because human
> affairs are conducted in more orderly fashion if each is charged
> with taking care of some particular things himself, whereas there
> would be confusion if everyone had to look after any one thing in-
> determinately. Thirdly, because a more peaceful state is assured
> to man if each one is contented with his own. Hence it is to be ob-
> served that quarrels arise more frequently where there is no division
> of the things possessed.

Thomas does not detail the difficulties caused by the confusion noted in his second concern, but they seem to be either ineffectiveness in the use of the exterior thing in question or other things, or the quarrels to which the confusion might lead—the bad effects of his other stated concerns. He seems to have thought, therefore, that, without dividing exterior things so that some people are definitely in charge of some things, the value of exterior things will not be effectively utilized, and the social costs will compromise basic elements of the common good, in particular, social peace.

Thomas does not specify what makes some item become the property of one and not another beyond specifying some obvious ways in which that cannot happen—by fraud, stealing, and so on. Presumably, he would accept that much of the rest is to be settled by conventions, including any within the *jus gentium* that might apply, for example, coming to own something one finds without evidence or claim of ownership by another, or coming to own a piece of unoccupied land by improving it.

Thomas's account is meant to preserve the ethical primacy of the common possession of external things by human beings. He does this by distinguishing their use from the discretion about how to use them, the *potestas procurandi et dispensandi*, which I would render as "the authority or discretion" over how they are used. This is what the three arguments for ownership support. However, Thomas says that the use of what is owned should be common, not proper to the owner. He clarifies the sense of this by the example that "someone might readily communicate them [the exterior things] for the necessities of others." The arguments for dividing the authority over an item require a qualification: that the owner's legitimate use has priority over others' claims (cf. *ST* 2-2, q. 66, a. 2, ad. 1). Still, the goal of property conventions is the fair, efficient, and peaceful use of external things to serve human benefit generally, that is, as far as those dealing with external things can make them serve this purpose.

It is important not to over-moralize Thomas's account. He recognizes that owners are not always responsible in using what they own; indeed his view is compatible with thinking they usually do not. Property division is partly for the sake of fostering the effective use of the things owned; that efficiency provides a human empowerment that can be used for good, for example, to carry out the owners' particular responsibilities to his or her family and community. Owners' irresponsibility does not remove the empowerment their ownership provides, and if a society did abolish the empowerment of ownership, it is not clear that any replacement would be less easily abused. Thomas's argument is not that the use of property is inevitably upright, but that the convention is necessary for human life.

This natural-law account of property provides some categories for thinking about what kinds of things can be owned and in what amounts, but gives no short answer to these questions. Any naturally given or produced thing that can be used for human benefit can be owned if ownership serves its good use, the effective and peaceful use. That good use necessarily involves its efficient use to serve the needs of those who can benefit from it. Extensive property holdings, for example, by corporations, often make possible effective uses of resources that individuals or less wealthy companies cannot realize. If such holdings serve consumers, employees, and others in a fair way, the extent of the holdings is not a moral disqualifier. Still, the benefits of property are justly used only for the common good, not simply for the individual benefit of the owners who have discretion over the undertaking.

The natural-law rationale for property unfolds more readily and directly toward the judgment that some minimal level of property holding by all capable persons is morally required. This is an implication of the reasonable use of exterior things for human benefit. The unhappy condition that would exist if people did not have discretion over the things most central for their daily living and vocational undertakings would make their own meaningful action all but impossible, and would render them at best passive in respect to the actions of others concerning all the particulars of life. What this judgment practically requires will be variable over societies and forms of social and technological organization, but outside extreme cases of lawlessness or natural catastrophe, protecting and promoting minimal ownership—and the personal discretion and control of one's life that such ownership makes possible—seems feasible. In developed countries today, minimal ownership probably does not require home ownership or any short list of possessions, but does seem to require reliable financial support that one can make use of as one sees fit.

The permissible size of the gap between the ceilings and floors just discussed is not based on its size—that is, on the measurable difference in wealth—although the sheer size of a great gap can provide a sign that the difference measures a failure in justice. Two conditions seem especially important: that great wealth be justified by its effectiveness in making some exterior things useful, and that it serve this use by human beings in a fair way. When these conditions are met, the size of the difference between the holdings of the wealthy and that of the poor are, as such, unimportant. Of course, in practice that size often causes or is embedded within a set of conditions that favors the social power and indulgence of the wealthy, and does not provide the economic empowerment and discretion poor people need to live their lives. In such cases, the size signifies that the wealthy act unjustly, and calls for remedy.

That remedy is the responsibility of all the parties to the social cooperation of a community. It particularly includes the responsibility of owners to use their property, and any advantages it gives them, for the common good. Other persons in the community have responsibilities not only to provide what they can to those in need, but to speak on their behalf. The relatively poor who are able also have a responsibility to seek redress and to cooperate to change the unjust arrangements by such things as labor actions and political initiatives. Political leaders have responsibilities to regulate the economy so as to prevent or remove harmful inequities. Political leaders also have welfare-based political responsibilities, as I will argue below in the section on taxation.

Natural Resources

Natural resources are an important kind of external things, naturally given materials or things that humans can improve or use for their purposes. Indeed, natural resources provide what is probably the focal case of "external thing" in Thomas's vocabulary. Ownership of a natural resource is, therefore, justified when it makes for effective, fair, and peaceful use of the resource. Some of the differences among natural resources are relevant to the justice of the arrangements adopted for their exploitation and use.

Some natural resources such as air and large bodies of water are not easily or generally divided into property owned by private persons, and such divisions as are possible do not clearly serve the effective, fair, and peaceful use of such resources. Ubiquitous resources such as air and sunlight seem to be inherently common goods, whose fair common use is not amenable to division into owned parcels; the guarantee of the cleanliness of the air and the regulation of buildings that shut out sunlight seem best secured not by private ownership of some part of the atmosphere but by direct government regulation.

Similarly, oceans, rivers, and underground aquifers that affect people over wide areas are not easily or rationally divided. Although the effective and fair use of such resources, including for human transportation and commerce, requires authoritative discretion and regulation, governmental action or international agreements appear to serve their common use better than private ownership could.

The extraction from bodies of water of renewable resources such as water itself or fish obviously requires regulation—for example, licensing to prevent resource-destroying actions (e.g., overfishing) and to provide for fair and orderly competition among those wanting to extract resources from these bodies of water. The resources they legally extract are reasonably taken to be owned as their property.

The extraction of non-renewables—for instance, minerals and crude oil—from such bodies of water also requires regulation, including licensing. Here the specific moral issues seem to be safety and conservation. The risks and other harmful side effects of extraction and the transport of what is extracted, together with the duty to preserve some non-renewables for future use, do not exclude extraction, but do require authority over the body of water and the conditions of the extraction. Given the difficulties in division of bodies of water, this authority must be public. So, the good use of this kind of resource involves allowing extraction, but on terms clearly short of private ownership, since such a regime, including both licensing and ownership of the resources legally extracted, protects the discretion needed for effective extraction and the common interest in regulating renewal resources and conserving non-renewables for future use.

In addition to resources whose importance for humans arises from their inherently common character, modern societies deem some resources to be public goods that are to be preserved for the general, non-consumptive use of all the members of society. Resources such as some forests and beautiful landscapes are reasonably protected from extensive industrial activity and resource development by the government to guarantee fair access by all.

Other resources, such as fertile fields, grazing lands, and forests, are also inherently stationary. Their good use does seem to require ownership, or tenancy very like it—or, in the case of extractable resources within such lands, licensing. The cultivation of these resources requires discretion and confidence that one's investment in it will not be lost. However, the fruits of cultivation are transportable, and indeed successful transport to market is usually necessary for the good use of the products of all these stationary resources—necessary in most cases other than those of subsistence farming, herding, and hunting. So, ownership of such resources as land and its fruits plausibly does secure their good use and availability for use for the benefit of others. That arrangement need not be unfair, even when that involves the ownership of considerable assets. However, the side effects of modern agriculture, such as pollution and excessive use of antibiotics, and the effects on climate of the destruction of large forests, seem to imply that common use is incompatible with the most robust forms of ownership. The temptation of owners to favor themselves and not to share reasonably with others is a common human failing, not distinctive of the ownership of stationary resources and their fruits.

Products

Products are an important class of exterior things; they are not simple materials given by nature but improved by human initiative for human purposes, and often imbued with symbolic or cultural meaning. Tools and artifacts, including housing and clothing, are products. This suggests that some products, at least very generically described, are among the things that all people reasonably should have as their own, and will be widely owned if a community is in a position to provide them. Still, this is not to deny that some products take on a special significance in some cultural and technological contexts. Certain specifically characterized tools are needed for human beings to succeed in some contexts, distinctive weapons for hunting; tools for farming, herding, or fishing; storage facilities; calculation and recording devices; and so on. The claim of a member of a group to hold on to or fairly acquire such a product as his or her own would be very strong if the person's chance to live his or her life decently depended upon owning the item. Such a claim would not rest on the person's desire for the item, but his or her need in a context, and the capability of the community to provide the essential item. If the item were generally needed and not widely available, natural law would require considering whether any reason favored providing it to some and not others. Absent such a reason, a randomizing procedure is the best one can do, and that is preferable to denying the chance for someone to make good use of the product.

Of course, in a consumption-oriented society such as much of the developed world has become, the problem for reasonable use of products lies not so much in the required minimums but in the indefensible excess of products that are often not well used by those who have them and might be better used by others—or, in some cases, not produced at all, in favor of products that more centrally contribute to human good. This moral challenge results from elements of developed economies that are deeply embedded. Action by public authority is therefore unlikely to be taken.

But this does not remove the more fundamental responsibility of those who create products to make them to address human need and to facilitate human good. Those who buy and use products have a corresponding responsibility, and the further responsibility not to accumulate things beyond one's need for them, and to share the extra with those who have a similar need.

Wealth, Income, and Employment

Wealth

Wealth, income, and employment are closely connected. The noun *wealth* and especially the adjective *wealthy* refer to an abundance of assets, but wealth is also a name for the total of a person's or a group's valuable assets—property, possessions, and money. The abundance of wealth raises questions of justice, when many are relatively poor and some at least are poor in the more absolute sense of lacking the wherewithal for living a good life or even the necessities of life itself. But wealth understood as the sum of one's assets provides a useful category of exterior things. One can distinguish wealth from income, which makes reference to receiving something of value—money or goods one can make use of for one or more purposes, whether from employment, pensions, investments, gifts, or welfare. The goods received as income can be used immediately—for example, many people who live "paycheck to paycheck" have no choice but to spend their income immediately. That is in contrast to those whose income is not immediately spoken for and who can maintain it at least for a time as wealth. In other words, income empowers earners to support themselves and others, and perhaps to do other good things. But the empowerment of wealth is substantially greater, because it allows discretion over time and the ordering of affairs, which income used immediately does not allow.

This empowerment defines the human interest in acquiring and maintaining wealth.

Having wealth is beneficial because it offers opportunities for planning, for providence in providing for future needs and contingencies, and for creative use of assets that is impossible when they must be immediately and urgently used and consumed. These benefits of wealth are broadly instrumental and will be morally justified in any particular case by their use to facilitate the realization of the human good. The inheritance within a family is an aspect of this instrumentality, and its justice in general and in particular cases is to be assessed by the same standard.

The power wealth includes is not inevitably misused but its good use is not automatic, since it can be used for such things as dominating others and creating a sense of false security against life's contingencies. Even if one holds wealth for morally acceptable reasons, however, the justice of doing so is not guaranteed. For even if one uses one's wealth to facilitate genuine goods that can be realized in one's life, or to discharge genuine responsibilities to one's family or one's community, one might realize these goods and fulfill these obligations with less attention to maintaining a particular level of wealth. One might use one's wealth in ways that better serve the needs of others. Most who have wealth know, or should know, that they could choose to use their resources differently than they, in fact, do, and sometimes that, if they choose differently, they can make part of their resources available to meet others' needs. Ignoring such possibilities is a failure to make use of the Golden Rule techniques for securing fair-mindedness.

In short, the justice of holding wealth, any amount of wealth, is the compatibility of that particular holding with the purposes of ownership generally. Holding more than is immediately needed for immediate use is an important empowerment that can be sought for genuine human benefit, and this use of exterior things is not inevitably unjust, although its fairness for "common use" is hardly guaranteed.

Philanthropic use of some wealth is obviously one way a person could make use of the advantages possession of wealth allows; it directly addresses the need to share the results of one's discretion and authority over things with those who could benefit from them. But philanthropy is not necessary to justify holding wealth, and philanthropy by the wealthy does not provide a bar to redistributionist taxation. For philanthropy responds to the responsibility of owners to use their property for the benefit of all who can reasonably benefit. The use of the public authority to tax can facilitate carrying out this very responsibility, as I will argue below.

Income

There are perhaps a few people in most societies who can survive and even thrive by drawing down their wealth. For everybody else, income is necessary for survival, and it is certainly necessary for living a fulfilling life. Income includes, but is not limited to, the fruits of one's labor, broadly understood. It might also include inheritance, other gifts, welfare from philanthropy, and so on. Because of the necessity of income, providing the amount needed for survival, and also for the opportunity to live well when that is feasible, is an ethically urgent implication of the requirement that exterior things be used for common benefit. Consequently, if owners of productive things can share them or their fruits to serve this end, then they are bound to do so. Most owners cannot do this for all in need, but cooperatively, at least in developed societies, and probably more widely in a globalized world containing some very rich societies, there is enough capacity to address this need that it becomes obligatory for many communities and their citizens. Clearly, that obligation can be carried out adequately only by coordinated public action within a polity, and by a combination of public and private action to assist those outside a nation's borders.

Consequently, although the precise terms of the entitlement depend on circumstances, the natural law implies a right to an income sufficient to live, and if those having the duty generated by that right have the capacity to provide income that will generate the greater empowerments of having a minimum level of wealth, that, too, is required. This reasoning is based on the requirement of common use that is foundational to the natural-law account of the use of exterior things. Consequently, although the duty corresponding to the right to an income sufficient for life varies over individuals and communities, depending on circumstances such as their capacity to help, and any special obligations to some of those needing this help, the duty itself is common to all having authority over exterior things and the capacity to provide the benefits of their use to others who cannot do so themselves.

This reasoning does not have a similarly robust and clear implication for upper limits or ceilings on income. The incomes of a number of people in developed countries are so great in comparison not only to average incomes of others but to any apparent connection to a reasonable authority over resources—that is, authority that can serve their good use for the high-income earner and others. Perhaps that appearance is deceptive and some high-income earners have responsibilities of which outsiders are unaware, and undertake valuable philanthropic or commercial projects that require the resources high income delivers. This suggests that such earners have a serious responsibility to guarantee that their income is used well, and not simply to serve one or another of the morally dubious goals having wealth often serves.

This moral reality does not settle, however, how or even to what extent their responsibility can be enforced by public authority. There seem to be natural-law considerations on both sides of this enforcement issue. Preservation of a regime of ownership in societies where the market determines prices, including income for work, allows for the possibility for some to have a very high income. In such societies, an all-purpose prohibition of income beyond a certain level seems incompatible with respect for the reasons supporting ownership, particularly with the motivational rationale that people will work more effectively on what is their own, as extended to the motivation for earning high compensation. The rationale for the empowerment of ownership holds even when owners act irresponsibly, and that rationale seems to embrace income in a market economy.

That said, unless the requirement of common use is widely understood to be furthered by the extra income of the high earners, the social peace secured by an ownership regime is vulnerable. The reasonable needs of those whose income is inadequate should be addressed by the use of the resources of those having superabundant income or wealth. The legitimacy of that ownership is rightly called into question when common use is ignored. In the extreme case of necessity, natural law holds that taking what is conventionally designated as another's is morally legitimate (*ST*, 2-2, q. 66, a. 7). Even in societies where strict necessity is not the condition of a large group of poorer people, great discrepancies in the capacity of fellow citizens or fellow workers to meet important needs are bound to incite resentment. Political society can, within limits, contribute to removing this form of social antagonism by ensuring fair rules for distributing the various elements of income, and by using redistributionist taxation to secure a decent minimum of income for all.

Employment

Employment has a more active connotation than income. One who is employed by self or another engages in some activity, does something that has value. That is true even when a person is employed without compensation in volunteer activity or in a program of apprenticeship. Much employment involves drudgery or routine actions, but even this kind of employment involves action, which, in turn, involves activating some human capacities.

That, in turn, can involve actions that realize basic human goods, for example, cooperation with others and excelling in work. Supposing that human beings have equal human status, the work of any person has a quality that is not reducible to the elements of a mechanical process. Workers are not simply ingredients within the array of exterior things humans organize for human benefit—neither cogs in a machine nor draft animals. Workers' actions, independently of the value of the products they make, exercise their capacities and develop habits of attention, skill, problem-solving, and cooperation with others. Consequently, the work involved in employment has a significance lacking in receiving income, which is important for providing necessities and opportunities for more significant agency, because in working one acts, exercises human powers, and develops capabilities. Consequently, the actions of workers, although often immediately productive of artifacts and other instrumental goods, are important to them and others for more basic reasons. Drudgery in which a worker's initiative is limited is sometimes unavoidable, but bearing those burdens is surely a factor in determining what is due overall to such workers.

According to natural law, therefore, the rationale for employment is distinct from that for income. To the extent possible, both are required for a good human life: if necessity requires providing income, then that is required; if employment is also possible, that, too, is required. This logic suggests the affinity between a natural-law ethics of development and the capabilities approach associated with Amartya Sen's work.[9] Although contributing to developing capabilities gives those helped empowerments that are not so easily measured, they are more closely connected to the basic human goods that can be realized through economic activity. Moreover, there is no principled contradiction between developing capabilities and addressing basic welfare needs, as there is no contradiction between recognizing the responsibility to address basic needs by providing income and also to help people develop more active empowerments through the work of employment.

The difference between income and employment raises the question whether employers are obligated to provide a minimum wage. The natural-law verdict on basic income is clear enough, but natural law does not imply that basic income must be entirely provided by wages. Other sources of income are available, notably those of private charity and public welfare. Of course, employers have a responsibility to contribute to the welfare of their employees, but lacking the capacity to provide all the basic income needed does not require that the employment be foregone. The latter has value not reducible to the former.

The fact that a minimum wage is not a strict requirement for employers does not imply that levels of compensation are entirely at their discretion. The benefits of a cooperative action, such as a business, must, as a matter of justice, be shared among those involved in the common action. Those responsible for maintaining an enterprise reasonably compensate employees on the basis of qualifications, productivity, and so on. But this does not allow wage discrimination on the basis of personal characteristics that are irrelevant to the enterprise—race, gender, merit unconnected with the enterprise, and so on. These discriminations ignore the equal moral status of workers.

Issues of fair treatment in the workplace require public oversight of businesses. That oversight is not likely to be sufficient unless workers have a say in the decision-making of the enterprises to which they contribute. Workers' associations and unions are, therefore, a virtual requirement of modern economic life, and constitute a just instrument for securing the benefits of common use for employees. Antagonism and strife are avoidable evils of this arrangement, but the adversarial character of modern unions is justified.

Taxation

Natural law justifies taxation, at least insofar as taxes are used for the costs of running political society, as well as to finance other actions governments legitimately perform, such as regulating contracts and enforcing property rights, maintaining a court system, police, basic infrastructure, and so on. Natural-law theorists have cautioned that this justification does not guarantee the just use by public officials of the power they have, especially their use of political power coercively to expropriate citizens' property. Partly because of this concern, there has been no unanimous position on the legitimacy of redistributionist taxation among natural-law theorists. For example, Cicero limits the function of political society to protecting possessions (*De Officiis,* book II, xxi, 73, 79) and expresses concerns about the socially destabilizing effects of governmental expropriation and redistribution.

Cicero's view of property does not depend upon an individualistic conception of property. He accepts a Stoic version of Thomas's thesis that all that the earth produces is for human use, and that use should include mutual help among people (book I, vii, 21–22). But his limited conception of political authority and his concern to avoid the social disruption caused by expropriation dominate his views on redistribution; the result is that the socially virtuous use of one's goods remains essentially a non-political matter. It is a matter of personal fair-mindedness in one's dealings, and generosity in sharing one's wealth. Some within the natural-law tradition continue to follow Cicero's conception of political society as limited in a libertarian direction.[10] However, especially among Catholic natural law theorists since the beginning of "Catholic Social Teaching" in the late nineteenth century, a natural-law argument for redistributionist taxation in the service of providing welfare to the needy of a society has been developing.[11]

Here I will articulate a strand of that argument that begins from Thomas's recognition of the responsibilities of owners to others, which is contained in his thesis of the common use of exterior things.[12] Thomas's thesis is that although owners are in charge of their property, the benefits of that property, beyond those needed for the owner, are for human use generally. That involves a responsibility on the part of owners to provide for the needs of others.

This responsibility is often thought to be supererogatory, a work of charity, and not a strict moral obligation. However, Thomas's argument for ownership does not imply that "charity" is optional. What it implies is discretion about how to carry out the responsibility of common use. That discretion is in the service of using one's resources well for oneself and for others; it is logically distinct from the claim that ownership justifies any indifference to using one's surplus to assist others.

The significance of this is that it points to a moral ground for redistributionist taxation prior to the political action of taxation. The political action is a public instrumentality for carrying out part of that responsibility; it is not simply creating an obligation by political fiat and imposing it coercively through taxes. The issue concerning redistributionist taxation, therefore, is not whether it responds to a responsibility or is an arbitrary, coercive imposition. Since it does respond to a responsibility on the part of those taxed, it is not arbitrary, unless it is an obligation that is inappropriate for political society to enforce.

To address this reformulated question, I begin with the idea of "subsidiarity" that developed in Catholic natural law theorizing in the twentieth century. The word *subsidiarity* is derived from the Latin word for help or assistance, *subsidium*. The idea is that political society has various powers and legal authority to coordinate the life of the community; these powers are not reducible to those of private individuals or groups, and can be used for the community's common good by providing assistance to individuals and groups within the polity. Providing such assistance is intended to assist individuals and groups in carrying out their responsibilities and in pursuing the goods defining the common actions of the groups and the vocational pursuits of individuals. That help promotes the common good of the society as a whole because the self-perfecting acts of citizens are constitutive of it. The idea of subsidiarity, in short, provides a ground for political action beyond common security and legal adjudication, and also the limitation on the ground—namely, that political society should not take over these responsibilities or remove personal initiative but help citizens carry them out.[13]

Subsidiarity provides an important natural-law strategy for thinking about the role of political society in developed societies requiring complex regulation of commercial transactions and ownership relations, infrastructure that is not well directed by private ownership, educational requirements whose costs are not easily met by many families, and the existence of a large number of people dependent on others for the basics of life, yet sometimes exploited by them. In all these areas, coordination of individual behavior by public authority appears reasonable and is often simply necessary. Subsidiarity, in other words, is not an ad hoc conception for justifying redistribution of wealth through taxation for purposes of welfare for the poor; it applies quite generally to the regulatory activities of developed society, and to community initiatives—for example, providing social security for retirees and insurance for basic needs such as health care. Even without the welfarist elements such initiatives usually include, these seem to be justified by the fact that the cooperative actions of the community as a whole, coordinated by public authority, can provide the sought empowerments more effectively than can private action.

These considerations suggest a necessary condition for any governmental initiative justified by appeal to subsidiarity: the actions that are socialized and coordinated by public authority must be more effective at realizing the benefits—usually empowerments such as organizing pensions, employment insurance, and access to necessary services—than individual action could be. This clearly happens when social coordination allows obvious savings and convenience, and avoids social problems like free riding and moral hazard in comparison with private action. In some of these matters, public authority provides what individual ownership and discretion cannot.

But this condition is not sufficient for invoking subsidiarity, since the outcome of the public action must not be to take over personal initiative and responsibility, but to facilitate the actions of individuals, families, and voluntary associations in acting and in living well. For that is where the common good of a society is instantiated. I believe that these two conditions are together sufficient for justified subsidiary actions by political society.

I believe that redistributionist taxation for the sake of welfare for the needy can meet these conditions. In the large, complex societies characteristic of the developed world, the reach of government in coordinating and guaranteeing welfare for the needy is far greater than any charitable organization could provide. Moreover, by taxing the population generally, the demoralizing avoidance of this obligation by the selfish can be minimized. Although governmental agencies need not directly provide the help to the needy, the public action guarantees its fair and efficient provision. So, at least in respect to the funding and coordination of welfare efforts, the public action can do what private agents, acting without public action, could not do.

The second condition is not so obviously met. It cannot be met unless the taxation regime allows citizens who are taxed for this purpose to remain in control of their lives. Redistribution of the results of a person's labor and wealth is not morally justified if that removes the person's discretion over exterior things to the extent that they cannot be used for the reasonable goals that person has in making use of them. A taxation regime that does not respect that discretion would undercut its moral grounding in common use. So, a welfare-based redistributionist tax regime must bear lightly enough on citizens that they can continue to meet their other political and pre-political obligations. This points toward a progressive taxation regime, for those with great wealth have more available for sharing with others without significantly curtailing their discretion and capacity to live well, unlike those whose wealth hardly allows them to live well. It seems, in short, that this aspect of the condition of respecting individual action and initiative can be met by redistributionist taxation, although care is needed to guarantee that it does so.[14]

But many people think that an important aspect of personal initiative is missing from governmentally provided welfare: namely, the personal involvement with the needy, which allows face-to-face interaction and possibly greater significance in religious terms as an expression of mercy.[15] It is true that active engagement on the part of one helping a needy person usually involves something beyond the provision for the necessities for living. Often there is respect for the dignity of the needy person and encouragement for a better life, solidarity, and the beginning of friendship. Moreover, the help characteristic of a capabilities approach can more easily emerge when individuals and voluntary associations reach out to the needy.

But the truth that more is possible does not imply that providing for necessities widely and efficiently is not also valuable; indeed, providing resources to the needy is a central component of what owners are generally in a position to do for those they cannot employ in profitable activity. For most of us, in short, what we do for others is very substantially to provide them goods, usually money, so they can meet their basic needs.

The implication of this reflection is that owners have obligations to the needy in their society that go beyond what public welfare, and taxation for that purpose, can rightly demand. That does not undercut the rationale for public assistance, but shows instead that it cannot provide all of what is owed. That fact is consistent with the limitation on redistributionist taxation required by respect for the discretion protected by ownership. The just requirements of helping others are justly supported by political action, but that support cannot completely fulfill the responsibility, which people have independently of political action.

Notes

1. This is the standard way of referring to Thomas Aquinas's works, common to all editions and translations. The reference here is to the *Summa Theologiae,* first part of the second part (dealing with ethical issues), question 94, article 2. For Cicero's list, see *De Officiis,* book I, iv, 11–15; this is one of the most widely read works in the natural-law tradition, from antiquity until the Enlightenment. See also Germain Grisez, "The First Principle of Practical Reason: A Com-

mentary on the Summa Theologiae, 1–2, Question 94, Article 2," *Natural Law Forum* 10 (1965), 168–200. This is the founding work in what was later called the "new natural law" theory. I follow his interpretation in this paper. Grisez exhibits and criticizes Thomism, the form of natural law favored by neo-scholastics before 1940.

2. See John Finnis, *Reason in Action: Collected Essays: Volume I* (Oxford, Great Britain: Oxford University Press, 2011), 216–217. This is the approach I take. See also my "On the Most Fundamental Principle of Morality" in John Keown and Robert P. George, eds., *Reason, Morality and Law: The Philosophy of John Finnis* (Oxford, Great Britain: Oxford University Press, 2013), 56–72.

3. See Germain Grisez, *The Way of the Lord Jesus: Volume III, Difficult Moral Questions* (Quincy, Illinois: Franciscan Press, 1997), 849–870.

4. See John Finnis, *Natural Law and Natural Rights*, 2nd edition (Oxford, Great Britain: Oxford University Press, 2011), 107–109.

5. See John Finnis, *Aquinas: Moral, Political and Legal Theory* (Oxford, Great Britain: Oxford University Press, 1998), 170–172, for an exploration of some of Thomas's key texts on this. Sherif Girgis, "Equality and Moral Worth in Natural-Law Ethics and Beyond," *American Journal of Jurisprudence* 59 (2014), 143–162, argues against Finnis and others that human equality is purely formal and carries no justificatory weight. I have tried to formulate the equal humanity norm so as to avoid his critique.

6. See John Finnis, "Equality and Differences," *American Journal of Jurisprudence* 56 (2011), 18–20, for a fuller statement and the start of a defense of the view. The thesis of equal moral status implies that the idea is binary, not something one has more or less. I begin an argument for this thesis in the preceding paragraphs, based on the ways in which basic human goods are common to human beings.

7. Finnis, *Natural Law and Natural Rights*, 163.

8. My reasoning in this paragraph tracks that of Aristotle in *Politics* I, 1256b29–1265a20. He does not state the conclusion I draw.

9. See Sabina Alkire, *Valuing Freedoms: Sen's Capability Approach and Poverty Reduction* (Oxford, Great Britain: Oxford University Press, 2002). Alkire relates the capability approach to Finnis's version of natural law.

10. For recent examples see the works cited in my "Fairness in Holdings: A Natural Law Account of Property and Welfare Rights," *Social Philosophy & Policy* 18 (2001), 214–215.

11. See John Ryan, *Distributive Justice*, new and revised edition (New York, New York: Macmillan, 1939), 87–113, 268–281; Johannes Messner, *Social Ethics: Natural Law in the Western World* (St. Louis, Missouri; London, Great Britain: Herder, 1949), 646–655.

12. Finnis highlighted the key texts of Thomas as well as relevant conceptual issues in *Natural Law and Natural Rights*, 186–187, 192, 463; and in *Aquinas*, 195, 222–252. Finnis's interpretation is disputed in Christopher Todd Meredith,

"The Ethical Basis for Taxation in the Thought of Thomas Aquinas," *Markets and Morals* 11 (2008), 41–58. I will not enter here into the strictly interpretative debate.

13. See Finnis, *Natural Law and Natural Rights*, 144–147, 159, 194.

14. I have developed the reasoning in the preceding paragraphs in "Fairness in Holdings."

15. The significance of the difficulty addressed here is underlined by the fact that Pope Leo XIII expressed this concern in his teaching on the rights of workers, a teaching that began the movement called "Catholic Social Teaching," and the natural-law thinking that involves. He responded, as follows, to those who favor a "system of relief organized by the State": "But no human expedients will ever make up for the devotedness and self-sacrifice of Christian charity" (*Rerum Novarum* [1890], para. 30). But I do not see that publicly organizing help to the needy need be in any respect irreligious.

Christianity

CHRISTIANITY AND ECONOMIC INEQUALITY

D. STEPHEN LONG

Introduction

Before you, the reader, and me, the author, lies an impossible task—a presentation of the Christian perspective on economic inequality. The task is impossible because it brings together three contested disciplines: Christian theology, economics, and ethics. Agreement on the core principles of each of these disciplines is seldom found among its practitioners, let alone a consensus that brings all three together. Ethics is a discipline older than Christianity, and it has as many branches as Christianity has churches. Ethics can take shape as Platonist, Aristotelian, Stoic, utilitarian, Kantian, sentimentalist, feminist ethics of care, natural law, and many others. Some version of Christianity has adopted nearly every one, or more, of these ethical theories. The same can be said of economics. Christian theologians, bishops, clergy, laypersons, and/or churches have been Rawlsian or Nozickian liberals, Marxists, socialists, capitalists, fascists, distributivists, even mercantilists, feudalists, and slavocrats. There is no single "Christian perspective" on economic inequality, any more than there is a single "ethical" or "rational" perspective. To bring this impossible task into a manageable order, the following essay begins with an all-too-brief map of Christian approaches to ethics, being attentive to how it bears on economics. It then proceeds by adopting an approach that considers economics through the practices of the church, its doctrines, liturgies, Scriptures, and faithful exemplars, what I have called "ecclesial ethics." Although most of these practices were forged prior to the development of the modern economy, they will be mined in the third section of this essay to answer questions specific to the modern economy: topics of equality, property, natural resources, wealth, income, employment, and taxation. The fit between what Christian ethics offers and these questions will not be exact. Christianity is not a macroeconomic theory for the production and distribution of resources, but it does offer practical wisdom on economic ethics.

Guide to the Discussion

One of the most significant attempts to bring Christian theology into conversation with modern economics was Pope Leo XIII's 1891 encyclical, *Rerum novarum*. The Latin title means "on new things," and the "new things" that emerged in the latter part of the nineteenth century were new forms of economic arrangements. Leo XIII, like most Roman Catholic moral theology at the time, approached the task from a theology known as neo-scholasticism; it built on the scholasticism that arose centuries earlier from the works of Cardinal Thomas de Vio Cajetan (1469–1534). For Cajetan, scholastic ethics set forth a "twofold end," or purpose, to ethical action interpreted in terms of natural and supernatural ends. Justice in society is a natural end; it is not informed directly by Scripture or church teaching; it is universal, grounded in the right use of reason and available to anyone. Supernatural ends are for salvation, known primarily by revelation and present in the church. Economic ethics is pursued primarily in terms of natural ends. Pope Leo XIII's famous encyclical drew on an updated version of scholasticism. It did not primarily address Catholics or Christians, but all people of good will with basic natural principles concerning the "rights and duties" of owners and workers, including the right to own private property, to receive a just wage, and the need for owners and workers to live in "concord" rather than conflict and competition. Roman Catholic "natural law" ethics tends to assume there is a realm of nature that can be identified and presented in order to make clear the rights and duties involved in economics. However, what constitutes this "natural law" is contested among its adherents. Are the principles of the free market—pursuing self-interest within a competitive system and a level playing field—natural or cultural? Most official Roman Catholic teaching refuses to find them "natural," but some Roman Catholic theologians and ethicists do. For instance, a few U.S. Roman Catholic theologians chastised the U.S. bishops' pastoral on economics for drawing primarily on Scripture and thus criticizing the principles of the free market on the basis of biblical teaching rather than defending those principles based on the natural law.[1] Although much of Roman Catholic moral theology proceeds on the natural law, the inability to find agreement on what is natural when it comes to economics has made this approach unconvincing to many. Both Benedict XVI's encyclical on the economy—*Caritas in veritate* (2009)—and Pope Francis's *Laudato si* (2015) draw on a more biblical and ecclesial ethic to approach economics, an approach that emerged from Vatican II (1962–1965).

Modern Protestant theology tends to be suspicious of natural-law approaches to ethics. One influential Protestant approach to economics is neo-calvinism. Originated by the Dutch Reformed theologian Abraham Kuyper (1837–1920), it emphasizes "spheres of sovereignty" and "common grace." God creates distinct spheres of life, each with its own autonomous responsibilities, authorities, and competencies such as politics, economics, family, morality, education, culture. Because each sphere is autonomous, it should not fall under the rule of a different sphere. No pope, secular ruler, or overarching rationality holds authority over all the spheres. Economics, then, proceeds in terms of those entrusted with authority and competency for it. Although it is similar to Roman Catholic natural law, neo-calvinism rejects reading of moral norms from nature because of the Reformed doctrine of total depravity. It makes continuity between human nature, now corrupted by the fall, and graced nature, redeemed by Christ, difficult. While Catholics can speak of "grace perfecting nature," Reformed Protestants find grace and nature discontinuous and related dialectically. What allows for the autonomy and cooperation among the spheres is not "nature" but "common grace." It is a general grace God gives in each sphere of sovereignty that makes morality possible. Neo-calvinist approaches continue to have an important role in contemporary discussions of Christian economic ethics. They have made common cause with Roman Catholic natural law approaches, and usually do so by affirming the present capitalist economic order.

Liberal Protestant approaches to economics tend to mediate Christianity through social sciences in order to produce a synthesis of Christianity and contemporary economic science. Ernst Troeltsch (1865–1923) undertook one of the first and most influential analyses of the social teaching of Christianity. He argued that Christianity in itself is not a social ethic but a religious idea. Jesus proclaimed the Kingdom of God, but Troeltsch stated, "This Message of the Kingdom was primarily the vision of an ideal ethical and religious situation, of a world entirely controlled by God, in which all the values of pure spirituality would be recognized and appreciated at their true worth."[2] Christianity contains no intrinsic social teaching because it provides no specific platform for the economic distribution of goods and services. There is, at most, a "Christian ethos," which Troeltsch defined as "absolute individualism and absolute universalism." Because Christianity is religious rather than social, it must look for a social ethic. The early church adopted a Stoic ethic. Troeltsch did not explicitly state this, but an implication of his thought, and one that has been influential in Christian ethics, is that the social task of Christianity is to seek out the best social ethics in each generation. After Troeltsch, the task of many Christian ethicists was to figure out which was the best social ethics that they could affix to an essentially asocial Christianity.

Liberation theologies emerged in the late 1960s and early 1970s. They also mediated Christianity through sociology, but they tended to do so by using socialist categories. Whereas the neo-scholastic and neo-calvinist approaches noted above find allies between Christianity and capitalism, liberation theologians resist capitalism and advocate socialism.

Given the different approaches to ethics noted above, how should we proceed? It might seem to be appropriate to lay out the various ethical theories on something like a "periodic chart" of ethics, along with their relationship to Christianity and economics, and ask readers to "choose" an ethic of their own liking. While that may appear innocent, the very idea that ethics is about choice, and subjective choice at that, is only one ethical approach among many—an ethic that understands human agency in terms of "choices." Although such an ethics might appear neutral, it actually invites the reader into one among many competing ethics and the sociality that undergirds it without acknowledging the underlying social formation that renders that ethics intelligible.

At the end of modernity, universal moral norms that float free from their embodiment in some community that sustains them has increasingly been called into question. Every ethics, suggests Alasdair MacIntyre, implies some underlying sociality.[3] Utilitarianism (the greatest good for the greatest number) and its ethics of choice make sense in a free market–oriented society with corporations that formed it, such as the Dutch East Indies Company. Deontology (an ethics of binding obligations) arises within constitutional democracies that formed modern nation-states. If MacIntyre is correct, the question of ethics becomes a social question. Rather than assuming ethics is something a subject chooses, in what follows I adopt the broad contours of a *theological* approach to ethics that has its sources in a Catholic theology known as *nouvelle théologie* and a Protestant one that arose from the work of Karl Barth (1886–1968).[4] Both were mid-twentieth-century theological movements in which Christian ethics increasingly drew on specific theological sources such as Scripture, Christology, Trinity, Ecclesiology, and worship to make sense of, and reflect on, human action. This approach assumes that what renders Christian ethics intelligible is its location within the church. Not everyone who affirms ecclesial ethics does it the same way, but most disagree with Troeltsch that Christianity must adopt a social ethic because it does not have one of its own. They also tend to be suspicious of natural law or neo-calvinist ethics. The Methodist ethicist Paul Ramsey (1913–1988) thought natural law approaches to ethics tended to overly emphasize justice and downplay Jesus' command to love. He sought to unite love and justice, bringing the supernatural to bear more directly on the natural.[5] Likewise, the Anglican theologian Oliver O'Donovan challenged "natural law ethics" in favor of an "evangelical" ethic that sets ethics "within the history of divine action" and its "vindication of creation."[6] Both Ramsey and O'Donovan, similar to Karl Barth, develop what is known as a Christocentric ethic; rather than abstracting from the specifics of Christian doctrine, its center—Jesus Christ—must be brought to bear on it. Their work differs from that of Stanley Hauerwas, who has most fully developed an ecclesial ethics, but they would agree that Christianity looks to its particular social reality to render ethics intelligible. In opposition to Troeltsch, Hauerwas has stated, "The church does not have a social ethic; the church is a social ethic."[7]

This statement does not mean the church rejects ethical wisdom wherever it is found. Nor should it be interpreted to suggest that the church is a complete political or economic society. It suggests that Christian ethics should begin with the social reality that makes sense of it in the first place: the church. The next section explains an "ecclesial ethic" and the sources it draws upon, sources such as worship, Scripture, and holy exemplars.

Ecclesial Ethics: The Church as Social Ethic

Ecclesial ethics emerged from the theological movements that produced the revisions to moral theology at Vatican II and that reenergized Protestant theology after the work of Karl Barth. Both were, as Barth put it, forms of a "Christological renaissance." Rather than nature or sociology providing the means for a Christian ethics, theologians sought to develop ethics by focusing on what makes Christianity distinct: Christians worship Jesus as God without confusing humanity and divinity. This act of worship forms the heart of Christian ethics, but it does not exclude gathering ethical wisdom from other sources inasmuch as they do not conflict with the center of Christian worship. The work of Daniel Bell brings an ecclesial ethics to bear on economic justice.[8] His work on justice begins with the "startling" claim by Saint Augustine that "true justice is found only in the City of God, the Church whose ruler and founder is Christ."[9]

Augustine's startling claim does not necessarily contradict theories of justice present beyond the borders of the church. For instance, it does not reject Ulpian's ancient understanding of justice known as the *suum cuique*— "render to each what is due"—nor does it oppose modern forms of justice founded upon equality. However, it sets forth an understanding of "what is due" that at least reconfigures ancient teachings on justice and sits uncomfortably with modern notions of justice based on rights and proper procedures. Ancient teachings have a distinct hierarchy of what is owed based on status, whereas modern teachings flatten that hierarchy, ascribing rights to individuals grounded in fair procedures that seek to treat everyone equally, in terms of either opportunity or outcome. Bell's ecclesial ethics is for and against both teachings. On the one hand, Christianity affirms a hierarchy in which God is owed worship and praise; there can be no true justice without proper worship. On the other hand, by first rendering our due worship to God, every other creature stands before us in a relationship analogous to the one we have before God. Each creature has a claim on, and responsibility to, the good of all other creatures patterned on divine mercy and generosity.[10]

In ecclesial ethics, the primary act of worship known as the Lord's Supper, Communion, or Holy Eucharist establishes the basic pattern of economic justice. God gives God's self to creation through a liturgical act in which bread and wine become the body and blood of Christ. Its consumption makes participants the "body of Christ" in the world called to enact His "Kingdom." Each wafer or piece of bread is the entirety of Christ's body so that all consume equally and in turn are equally consumed.[11] Saint Augustine explained this basic form of exchange in his *Confessions*: "I heard your voice calling from on high, saying, 'I am the food of full-grown persons. Grow and you shall feed on me. But you shall not change me into your own substance, as you do with the food of your body. Instead you shall be changed into me."[12] This mystical exchange provides practical instruction in a Christian economic justice. Daniel Bell notes two consequences that the act of worship has: first, justice "is about the communion of humanity in God." Second, such a justice is "no longer a human achievement but is a divine gift, the logic of which is distinctly liturgical."[13] Worship and ethics are inextricably linked.

"Communion of humanity in God" is the goal for Christian economic justice. Communion takes up the most basic economic reality, the consumption of food, and transforms it into a means through which God communes with creatures, creatures commune with God, and creatures commune with each other. Through this communion, our lives are implicated in each other and transformed into a community that is more than equality. What one does affects all others. As the cultic-ethical pattern for all human action, communion radiates outward to render intelligible every form of economic exchange. Each exchange should be open to, and measured by, communion. Once this form of economic justice is in place, then exchanges are confronted with this question: do they foster community, or do they disrupt it? Economic justice requires more than a just distribution of resources; it also asks what those resources that are justly distributed are doing. Christian economic justice does not begin with the question as to what global economic system should be implemented in order to ensure the best outcome. Instead, as William Cavanaugh has put it, "The Christian is called not to replace one universal system with another, but to attempt to 'realize' the universal body of Christ in every particular exchange."[14]

The realization of the body of Christ includes participating in the communication of Jesus' life by his words and deeds. Ecclesial ethics turns to Scripture for ethical wisdom about economic justice. The Sermon on the Mount (Matthew 5–7) is a major element in shaping a Christian understanding of justice. It refers to a "greater righteousness" (or justice, *dikaiosune*) that is required for those seeking the "Kingdom of God." A distinctive contribution Christian ethics makes to justice is found in Jesus' admonition to love one's enemies, and thus become "children of your Father in heaven; for He makes His sun rise on the evil and on the good, and sends rain on the righteous and on the unrighteous" (Matthew 5:45). God's generosity is not founded upon merit; those who imitate God are to be lavish in their generosity and open in their receptivity. Jesus concludes by telling his followers that in such actions they imitate God. "Be perfect, therefore, as your heavenly Father is perfect" (Matthew 5:48). Justice is associated with the important theological word *teleiosis*—perfection, completeness, or wholeness. As God is perfect in God's generosity, Christians are called to emulate that generosity.

Justice is a demand to be forgiving as God is forgiving; in this practice divine perfection is found. The Lord's Prayer, a prayer taught in the Sermon on the Mount, offers counsel on how to orient one's life toward divine perfection. Jesus teaches his disciples to pray: "Your kingdom come, Your will be done, on earth as it is in heaven. Give us this day our daily bread. And forgive us our debts, as we have also forgiven our debtors" (Matthew 6:10–12). Once again, this prayer displays a concern for the most basic economic reality—daily bread. The unity of earth and heaven is found in a generous distribution of daily bread that includes the forgiveness of debts. What we owe each other, then, is forgiveness. Bell explains how forgiveness reconfigures justice: "Justice and mercy are not opposing logics; rather, they share a single end: the return of all love, the sociality of all desire, in God."[15]

Once communion is the basic pattern of justice, economics is loaded with a high ethical burden. This demanding burden is itself part of a Christian economic ethic with its odd notion of gift. Bell presents justice as a divine gift, mediated liturgically. To think of ethics as a divine gift puts pressure on the very notion of ethics. It is usually considered the science of human action alone. Christianity, however, has a long tradition of conceiving ethics not primarily in terms of what the human will alone creates, but as an invitation to participate in what God has done, is doing, and will do. To find ourselves involved in exchanges producing communion is, then, a cause of thanksgiving and joy. To find ourselves involved in exchanges destroying community is a reason for repentance as we wait on the coming of God's reign. Jesus announced that God's sovereign rule had broken into history and that he was its manifestation. This sovereign rule required the "greater righteousness" or justice found in the Sermon on the Mount. It comes as a gift in which we at most participate by actively seeking and not resisting it.

Christian Ethics and Modern Economics
As the above discussion demonstrates, Christianity does not provide a coherent macroeconomic system, but it does offer an economic ethic. Its basic elements are found in Scripture, developed in tradition, speak primarily to those in the church, and secondarily to all persons of good will. It does not provide definitive answers to economic questions; Christian ethics is not a deductive, logical system, but it offers practical reason in order to guide first the church in its witness and second all persons of good will, in seeking communion. It does so by attending to Scripture in the light of its reception in tradition, and drawing upon ethical wisdom wherever it is found so long as it is consistent with the worship of God. From this practical perspective, the following economic matters can now be taken up: equality, property, natural resources, products, wealth, income, employment, and taxation. Each will be examined by considering them in terms of Scripture, church doctrine, or faithful exemplars who assist us in understanding what is at stake in the question.

Equality

The first book of the Bible—*Genesis*—teaches that all creatures are made in the image of God (Genesis 1:26). The New Testament teaches that in the renewed creation, creatures are given a diversity of gifts and vocations (Romans 12:3–8). They are not equal in the sense of possessing the same opportunities or capacities, and we should not strive to make them so. Christianity, like Judaism, affirms what has been called "the scandal of election." Some are elect for special vocations and given gifts and capacities for those vocations. Others are asked to provide resources to support those special vocations. Abraham and Sarah were elect for a particular mission and equipped to fulfill it. Mary, the mother of Jesus, was likewise given a special calling concomitant with the graces necessary for it. Prophets, apostles, saints, martyrs, and others are also elect. Christianity assumes that these exemplars "fix the reference" of the good, just, and wise person.[16] These exemplars provide conceptual clarity without systematic totality. They are given higher regard in that they are to be imitated as they have imitated Christ.

Because human beings cannot will themselves into a relationship with God, the doctrine of election means God either initiates or is solely responsible for a just relationship between God and creatures and among creatures. The doctrine of election, with its inequality of capacities, has had negative outcomes when it is applied to wealth. Max Weber interpreted the doctrine of election in Calvinism as suggesting wealth became a sign in Christianity that a person is of the elect, and thus it was a motivating force in the accumulation of capital. Medieval Catholic and Lutheran Christian ethics did not have such a strong doctrine of election, so Weber suggested, and viewed wealth with more suspicion. For them, work was understood as a necessity after the fall, but not a place in which one worked out one's salvation. Calvinists also had a suspicion of wealth, but they viewed their work as a calling that could be an indication of election if it were rewarded. In other words, riches imply that God has blessed someone, and this blessing is an indication that they are elect. It leads to a justification for economic inequality.[17] Weber's interpretation has been widely criticized, but there have been aberrant Protestant teachings, such as the "prosperity gospel," that do equate wealth and election. They were not present among the formative Protestant theologians in the sixteenth and seventeenth centuries. Economic justice as communion pared with elect exemplars suggests an inequality of capacities, but it does not suggest that the possession of wealth is a sign of election or that unequal economic outcomes are justified.

Election should result in a sharing of goods that is not a strict equality, but at a minimum ensures no one lives in poverty. Abundant wealth is not a sign of election; instead Scripture states that a sign of divine election is that "there are no needy among you" (Deuteronomy 15:4). Two passages from the sequel to the *Gospel of Luke*—*The Acts of the Apostles*— became a source for this Christian understanding of equality. *The Acts of the*

Apostles presents Jesus' disciples continuing his mission after his death and resurrection. It begins with the story of Pentecost, when the Holy Spirit descends upon Jews "from every nation" and unites them in a common language, undoing God's division of peoples in the myth of Babel. The unity they have is not only the ability to communicate with language, but also with their goods. Both in Acts 2 and Acts 4, a consequence of the outpouring of the Spirit is that persons sell their possessions "and distribute the proceeds to all, as any had need" (Acts 2:45) with the result that there are no needy among them (Acts 4:34). The latter is a sign that God's reign has come upon human creatures; for when it occurs, poverty will be eradicated. If the Kingdom has come, then there should be signs of it. *Acts* finds them in these early Jerusalem Jewish-Christian communities. Justice occurs through the sharing of possessions in which poverty is eradicated.

The messianic expectation of possessions held in common provides practical insight into a Christian understanding of what should be equal and what should not. Each person is given a gift to be cultivated. Capacities must be identified and brought to their fullness, and each person is unique in the capacities given. Resources should be shared in the cultivation of capacities, and that cultivation allows for diversity of capacities, including those who lack capacities for mainstream forms of economic productivity. Every human creature has a gift, including the differently abled, the young, the sick, the elderly, and the dying. Christian communities such as *L'Arche* "provide homes and workplaces where people with and without intellectual disabilities live and work together as peers."[18] They are signs of economic justice as communion. Distribution is made not on merit, but on need.

Christianity does not assume strict equality in which everyone is reduced by fiat to the same level, or lack, of ownership of goods. It encourages communities such as religious orders, Anabaptist communities, and lay monastics, in which common ownership is practiced at the level of proportional equality. In some of these communities, persons contribute their earnings to a "common purse," which is then distributed based on need. These communities are understood as voluntary arrangements that point to God's realm, and they are to influence how all Christians hold their property, but they are not understood to be an economic blueprint that one should force on one's neighbors through state intervention.

Economic justice as communion focuses more on need than on equality of inputs or aptitudes. It affirms differences in productivity but does not assert that inequalities in inputs or aptitudes should have a disproportionate share of the profits. The term "social justice," originally set forth in Pius XI's 1931 encyclical *Quadragesimo anno*, had a specific meaning related to profit-sharing among workers and owners. Like much present in Christian economic ethics, Pius XI did not reject owners' right to profit from the employment of their property, but he also insisted that workers could not be "excluded" from "sharing in the benefits" that the social relationship between owners and workers produced. The proper understanding of that relationship was termed "social," or sometimes "contributive justice." Workers were entitled to a sustainable wage and sharing in benefits such that they, too, had the ability to contribute to the common good. Because the distribution of goods should serve the "perfection" God intends, and that perfection includes everyone having the wherewithal to give alms or share their possessions, owners who profit from workers by excluding from them the surplus necessary to contribute to the common good commit an injustice against them.[19]

Economic justice as communion also requires an equal sharing in risk. The traditional "usury prohibition," understood at its best, was to ensure that risks are equally shared by everyone involved in an economic exchange. Most modern economists claim that this teaching was incoherent and a roadblock to a rational economy (John Maynard Keynes was an exception).[20] The usury prohibition is often condemned for imagining economics was a zero-sum game: someone could profit only at another person's expense. However, a cursory examination of the teaching demonstrates the error in that judgment. The usury prohibition allowed for a legitimate profit through "titles" known as *damnum emergens* and *lucrum cessans*. The first title allows for compensation on a loan from actual losses suffered by the one or ones who made it. The second allows for compensation from profits one could have expected in the employment of a loan, although they were not actual losses suffered. Both were permissible titles for compensation. However, both assumed that the risk was borne by all participants involved. Reasons had to be given as to why one had a claim on profit. It was insufficient to argue that one had a "right" to it only because one's capital had been used by others. How it was used, and the risks attendant on its use, were to be equally shared by all. As will be demonstrated below, these titles, along with the "universal destination" of property, set a standard of justice for what could be owned, bought, and sold.

Property

Jesus' teachings on property are some of his most difficult and confusing. He views possessions as a future promise for those who have none, as a present indictment for those who do, as a sign of proper use, as a threat for improper use, and as a sign of God's generosity independent of use. Mary's opening proclamation in the Gospel of Luke sets the tone for what follows. Jesus will "fill the hungry with good things and send the rich away empty" (Luke 1:53). This opening announcement sets the agenda for much that occurs in the Gospel. Jesus fed five thousand hungry persons with five loaves and two fishes (with clear allusions to the Lord's Supper or the Eucharist, Luke 9:12–17), and sent the rich away empty (Luke 18:18–25). He pronounces eschatological blessings on the poor (Luke 6:20–21), and condemnation upon the rich: "But woe to you who are rich, for you have received your consolation" (Luke 6:24–25). This condemnation is all the more striking because of the term "consolation." The "devout and righteous" Simeon had been looking for the "consolation of Israel" and he found it in the infant Jesus (Luke 2:25–32).[21] The poor will receive this consolation, but not the rich. A major teaching is that those who do not have will receive not only possessions but Jesus' consolation, and those who already have possessions will not.

Denunciation of those who have possessions is not the only approach Jesus takes toward them. He also affirms their proper use. It is affirmed and rewarded, while improper use is a reason for loss. In Luke 12:48, a servant is put in charge of more possessions because of his faithful use. Then Jesus states, "From everyone to whom much has been given, much will be required; and from the one to whom much has been entrusted, even more will be demanded."[22] Proper use is defined by its service to God's reign. Another teaching on possessions is that they are given regardless of proper or improper use. The prodigal son squanders his wealth and yet receives possessions, while the faithful, dutiful son is no more or less rewarded than the dissolute, prodigal one.

Taken as individual ethical commands, Jesus' teaching on possessions is confusing. A second major category of his teachings, however, is clear and coherent. Jesus unequivocally teaches the importance of offering alms or charity and sharing one's possessions. He tells not only his disciples but whomever listens to him to "give, and it will be given to you" (Luke 6:38). He admonishes them not only to give alms, but to do so by selling possessions: "Sell your possessions and give alms. Make purses for yourselves that do not wear out, an unfailing treasure in heaven, where no thief comes near and no moth destroys. For where your treasure is, there your heart will be also" (Luke 12:33). Giving becomes a sign of God's rule. Of course, there can be no giving without receiving, and Luke's gospel also affirms the importance of receiving. The women traveling with Jesus and his disciples "provided for them out of their resources" (Luke 8:1–3). Jesus' mission is possible because they give and he is willing to receive. The story of the Good Samaritan emphasizes that giving to those in need and being willing to receive from even unlikely sources obeys the law to love God and one's neighbor (Luke 10:25–37).

Private property receives a mixed review in the Scriptures. On the one hand, it is a sign that something has gone wrong. On the other, possessions can be properly used to care for the poor and to further Jesus' mission to restore creation. This mixed review led the majority of the Christian tradition to claim that private property, like war and slavery, were signs of the fall. They were not present in the Garden of Eden. They are *post lapsum* (after the fall) realities that could be used for good in the time between Christ's first and second comings, the time known as the *saeculum*. As *post lapsum* realities, they have a relative function. They are always means and should never be an end. Fortunately, slavery, although still widely practiced, is no longer acknowledged as a necessary *post lapsum* reality. War and private property are still understood as such by many but not all Christian ethicists. The difference among Christian ethicists has to do with the extent one should assume creation has been restored in Christ's incarnation, death, resurrection, and ascension. Although the Kingdom of God has not yet come and must still be prayed for, its first signs are present in history, and the task of Christian ethics is to witness to those signs. How Christians use property is the test of that witness.

Joan Lockwood O'Donovan has aptly developed the ambiguous character of private property for a contemporary Christian social ethics. She suggests that it should not be understood in terms of rights and property.

The modern notions of "subjective natural rights" are inadequate, because they are always associated with "property."[23] They view creation as "unowned resources" and ask who possesses rights to which resources under what conditions, including a right to own one's self. Rights, then, are proprietorial. Oliver O'Donovan makes a similar argument: "The curiously abstract thought of unowned resources in search of the right owners is simply the shadow of a proprietorial idea in which everything susceptible to just treatment is owned already."[24] The patristic and medieval Christian understanding of property was not that one had a right to it, but that all other creatures had a "claim" on the goods one owned. Lockwood O'Donovan refers to this as a "non-proprietary community of rights." It differs from our own modern understanding of rights on two essential points: (1) "Of all creatures, but especially of human individuals, this [nonproprietary] ethic affirms that they *are claims*, not that they *possess rights*: as objects of God's self-communication in Christ persons are claims upon the wills of one another"; (2) "A second insight of the non-proprietary ethic is that righteous human lordship is communal chiefly because it is spiritual: that is, righteous human community is a sharing in or communication of spiritual goods before physical goods."[25] Her non-proprietorial community of rights is seldom at the center of Christian economic teaching today; she acknowledges that it would need to be retrieved in the face of the dominance of modern rights and a proprietorial ethic. However, in both Protestant and Catholic teaching, this non-proprietorial ethic can still be found. Both traditions teach that individuals do not have an inalienable right to property; it should be held for specific ends. All property is a gift from God and thus it has a "universal destination." The latter term refers to the teaching that once a person has sufficient resources to care for her or his family, any surplus should be directed toward the common good. God has permitted private property in the time between the times for the preservation of our own life first, and then that of our neighbors, and then of all God's creatures. If those ends are violated, the ownership of property becomes little more than theft.

Property oriented toward the universal destination of goods conflicts with modern, Lockean understandings of inalienable property rights. The exercise of one's labor does not entail an inalienable right to property. Take, for instance, Thomas Aquinas's explanation of the biblical commandment against stealing. Stealing is not simply taking something from someone else. If someone is wealthy and another person is destitute to the point of being unable to sustain the life of his or her family, then the poor person does not steal in taking from the wealthy person even if he refuses to give. For his property, like all property, is a patrimony to be used for the good of all, with a "preference" for the poor. Latin American liberation theology takes this long-held teaching of the preferential option for the poor as its central organizing theological theme. Theologians and church leaders have suggested ownership can be relinquished when these ends are dishonored, although how it is relinquished and to whom is not specified. Few argue for a non-voluntary seizure of property by an empire or state.

The universal destination of all our goods does not give precise information as to what constitutes a maximum amount for what people can own, or how much can be earned. In some Christian traditions, there is no such maximum. For instance, the eighteenth-century Anglican and founder of Methodism, John Wesley, gave this counsel: "Earn all you can, save all you can and give all you can." Such counsel is not unique; it is present in much of Christian tradition. Seldom has it suggested a maximum on what can be earned or saved. The limitation on owning is found in the third part of the counsel. If one earns and saves in order to give, then the limitation on what can be owned depends on the needs of those who should be the recipients of one's gifts. A standard understanding of this limitation is that all superfluities and luxuries rob the needy of their due and violate economic justice. What constitutes superfluities and luxuries has been variously defined.

The universal destination of all our goods tolerates some economic inequality, but nothing as drastic as what is present in contemporary society. A fixed number cannot be given for an acceptable inequality, but any inequality that leaves some struggling to meet their basic needs and others able to meet their needs and much more is a sign of economic injustice. Recall that social justice requires that all working persons should be able to care for their families *and* make a contribution to the common good. Everyone should be able to use her or his possessions to fulfill the universal destination that God intends for our property.

Natural Resources

The majority Christian tradition permits private ownership of most natural resources, but rather than "natural resources," water, air, land, plants, animals, minerals, and so forth, should first and foremost be considered as creatures. Once they are, then it challenges thinking of them only as resources that can be used for the purpose of human existence. Water and air, for instance, are creaturely goods necessary for human and animal creatures. Poisoning wells even in times of war was understood as a grave injustice committed not only against other creatures but also against God. Water is to be held in common even among enemies. Creation is good in its own right. Can it be owned? Can one creature own another? There is a hierarchy of goods that allows for private ownership as a *post lapsum* reality. In its worst ethical manifestation, this hierarchy permitted slavery and underwrote patriarchy. After the nineteenth-century abolition of slavery, the hierarchy of creaturely goods no longer extends to one race, nation, or culture of human creatures owning another. A few Christian ethicists suggest the abolition of hierarchical ownership should now be extended to animal life. None have argued that plant life cannot be cultivated and owned.

Christianity shares with Judaism a mission that helps make sense of the relationship between resources necessary for life and their transformation into products useful for all. The mission is found in Genesis 12:1–3; it is a mission God gives to Abraham and Sarah: "Go from your country and your kindred and your father's house to the land that I will show you. I will make of you a great nation, and I will bless you, and make your name great, so that you will be a blessing. I will bless those who bless you, and the one who curses you I will curse; and in you all the families of the earth shall be blessed." Abraham's mission is to not be like the other nations for the sake of the nations. The distinctive, particular identity is in order to be a blessing to everyone. These norms of proximity and universality guide ethical judgments about natural resources. Societies have responsibilities for resources proximate to them in order to first ensure their communities are sustainable. They also have responsibilities to use those proximate resources for the good of all. Workers turning lobsters into a commodity for the global market should not suffer from malnutrition because they lack the financial wherewithal to purchase a product they themselves have created. A rich copper mine in the Andes in Colombia should primarily sustain those closest to it. At the same time, a local community should not hoard local resources needed by all.

The tension between a particular, proximate identity for the sake of universal blessing provides a basic moral norm that is sometimes called the "principle of subsidiarity." Inasmuch as it is possible, judgments should be left to a local level, but the judgments made, especially for economics, should have a universal destination. Proximity to resources entails claims to, and responsibilities for them, but the proximity to "natural" resources also serves the universal mission of humanity-in-communion.

Humanity-in-communion can be furthered at the local and global level by maintaining common spaces. Christianity has a long tradition of "the commons." It is a shared space that cannot be privately owned inasmuch as everyone in a locality depends upon it for sustenance. The commons could be a forest, the fish in an ocean, natural plant life, etc. "The commons" assumes there are creaturely resources everyone has a stake in, in order to sustain life. Their sustainability assumes economic justice as communion. Persons must voluntarily consent to use common resources based on need and not for individual profit. An economic theory known as "the tragedy of the commons" suggests that some will violate the commons and use it for their own advantage to the detriment of others. Government intervention by parceling up the commons into privately owned resources ruled by law and contract supposedly prevents the tragedy of the commons. Such intervention has been commonplace since the eighteenth century. Thus, private ownership in modern economics greatly diminished common spaces. However, they continue to exist: roads, parks, forests, water, and air are still de facto common spaces in many places. Much of modern economics seeks the transformation of common spaces, now increasingly rare, into privately owned natural resources. Christian economic justice moves in the opposite direction. It seeks to extend common spaces as far as possible.

On the one hand, common spaces require "proximity." Those closest in proximity to the resources have a priority in their use and/or ownership. They will know and love them more so than distant owners who view them primarily for their use or as profit. On the other hand, the priority of those in proximity to resources should not come at the expense of the global. Local communities can be myopic and seek their own interests at the expense of the universal destination of our goods. In our present situation, a situation that has existed since colonialism, the global has taken a priority over the local, which jeopardizes the sustainability of local common spaces. For instance, the legacy of mining for natural resources has created a situation in which local communities speak of the "curse" of those resources. Rather than enriching and sustaining local communities, mining for minerals has destroyed them. Mountains are reduced to rubble, profits are taken globally, and local communities have been abandoned. This legacy creates an unstable economic situation that some international mining corporations have acknowledged.

In 2013, the International Council of Mining and Materials (ICMM) met with Pope Francis and the Pontifical Council on Justice and Peace in order to seek the counsel of the church to assist with their troubled legacy. In 2014, they held a second conference, at Lambeth Palace, with Anglicans and Methodists.[26] The mining companies that comprise the ICMM acknowledged the problematic legacy of mining and sought the counsel of Christian churches to assist them, recognizing that Christian churches have been one place in which the extraction of local, natural resources by global corporations has been challenged. The ICMM implemented ten principles of sustainable development to address this legacy, and required all their members to abide by these principles.[27] One principle is to "uphold fundamental human rights and respect cultures, customs and values in dealings with employees and others who are affected by our activities." They have asked churches to hold them accountable to their ethical principles.

A central role for the Christian church is to hold corporations accountable to economic justice. In so doing, the church acknowledges a place for private ownership but also seeks to limit that ownership by asking how it serves both the local and global realities of human existence. Mining companies have the capital resources to move tens of thousands of people into remote areas, remove whole communities from traditional lands, and create industries that increase traffic, pollution, and put pressure on local resources beyond those of the materials being mined. They have more power than local, and sometimes national, governments. Christian economic justice requires limitations on ownership of these resources based on their proper use. Morally licit private ownership of natural resources, if it is to be tolerated, should not only share profits with workers but also demonstrate how such ownership enriches the life of the local populations and the global community.

The Christian tradition has been attentive to legitimate and illegitimate forms of profit of creaturely resources. Some things can be owned; others cannot. Once again, the traditional teaching on usury has some relevance. Opposition to unjust profit in terms of "usury" goes back to the Council of Nicaea in 325. It was an extension of Old Testament passages such as Exodus 22:23, Deuteronomy, 23:19–20, Leviticus 25:36–37, Psalms 15:5, coupled with Luke 6:35. It also affirmed Aristotle's prohibition of usury based on his teaching that "money does not fructify." The prohibition, however, was not made imperial law until the Carolingian period (eighth century).[28] Making money from money was viewed as illegitimate because it wrongly described business practices; money obviously cannot make money without being employed in productive enterprises. To claim that money made money was another form of mendacity. It was also assumed to sell something that only belonged to God—time. Time is not a "natural resource" that can be sold. Judgments must be made on the justice of those enterprises; the role of the Christian church is to function as a transnational community that makes judgments on the justice of profits and the appropriateness of "resources" that can be turned into commodities and traded.

Products

The term *product* assumes the cultural transformation of natural resources into commodities serviceable to human needs. If by "natural" is meant something that is neutral to theological or ethical evaluation before it becomes a product, then Christian economic justice has no category known as "natural" resources. Such a neutral account of "nature" is often present in the modern fact/value distinction present in introductory economic textbooks. The fact/value distinction assumes that neutral, non-ethical facts are objectively present waiting for subjective ethical evaluations only after they have become products. A forest, mountain, or mineral is just an inert potential input waiting for human productivity to give it meaning or purpose by transforming it into a commodity. Of course, Christian economic ethics knows categories like trees, mountains, and minerals, but it cannot begin by viewing them as "resources" to be made into products.

Not everything can be turned into a product. Basic realities for human subsistence—time, water, air, sexual reproduction, body parts—are turned into tradable commodities only by violating creation as God's gift. A kidney is not like a mineral. It cannot be turned into a commodity and traded on a futures market. Minerals, however, are necessary for human flourishing and can be traded. Everyone needs them. Christian ethicist Esther Reed explains how all our lives are implicated in mining. "Anyone with a mobile phone or washing machine, who uses electricity that travels down copper wires, rides in cars with emission control devices made of platinum, handles coins that contain nickel, has had restorative dentistry involving a gold alloy crown, uses buildings with ceramics optimized for stability and strength with zircon, toothpaste and sun-screen, and much more, benefits from the products of mining."[29] The transformation of natural sources into such necessary products does a service to the global community.

Human creatures are entrusted by God to use non-human creatures for specifically human purposes. They are given "dominion" over them, but dominion does not mean domination or exploitation. Take, for instance, the relationship between human and animal creatures in the Bible: eating animals is itself another sign of the Fall. Plant life sustains animal and human life. The first story of creation in *Genesis* states, "God said, 'See, I have given you every plant yielding seed that is upon the face of all the earth, and every tree with seed in its fruit; you shall have them for food. And to every beast of the earth and to every bird of the air, and to everything that creeps on the earth, everything that has the breath of life, I have given every green plant for food.' And it was so" (Genesis 1:29–30). Human creatures are not permitted to eat animal life until after the Great Deluge and the new covenant God makes with Noah. After the flood, animals and humans live in fear of each other. God tells Noah, "Every moving thing that lives shall be food for you; and just as I gave you the green plants, I give you everything." The animal life now consumed still belongs to God and taking it requires accountability. "Only, you shall not eat flesh with its life, that is, its blood. For your own lifeblood I will surely require a reckoning; from every animal I will require it and from human beings, each one for the blood of another, I will require a reckoning for human life" (Genesis 9:3–5).

Christian economic justice does not set a fixed ceiling or floor on what percentage of natural resources can be owned and turned into products. On the whole, it affirms that local governments make these determinations. However, the positive law affirmed by local governments must be held accountable to the natural and divine laws found in the purposes for these creaturely realities, including that all our "resources" are entrusted to us first as gifts.

Wealth

In *Naked Economics*, Charles Wheelan rejects the claim that wealth can have a limit. He first distinguishes wealth from money. Wheelan states, "To economists, money is quite distinct from wealth. Wealth consists of all things that have value—houses, cars, commodities, human capital. Money, a tiny subset of that wealth, is merely a medium of exchange, something that facilitates trade and commerce."[30] Once wealth is distinguished from money, it has no limit. Wheelan states, "Economics tells us there is no theoretical limit on how well we can live or how widely our wealth can be spread."[31] The lack of a theoretical limit to wealth is why the economists he cites are unconcerned about "income gap."[32] Christian economic justice is more suspicious about wealth. The accumulation of material wealth works against the mission for which possessions are given. Jesus' teaching on this is clear: "Do not store up for yourselves treasures on earth, where moth and rust consume and where thieves break in and steal; but store up for yourselves treasures in heaven, where neither moth nor rust consumes and where thieves do not break in and steal. For where your treasure is, there your heart will be also" (Matthew 6:19–21).

Jesus' denunciation of material wealth might not differ from Wheelan's affirmation of wealth. If it consists of "things that have value," then "treasure in heaven" could be construed as a thing with infinite value and thus it possesses no upward limit. True wealth is found in God, who is infinite, eternal, and thus inexhaustible. The conflict occurs with Wheelan's use of "things" in his definition. Wealth is for him an immanent and material reality. To argue that it has no limit is to fail to see the purpose of material possessions. As creatures, they are finite, temporal, and exhaustible. Rowan Williams, former Archbishop of Canterbury, argues that to learn to live within limits is what it means to become a moral subject.[33] Our temporal life itself is limited and requires us to make significant moral decisions on what matters most.

Wealth has a limit, in that it has an end. The end of wealth for an economic justice founded upon communion is mission. Based on the sayings of Jesus, Philip Goodchild has stated that for Christianity "wealth is service."[34] Service, or mission, is to foster humanity-in-communion. Anything beyond the wealth necessary for securing the basic goods for one's family and then contributing to the common good is viewed with suspicion. Anyone with such surplus wealth would need to justify it in terms of its appropriateness for mission.

Almsgiving and renunciation are two remedies for exorbitant wealth. In the Gospels, Jesus responds differently to his followers and would-be followers about their possessions. Some are affirmed for no longer defrauding and giving alms or charity, others are asked to do more. The rich ruler who has kept the commandments all his life is told he only lacks one thing: "Sell all that you own and distribute the money to the poor, and you will have treasure in heaven" (Luke 18:22). Others are also asked to renounce their possessions completely in order to follow Jesus. In a section on enemy love (also found in Matthew), Jesus accentuates his teaching on almsgiving so much that he renounces any possible gain from lending. "If you lend to those from whom you hope to receive, what credit is that to you? Even sinners lend to sinners, to receive as much again. But love your enemies, do good, and lend, expecting nothing in return" (Luke 6:34–35). This teaching became known as the evangelical law of perfection.

Irenaeus (130–200, bishop of Lyons) was one of many early Christian theologians who addressed the question "Why was the rich young ruler asked to give all and not others?" Irenaeus' answer became a standard response toward wealth. The particular sin of the rich young ruler was covetousness. As a healing for his particular sin, Jesus offered him the possibility of almsgiving. Almsgiving is not only necessary for relieving the plight of the poor; it is also a means by which the rich can ensure that avarice does not take root. The wealthy cannot simply claim a "spiritual" detachment from their possessions; they must also demonstrate it by a practical, material dispossession through sharing possessions and almsgiving.

If Irenaeus assumed the problem was not wealth per se, but one's attachment to it, Clement of Alexandria (150–215) made that assumption explicit. As Justo Gonzalez puts it, Clement's "Can a Rich Man Be Saved?" is "the first attempt at a systematic discussion of the relationship between faith and wealth."[35] Clement provided one of the earliest defenses of a limited form of private property. He argued that if the story of the rich young ruler were lived out by every Christian, then the faithful would have no goods to give and share and thus the command to do so could not be fulfilled. "Those who have nothing cannot feed the hungry or clothe the naked." He reads the story of the rich young ruler as an allegory where the "selling of all possessions" is equivalent to "ridding the soul of passions."[36] Nonetheless, ridding the soul of vice cannot be done spiritually without actually attending to material dispossession.

In the Christian tradition, wealth should not be gained from illicit means. As noted above, benefiting from what could not be turned into a commodity, such as time or body parts, was a grave injustice. Even if it would be Pareto-optimal, wealth gained from a futures market for body organs or surrogacy violates the basic norms of Christian economic justice. As will be noted below, Catholic teaching judges "degrading conditions of work" that treat people as "instruments of labor" to be intrinsically evil. The Catholic catechism teaches that keeping the Sabbath is a "protest against the servitude of work." It states, "God's action is the model for human action. If God 'rested and was refreshed' on the seventh day, man too ought to 'rest' and should let others, especially the poor, 'be refreshed.' The sabbath brings everyday work to a halt and provides a respite. It is a day of protest against the servitude of work and the worship of money."[37]

Money should not be made by fanciful financial instruments devoid of just productive enterprises. Reasons should be given for how wealth is produced based on proper use of God's creation. Some forms of transfer, such as inheritance or donations, have been understood as licit. They should not be prohibited by law. But to gain and keep wealth through these means without giving it to those in need, or for the sake of mission and service, places a suspicion on that wealth as well.

Income

How one earns one's living is as important for Christian economic justice as how much wealth one holds. In the early church, those preparing for baptism were asked to give up some forms of work. In his treatise "On

Idolatry," Tertullian argues that all sin can be traced back to idolatry; concupiscence, lasciviousness, drunkenness, vanity, and mendacity are all species of idolatry.[38] How someone earns a living can underwrite these forms of idolatry, so Tertullian takes great pains to explain how certain occupations must be avoided, such as gladiator, teacher, soldier, or artisan of idols, because they implicate one's life, and the life of the community, in idolatry.[39] Like many in the early church, he then asks whether all "trade" entails covetousness: "is trade adapted for a servant of God? But, covetousness apart, what is the motive for acquiring?" He answers his question carefully, not assuming that all trade and business only arises from a covetousness motive. He rejects those forms of trade and business that he finds particularly culpable of covetousness, but nevertheless suggests, "Let none contend that, in this way, exception may be taken to all trades."[40] Few of us have to worry today about the specific trades that troubled Tertullian, but his work signals that how one makes one's living is a matter of Christian ethics.

Few contemporary Christian ethicists are as specific as Tertullian on what vocations are permissible and forbidden for Christians. However, Vatican II's *Gaudium et spes* noted activities forbidden for Catholic Christians that are possible sources of profit in the contemporary market economy. In his encyclical *Veritatis splendor*, John Paul II cited this teaching for its ongoing relevance in terms of evil acts that should never be permitted: "whatever is offensive to human dignity, such as subhuman living conditions, arbitrary imprisonment, deportation, slavery, prostitution and trafficking in women and children, degrading conditions of work which treat labourers as mere instruments of profit and not as free responsible persons . . ."[41] Persons are not to be "instruments of profit." Catholic teaching does not explicitly identify what specific work should be permitted and prohibited, but profiting from child labor has often been understood as excluded. The latter has been a source of ongoing debate in that some economists and a few Christian ethicists argue global corporations that rely on child labor are permissible because the alternatives for children in those contexts are worse. That kind of utilitarian ethic is unusual in Christian ethics. If forms of work are evil because they reduce laborers to instruments of profit, how laborers are paid is a pressing ethical matter.

Employment

Labor has a mixed relationship in the Christian tradition. The difficulty
in producing goods from the earth was understood as a judgment by God
upon human sinfulness. The arduous character of Adam and Eve's labor
was a sign something had gone wrong, a sign of the "fall" that broke the
original communion between God and creatures that originally allowed
for a sharing of God's good creation among them. Arduous labor was
understood—like private property, slavery, and war—as something not
redemptive, but necessary. It will have no place in God's final reign.

Mission is more important than labor in Christian Scriptures. Work
oriented toward mission was affirmed more so than labor. There are admonitions as to how one should do his or her work. Along with his admonitions to give, John the Baptist admonishes those who came to him to fulfill
their work justly. Tax collectors are to take no more than their due, and
soldiers or police are not to extort. Jesus never rejects these themes, and
there are instances where he, too, demands the just exercise of one's labor,
but he also relativizes labor, affirming that those who leave their daily
work to join in his mission will still find provisions. Levi the tax collector
leaves his work for the sake of Jesus' mission (Luke 5:29), and several other
disciples leave their fishing occupation. His closest disciples are encouraged to set aside their labor because "life is more than food" (Luke 12:23).
Not everyone, however, is called to leave his or her work. The tax collector
Zacchaeus does not abandon his work but promises no longer to defraud
and to restore those he had defrauded fourfold (Luke 19:1–10). Jesus responds affirmatively, "Today salvation has come to this house, because he
too is a son of Abraham."

Although arduous labor is a necessary evil *post lapsum*, mission is a
vocation that redeems our labor. Everyone should be granted sufficient
income to sustain life. Whenever sustenance is violated, it is a sign that
God's reign has been violated. Pope Leo XIII set forth three principles
for proper remuneration that have wide agreement in Christian teaching.
First, "To defraud any one of wages that are his due is a crime which cries
to the avenging anger of Heaven."[42] His second principle helps understand
what is due to a worker. Wages are not fixed simply "by free consent."
The third principle states that "the remuneration must be enough to support the wage-earner in reasonable and frugal comfort."[43] Leo's principles

are repeated throughout Catholic social teaching and have been affirmed by many Protestants. They led to a tradition of a "just wage" that some cities have attempted to set in law. The church's teachings, however, are admonitions; they are not positive law, nor do they attempt to be so. Each city, village, or town would need to consider the best means by which to implement the admonition. Likewise, Christians involved in ownership, working, or profiting from a corporation would need to discern how best to embody these teachings given the realities of their workplace. Some have attempted to implement them by suggesting a ratio of 7:1—the highest-paid person should not make more than seven times the lowest-paid person. Few corporations have taken the church's teaching to heart through such practical policies. The best means to do this is through democratic forms of corporate governance among all those involved. It should also be the case that those who do not have capacities for productivity still must be given sufficient resources to sustain them and their families.

Taxation

In Scripture, the "tax collectors" were treated with suspicion and viewed as extortionists who took more than their due. Several of them became Jesus' followers, and in so doing gave up their work. Others were told to take no more than their due. They were not told to abandon their work. Such counsel suggests the legitimacy of taxation. However, Jesus addressed this question directly with an ambiguous answer. Some Pharisees sought to trick him into challenging the Roman Empire by asking, "Tell us, then, what you think. Is it lawful to pay taxes to the emperor, or not?" Jesus shows them the emperor's head on the coin and says, "Give therefore to the emperor the things that are the emperor's, and to God the things that are God's" (Matthew 22:21). Jesus' response has created an ambiguous tradition of taxation in Christianity. The question it raises is what belongs to Caesar (the state) and what belongs to God?

Saint Augustine was one of the most formative thinkers on questions of the relationship between the church and the state in the West. He never rejected a limited role for the state (or empire) in the pursuing of temporal goods. He did reject an ancient understanding of politics, that it could be used to perfect the human species. This opposition to a politics of perfection runs deep in the Christian tradition. Politics has a limited role in God's economy. Michael Bruno sets forth well Augustine's position: "Voting, the payment of taxes, military service, and obedience to the rule of law, are all to be undertaken by the Christian. Indeed, all of these tasks, as banal at times as they might seem, are opportunities to accomplish good by the exercise of virtue. However, none of these obligations must be seen as equal to the heavenly calling of the Christian, who must object to them if they threaten the ultimate end, heavenly citizenship."[44] Christian tradition has not opposed taxation, but it questions what is a legitimate extraction of taxes and what is not. Augustine's primary criterion for determining the legitimacy of taxation is: does it prohibit the proper worship of God? By proper worship, he does not mean only the liturgical act, but the ability to orient one's life to one's true end: the worship and praise of God.

Diverse Christian traditions find funding different social institutions by taxation to violate this true end. Most allow for funding education, although Catholics in the United States objected early that public education was Protestant education and tax money was going to fund religion. In response, they created their own schools, on occasion sought taxation for some services and have been rejected. Some evangelical Christians oppose taxation for public education in the present because of a perceived secular bias. The peace church traditions have opposed being forced to pay taxes to support military preparations for and during wartime. Roman Catholics and others have opposed forcing them and their institutions to pay for contraception or abortions in the Affordable Care Act. Despite these protests, few have advocated tax resistance by withholding taxes for what is found objectionable. Such tax resistance is present among Christians, but it is a minor tradition.

The Christian tradition has seldom rejected redistributionist taxation. Although the state should not assume its purpose is to make us holy or perfect us—that belongs to the church alone—the state can assist in the mission by ensuring a basic level of subsistence. Taxes can create a common space that secures the good for all persons. Little interest has been present in a strict assessment proportioned to use: roads, education, police, parks, welfare services are among some of the common spaces to which everyone capable has an obligation to contribute to support the needs of the common good. The central mission of the church to create "humanity-in-communion" before God cannot be accomplished by the state, but inasmuch as it creates the possibility for the cultivation of common spaces, it can accomplish the good present in creation. The Christian tradition has not had a specific proposal on tax rates; such judgments depend upon those entrusted with local government.

Conclusion

Property should be held for its universal destination. How we earn wealth, hold property, exchange goods, distribute resources, and profit from exchanges are all Christian ethical matters that reflect whether or not persons are imitating God's generosity or living against the grain of the universe by refusing to treat others as God treated them. For these reasons, money and wealth in the Christian tradition are not merely neutral elements. How one uses them are questions of salvation. Money is considered a temptation to evil; the love of money is called the "root of all evil" (I Timothy 6:10). Such a teaching led to a presumption against the accumulation of money. Luxuries and superfluities were condemned as robbing the poor of their patrimony. Making money on money was thought to be descriptively inaccurate and a violation of creation's goodness. In the Christian tradition, money was understood as a means of exchange, a store of value, and a unit of account. But to use it for speculation, especially buying a future that did not exist, and as credit that did not assume shared risk, was a sign of the "world" that is passing away; it is part of neither God's good creation nor redemption. Jesus' economic vision is related to his "eschatology"—his understanding of God's final work of restoring and completing creation.

Jesus began his ministry announcing the arrival of the "kingdom of God," and Roman imperial power putatively concluded it with his execution. Something about his life and teachings provoked Roman authorities to recognize him as a threat. In his trial as "king of the Jews," Jesus is brought before the Roman prefect Pontius Pilate, who asks the Jewish elders, "Shall I crucify your king?" To which the chief priests answer, "We have no king but caesar" (John 19:15). The New Testament scholar Raymond Brown suggests that this may give us authentic historical insight into the reason Jesus was crucified: concern about what Rome might think.[45] After his death and burial, Jesus' disciples and others claimed he was risen from the dead and this was the primary impetus behind the Christian movement. His disciples then continued to proclaim the presence of his "kingdom." As the above brief discussion illustrates, the coming of that kingdom anticipates an economic justice not easily embodied in this temporal life. However, Christianity privileges witnesses who begin now to live it, and encourages those inside and outside the church to follow their example.

The audience for a Christian economic justice is first and foremost those seeking to live the distinct way of life Christ calls them to live. Every ethic implies a social context, and the church is the primary social context for a Christian economics. Consistent with the mission of the universal destination of all our goods, the secondary social context is all of creation that seeks to live "with the grain of the universe." A late second-century letter, the "Epistle to Diognetus," explains this stance, and it does so in economic terms:

> For the Christians are distinguished from other men neither by country, nor language, nor the customs which they observe. For they neither inhabit cities of their own, nor employ a peculiar form of speech, nor lead a life which is marked out by any singularity. The course of conduct which they follow has not been devised by any speculation or deliberation of inquisitive men; nor do they, like some, proclaim themselves the advocates of any merely human doctrines. But, inhabiting Greek as well as barbarian cities, according as the lot of each of them has determined, and following the customs of the natives in respect to clothing, food, and the rest of their ordinary conduct, they display to us their wonderful and confessedly striking method of life. They dwell in their own countries, but simply as sojourners. As citizens, they share in all things with others, and yet endure all things as if foreigners. Every foreign land is to them as their native country, and every land of their birth as a land of strangers.[46]

The "Epistle to Diognetus" sets forth well the political and economic task of the early Christian communities. They did not seek to establish their own nations, cities, or economic systems. They acknowledged that they reside within other cities and economies and participate in them as fully as they can, but they do so by a "confessedly striking method of life." This epistle has a distinctly apologetic interest, but it displays the normative task of a "Christian economics"; it affirms what should be unique to its "method of life" while also participating as fully as possible in the good creaturely forms of life within which Christians find themselves.

Several centuries later, Saint Augustine offered counsel consistent with the "Epistle to Diognetus" in his influential *City of God*:

> The heavenly city, while it sojourns on earth . . . not scrupling about diversities in the manners, laws, and institutions whereby earthly peace is secured and maintained, but recognizing that, however various these are, they all tend to one and the same end of earthly peace. . . . [is] so far from rescinding and abolishing these diversities, that it even preserves and adopts them so long only as no hindrance to the worship of the one supreme and true God is thus introduced. Even the heavenly city, therefore, while in its state of pilgrimage, avails itself of the peace of earth, and . . . desires and maintains a common agreement among men regarding the acquisition of the necessities of life so far as it can without injuring faith and godliness.[47]

For both the writer of the epistle and Augustine, the task of a Christian economics is twofold. On the one hand, insofar as no injustice is done to faith or true worship, Christians participate in the "acquisition of the necessities of life" in harmony with all others. On the other hand, when the possibility of that injustice arises, Christians should attend to their "striking method of life" by refusing to cooperate. The wide diversity of cities or nations and their economies within which Christian churches find themselves, along with the wide diversity of Christian churches themselves, makes it difficult, if not impossible, to provide *the* Christian approach to economic inequality. Christians should not seek to impose their distinct way of life through state intervention. The "politics of perfection" is found in the church, not the state. Whenever Christians can cooperate with the state, civil society, neighbors near and far, in increasing common spaces, they should do so.

Notes

1. See Michael Warner, *Changing Witness: Catholic Bishops and Public Policy, 1917–1994* (Grand Rapids, Michigan: Wm. B. Eerdmans Publishing Company, 1995). Michael Novak's work has been at the forefront of Catholic efforts to pres-

ent the free market as consistent with the natural law. Contemporary Roman Catholic moral theologians retrieving a neo-scholastic natural-law approach would include Germain Grisez's *The Way of the Lord Jesus: vol. 1 Christian Moral Principles* (Chicago, Illinois: Franciscan Herald Press, 1983), 173–205; Steven A. Long, *Natura Pura: On the Recovery of Nature in the Doctrine of Grace* (New York, New York: Fordham University Press, 2010); and Jean Porter, *Nature as Reason: A Thomistic Theory of the Natural Law* (Grand Rapids, Michigan: Wm. B. Eerdmans Publishing Company, 2004); see also Joseph Boyle's essay in this volume. Although these moral theologians would agree on the importance of the natural law, how it works itself out in ethics does not find agreement.

2. Ernst Troeltsch, *The Social Teaching of the Christian Churches, vol. 1,* trans. by Oliver Wyon (Chicago, Illinois: The University of Chicago Press, 1981), 39–40.

3. Alasdair MacIntyre, *After Virtue: A Study in Moral Theory* (Notre Dame, Indiana: University of Notre Dame Press, 1981).

4. For a fuller account of these movements and their relationship the reader can consult my *Saving Karl Barth: Hans Urs von Balthasar's Preoccupation* (Minneapolis, Minnesota: Fortress Press, 2014), especially chapter 5, "The Realm of Ethics," and *Christian Ethics: A Very Short Introduction* (Oxford, Great Britain: Oxford University Press, 2010), 99–105.

5. See Paul Ramsey, *Nine Modern Moralists* (Lanham, Maryland: University Press of America, 1983), 1–8.

6. Oliver O'Donovan, *Desire of the Nations* (Cambridge, Great Britain: Cambridge University Press, 1996), 19. See also his *Resurrection and Moral Order: An Outline for Evangelical Ethics* (Grand Rapids, Michigan: Wm. B. Eerdmans Publishing Company, 1986).

7. Stanley Hauerwas, *The Peaceable Kingdom* (Notre Dame, IN: University of Notre Dame Press, 1983) 99.

8. Daniel Bell, *Economy and Desire: Christianity and Capitalism in a Postmodern World* (Grand Rapids, Michigan: Baker Academic, 2012).

9. Stanley Hauerwas and Samuel Wells, eds., *The Blackwell Companion to Christian Ethics* (London, Great Britain: Wiley-Blackwell, 2006), 182.

10. For a fuller discussion of Bell's account of justice within ecclesial ethics see D. Stephen Long, *Augustinian and Ecclesial Ethics: On Loving Enemies* (Lanham, Maryland: Lexington Books, 2018).

11. See William Cavanaugh, *Being Consumed* (Grand Rapids, Michigan: Wm. B. Eerdmans Publishing Company, 2008).

12. Augustine, *Confessions* (London, Great Britain: Penguin Books, 1961), 147.

13. Hauerwas and Wells, eds., *The Blackwell Companion to Christian Ethics,* 189–190.

14. William Cavanaugh, *Being Consumed* (Grand Rapids, Michigan: Wm. B. Eerdmans Publishing Company, 2008), 88.

15. Hauerwas and Wells, eds., *The Blackwell Companion to Christian Ethics,* 189.

16. See Linda Trinkaus Zagzebski, *Divine Motivation Theory* (Cambridge,

Great Britain: Cambridge University Press, 2004). Her "exemplarism" is a non-teleological virtue theory based on the premise that "We do not have criteria for goodness in advance of identifying the exemplars of goodness" (41). Exemplars, she notes, "fix the reference of the term 'good person' or 'practically wise person' without the use of concepts, whether descriptive or nondescriptive. An exemplar therefore allows the series of conceptual definitions to get started" (45).

17. Max Weber, *The Protestant Ethic and the Spirit of Capitalism*, revised 1920 ed. (Oxford, Great Britain: Oxford University Press, 2010).

18. See http://www.larcheusa.org

19. *Quadragesimo anno,* para. 57, at http://w2.vatican.va/content/pius-xi/en/encyclicals/documents/hf_p-xi_enc_19310515_quadragesimo-anno.html

20. See John Maynard Keynes, *The General Theory of Employment, Interest and Money* (New York, New York: Harcourt, Brace and World, 1964), 351–352.

21. In both places, the Greek "παράκλησιν" is used.

22. A similar teaching is found in Luke 8:18: "Then pay attention to how you listen; for to those who have, more will be given; and from those who do not have, even what they seem to have will be taken away."

23. Oliver O'Donovan and Joan Lockwood O'Donovan, *Bonds of Imperfection: Christian Politics Past and Present* (Grand Rapids, Michigan: Wm. B. Eerdmans Publishing Company, 2004), 74.

24. O'Donovan and Lockwood O'Donovan, *Bonds of Imperfection*, 193.

25. O'Donovan and Lockwood O'Donovan, *Bonds of Imperfection*, 93.

26. See http://www.icmm.com/news-and-events/news/ecumenical-day-of-reflection-on-mining

27. See http://www.icmm.com/our-work/sustainable-development-framework/10-principles

28. O'Donovan and Lockwood O'Donovan, *Bonds of Imperfection*, 100.

29. See Reed, "The Goods of Mining," at: http://blogs.exeter.ac.uk/theologyandreligionresearch/2014/10/19/the-goods-of-mining/

30. Charles Wheelan, *Naked Economics* (New York, New York: W. W. Norton & Company, 2003), 176.

31. Wheelan, *Naked Economics*, 115.

32. Wheelan, *Naked Economics*, 113.

33. Rowan Williams, *Lost Icons: Reflections on Cultural Bereavement* (Edinburgh: T & T Clark, 2000), 139–154.

34. Philip Goodchild, *Theology of Money* (Durham, North Carolina: Duke University Press, 2009), 202.

35. Justo Gonzalez, *Faith and Wealth* (Eugene, Oregon: Wipf and Stock, 1990), 112.

36. Clement of Alexandria, "Can a Rich Man Be Saved?" in Beech and Niebuhr, *Christian Ethics* (New York, New York: Alfred A. Knopf, 1973), 96–97.

37. http://www.vatican.va/archive/ccc_css/archive/catechism/p3s2c1a3.htm

38. Tertullian, "On Idolatry," in *The Ante-Nicene Fathers* (Grand Rapids,

Michigan: Wm. B. Eerdmans Publishing Company, 1989), 61.

39. Gladiator and artisan of idols are obvious examples. Teachers are potentially idolatrous for Tertullian because they are required to participate in the Roman cult.

40. Tertullian, "On Idolatry," 67.

41. Para. 80, http://w2.vatican.va/content/john-paul-ii/en/encyclicals/documents/hf_jp-ii_enc_06081993_veritatis-splendor.html

42. *Rerum novarum*, 9.

43. *Rerum novarum*, para. 21, 22, http://w2.vatican.va/content/leo-xiii/en/encyclicals/documents/hf_l-xiii_enc_15051891_rerum-novarum.html

44. J. S. Michael Bruno, *Political Augustinianism: Modern Interpretations of Augustine's Political Thought* (Minneapolis, Minnesota: Fortress Press, 2014), 296.

45. Raymond Brown, *The Gospel According to John XIII–XXI,* Anchor Bible Commentary (Garden City, New York: Doubleday & Company, Inc.,1970), 890.

46. http://www.ccel.org/ccel/schaff/anf01.iii.i.html

47. Saint Augustine, *City of God*, book 19, chapter 17, http://www.ccel.org/ccel/schaff/npnf102.iv.XIX.17.html

Judaism

JEWISH ECONOMICS

JOSEPH ISAAC LIFSHITZ

Introduction

Judaism is a juristic religion enshrined in canonical texts. Much of the normative energy of Judaism has been devoted to the interpretation of biblical law. Law looms so large in Judaism that the category of ethics is controversial. Does a notion of ethics exist in Judaism independent of law? Is ethics a subset or a way of reflecting on law? These are unsettled questions. Whatever the status of ethics vis-à-vis law, the two will always be tightly entangled. That is a strength of Judaism but also a kind of weakness. Using ancient texts from the Torah and the Talmud to reason about the normative dimensions of economic life can yield a detailed, focused discussion. But there can also be anachronism in this. Ancient texts, as rich as they may be, relate to a world that is very different from ours, culturally, economically, and politically. Nor do they present systematic, well-theorized perspectives. Jewish texts, especially the Talmud, which is the main source of Jewish law (*halakha*), are often collections of diverse opinions, records of ancient hermeneutic and substantive arguments. Thus, any contemporary claims about Jewish ethics and economic (or other) thought must be made with a sense of limits. Discussing Jewish ethics demands creative translations, adaptations, and selections from the vast store of ancient texts. It also will depend upon one's personal perspective. The texts are seldom univocal in meaning or implication. Systematizing them into a coherent moral point of view will always be an interpretive project.

Jewish law exhibits continuity and change over the centuries. Jews tried since antiquity to maintain judicial independence, despite their loss of political independence in Roman times. Their tradition of judicial autonomy never ceased until their emancipation and enfranchisement by European states in the late eighteenth and nineteenth centuries. This ongoing legal tradition, which governed the internal life of medieval and early modern Jewish communities, mitigated the effects of external forces. That is why major elements of Western notions of economic justice had a negligible effect on Jewish economic thought. Methodologically, a study of Jewish economic thought has to focus on Judaism's own traditions rather than on traditions and worldviews outside of Judaism. On the other hand, Jews did not live in an intellectual bubble. Some external norms—for example, the European rejection of polygamy—were absorbed by Jewish law. Since Jews were involved alongside non-Jews in the marketplace, it would be naïve to ignore entirely the influence of economic worldviews outside of the Jewish tradition. I will relate to the issue of influences later in the chapter.

Although tradition-oriented and aiming at continuity with a valorized past, Jewish law is also dynamic. On the one hand, Jewish law is connected tightly to its earliest sources: the Holy Scriptures and their rabbinic commentaries. These early sources were created in a rural economy. On the other hand, if Jewish law is to remain vital and pertinent, it had to adapt itself to market economies and modern states. The Jewish attitude of reverence toward the Holy Scriptures and their commentaries must qualify itself with a radical effort of translating principles drawn from a rural economy to a modern economy. Additionally, pervasive economic change has been accompanied by major political change. The modern state has assumed responsibility for social justice, education, health, and culture.[1] Such a change demands translating principles that applied to tribes or small communities to the legal environment of the modern state. Jewish legists constantly struggle to remain true to the sources while trying to apply them to novel, unprecedented problems.

In addition to economic and political (and technological) change, there is also the problem of moral change. For example, Jewish law, although it tries to mitigate slavery, nonetheless took shape in a world where slavery was widespread. It doesn't reject it out of hand. Dealing with the huge gap between ancient and contemporary moral views is itself an ethical problem. A Jewish legist has to balance respect for tradition and its internal norms with some measure of openness to moral change. Finally, the same is true for maintaining laws that were correct for a small-scale community but are insufficient for a state. I will elaborate more on the subject when I discuss equality.

Following Ronald Dworkin's distinction between principles and rules, Jewish law should be understood to consist not only of rules but of principles as well.[2] Let us then try to articulate Jewish law's own principles in the sphere of economic justice.

One of the most important principles is the sanctity of property rights, as an expression of divine justice. Property rights in Judaism are not given to the individual by the state, nor are they to be respected because of their contribution to society. They are perceived as an ethical right generated by the divine law. The right is expressed in the law in terms of prohibitions and obligations binding every person with respect to his fellow's dominion over his property. In many ways, the state stems from the property rights of every individual and not vice versa.

Yet, when studying the principle of property rights in Jewish law, an immediate objection seems to arise in the form of the principle of distributive justice. Isn't Jewish law committed to distributive justice? Many of the commandments seem designed to facilitate social justice, one might claim. Ownership is arguably subordinate to the needs of society.[3] Scholars point to Jewish law's commitment to principles of social justice, which allow the liberties of the individual up to a certain point but then oblige him to be socially responsible and to engage in give-and-take with others. Such claims are based on the limitations placed by Jewish law on personal ownership, the land-connected commandments of aid to the poor, and the custom of Jewish communities to enforce charity-giving. The prohibition against working the land in the Land of Israel during the Sabbatical Year, and the obligation to return land to its original owners during the Jubilee

Year, suggest that Judaism does not consider the individual to be master over his possessions.[4] Another root of the view that Jewish law endorses a principle of distributive justice is based on the rule of *kofin al middat Sodom* (literally: coercing due to the trait of Sodom). If a person exhibits Sodom-like traits, the economically salient example being unwillingness to help another person, he is overridden by a court of law—but only on the condition that he himself will not lose anything by complying.[5]

These considerations have led some interpreters to the conclusion that the Jewish concept of property ownership rejects the view that people are absolute masters of their possessions, since it limits the right to private property when a social cause is involved. Both the claim and the conclusion are expressed in the following quote from Rabbi Aharon Lichtenstein:

> Coercion over the trait of Sodom completely contradicts the widespread idea that man is the supreme ruler over his possessions, that his property is his to do with it as he pleases; as long as he is not causing direct damage to another person, no one can hinder him. Jewish Law has a different spirit to it . . . In Jewish Law there is almost none of the aversion to private property that the Church Fathers expressed . . . But Jewish Law never idolized this concept, and other moral necessities may occasion its limitation. Though Jewish Law is extremely removed from Proudhon's statement that "Property is theft," on the other hand, it refuses even to agree with the popular expression that "An Englishman's home is his castle." . . . We must differentiate between ownership for the sake of usage and ownership for the sake of sovereignty; we must agree with the first statement, and condemn the latter.[6]

An extension of this view is the claim that charity, the commandments relating to the Land, and the matter of forcing a person to help his fellow if he himself is not inconvenienced by it are all indications that Jewish law has a social-justice agenda. On this view, Jewish law is not satisfied with placing general limitations on the right to private ownership, but rather *commands* a distributive policy with the goal being to decrease poverty, or even do away with it altogether. Thus, Rabbi Shimon Federbush writes: "The basic direction of the Torah was to create in the Land of Canaan a model human society, in which human equality and equal economic subsistence will be ensured to all. This aspiration was expressed in the slogan, 'There will be no destitute people among you,' meaning that the political regime must engage in a fair distribution of property, in order to prevent the creation of a class of economically-destitute people."[7]

Proponents of this view see charity as an expression of a social-justice agenda for balancing class gaps. Its premise is that all property belongs to God; man is entrusted with it for his own use and for sharing it with the needy. A claim repeated time and again is that the word *tzedaka* (charity) and *tzedek* (justice) are one and the same: "Indeed, the term *tzedaka*, coined from the word *tzedek*, shows us that charity is not a matter of merely generosity or pity, but is seen as a matter of honesty and justice, and is an obligation placed on man. Not for nothing do we find the terms *tzedaka* and *mishpat* (judgment) together in many places in the Bible. And already when speaking of the descendants of Abraham our Forefather, it says 'And they will keep the way of God, to do *tzedaka* and *mishpat*.' "[8]

It must be noted that this claim is not completely accurate, for the word *tzedaka* in the Bible is merely a different form of the word *tzedek*, and is not the same as the term *tzedaka* in the language of the Talmudic sages and in Modern Hebrew.[9]

According to Tamari, who holds to a social-justice interpretation, the commandment to give charity stems from the individual's personal obligation to the society as a whole. The society is then permitted to collect funds from its members beyond the sum they are obligated to contribute as individuals. This is not only as a personal moral obligation, but rather a society-wide obligation to establish social justice.[10] Charity is proof of Jewish law's social policy, which is binding on the social organization and obligates it to engage in distributive policies according to equal basic needs determined by the society's culture and resources.[11]

There is, of course, a religious obligation to give charity. The views noted above claim that this militates against the sanctity of property. In response, I claim that charity, unlike other legal obligations, is not an "adversary obligation." An adversary obligation is one where one person's duty is another person's right. The needy do not have a right to demand charity under Jewish law. The obligation to give charity is an obligation of the wealthy, without a corresponding right of the needy. When the community demands charity from its members, *it demands moral behavior*. It does not and cannot demand money that belongs to one and give it to the other.

If there is an underlying aim here, it is the enhancement of empathy inherent in the giving of charity. Nonetheless, charity is not supererogatory; it is a genuine obligation. And because this obligation is coerced, I would not say that economic redistribution does not exist in Judaism. I rather say that it doesn't diminish or redefine property rights.

Understanding charity and, implicitly therefore, social justice as a way of enhancing empathy for one's neighbor, doesn't trivialize it or reduce its moral salience. As Maimonides says: "There are eight levels of virtue in charity; one is greater than the other. The highest value belongs to the one who supports the Israelite who is going under, and gives him a gift or a loan, or makes a partnership with him or finds him a vocation, in order to help him so that he will not become impoverished."[12]

By saying that, Maimonides demands openness to all types of charity, including giving a loan, investing, or even giving a job. He opens the door to a future welfare state. Indeed, Maimonides referred to an obligation on the individual, or even on a community to help the needy in any way possible. This empathy can be developed on a larger political scale. As I mentioned above, Jewish law must go through a historical translation, and that is why modern policy solutions for poverty are welcomed by Jewish legal authorities. In the same way that the Talmud developed a welfare community from the Bible's private efforts at charity, it is a duty of modern Jewish scholars to develop a state-level welfare system. Such efforts have recently been undertaken by several Jewish scholars.[13]

Equality

Equal treatment is, no doubt, one of the most important criteria of justice. Judging *correctly* means judging *equally*, and ruling correctly means ruling all citizens equally. Civil rights are equal rights. Each citizen deserves to receive equal benefits from his country. But does this mean that distributions should be equal? *People* are not equal, therefore distribution demands judgment that should take into account real needs and inherent differences. The complexity of the problem of demanding unequal distribution (affirmative action, etc.) aside, the question of equal distribution should be raised where it belongs—in the political sphere. When governments distribute, they should do so equally. Education, culture, social welfare, security, medicine—all should benefit from it equally.

Since the role of the state in antiquity was much more limited than in modern societies and didn't concern itself with education, culture, or medicine, the pertinent subject in Talmudic law is social welfare. Each community had a system of charity tax, of collectors and people who were in charge of distribution, and Talmudic law has regulations and rules of just and equal distribution for these communal welfare institutions. It created a combination of standard equality and proportional equality. On the one hand, the Talmud demands that only those poor who do not earn a minimum wage—two hundred Roman denarii a year, or own two hundred Roman denarii—deserve to receive food and other minimal necessities from the community.[14] A person who earned more did not deserve to receive charity from the community. At the same time, there was special attention for particular needs. As the Talmud says, in one case, the sages ordered the community to give a wealthy man who had lost his wealth "a horse to ride on and a slave to lead his way."[15] This was necessary to restore his honor. As Maimonides stated: "Whatever a pauper is lacking you have to give him. If he is lacking clothes, they will dress him, if he is lacking house utensils, they will buy him [. . .] if he was used to ride a horse and a slave ran before him, they buy him a horse to ride on and a slave to run before him, because it says (in the Bible) 'as he is lacking.' You are obligated to restore what he lacks. You are not obligated to make him wealthy."[16]

These two laws—the minimal two hundred Roman denarius wage of the poor, and the law of giving to the poor person anything he lacks—were perceived by the Jewish legal tradition as contradictory. The common opinion in Jewish law is that the minimum wage of two hundred Roman denarii is anachronistic. The definition of poverty is *relative*; it changes in every society. Later halachic deciders did not accept a precise poverty line.[17] They preferred following the Talmudic law that required giving to the poor man anything he lacks. The law that defines social welfare assistance as dependent upon the discretion of the community officials to give the poor what they judge to be necessary, but never more than what the poor person needs. They have "to support him, not make him a rich man."[18]

As mentioned in the introduction, the contemporary application of Jewish economic thought must translate principles developed in a rural economy into the setting of a modern economy. Any practical discussion of Jewish social welfare policy should be wary of anachronism. Jewish law envisions small-scale communities taking care of their own members. Getting from rules applicable to a community to the rules of a state is not just a matter of degree; it may be a difference in kind. Yet I would like to suggest that in the case of social welfare, the difference between community and state may be less categorical if we think of the state as composed of different subsidiary communities. The problem of poverty might be addressed by each community, which gets to define its own scale of poverty. The smaller the community, the more power of discretion may be given to its officials. Dividing society into small different communities, and giving each community its own scale of measuring poverty and manner of alleviating it, can help preserve the value of each person within his community. It seems to me that the closest definition among scholars today to that of Jewish law is Michael Walzer's *Spheres of Justice*. Thus, poverty is judged differently in every social sphere. Yet one has to be aware that such a solution leads to inequality. Wealthier and stronger communities will supply better welfare. A proper solution, therefore, must be proposed by Jewish scholars, especially in the Jewish state.

As argued above, charity in Judaism is a personal obligation and it is treated in a personal fashion. The Talmudic sages insisted that charity should always be given based on the needs of each individual. That is why communal charity was handed to community officials who were trained to collect the money from the community members, to judge each individual, and to examine his particular needs.[19] The Talmud, which raises the issue on several occasions, refers to these individuals as "people in authority," or people who are authorized to extract collateral from those who refuse to give to the poor, and to decide for each person in need how much and what he will receive from the community.[20]

There isn't an inherent distinction between the charity that an individual gives and communal charity. When an individual gives to those for whom he feels a special obligation, he expresses his empathy as a unique individual who takes responsibility for those around him. The same attitude should take place at a communal level. The officials who are appointed by the community should express their empathy as well.

This kind of giving, moreover, emphasizes the fact that we are not talking about an act of "justice," of satisfying the just claims of the poor against the wealthy, but about an act of personal obligation stemming from one's sense of responsibility for those around him.

Translating the halachic view of charity as a just way of distribution into the myriad distributive policies of the modern state is not an easy matter. I would argue that complexity, discretion, and fair judgment are much more important than achieving simple equality. That is not because simple equality is not an important moral factor, but because of the complexity of the concept of equality. Equality is very important, but applying it demands complex solutions that are not limited to simple algorithms.

Property

There are two definitions of property rights: the right *of* property (the right to hold property that is already held) and the right *to* property (the right to be an owner of property). Judaism, I argue, favors the former. Property rights in Judaism are not given to the individual by the state, nor are they respected because of their ostensible contribution to society. They are perceived as an ethical right, derived from divinely given law. They are constituted by prohibitions and obligations on every person toward his fellow's dominion over his own property. In many ways, the state's property right stems from the property right of every individual, and not the reverse.[21]

Jewish tradition takes a very positive view of both the institution of ownership and of the accumulation of wealth. It respects economic success, seeing it as both a blessing and as the basis of a flourishing life on earth—so long, that is, as it is obtained honestly and proper respect is shown for the social responsibility that accompanies it.

The reason for the positive view of the institution of ownership and the accumulation of wealth is theological. That man is created in God's image and that it is his consequent duty to exercise dominion over the world are the foundations upon which the Jewish concept of property rests. His inherent godliness sets man apart from all other creatures on earth: He is not merely flesh and blood, but rather a "portion from God above,"[22] an earthly being who contains an element of the divine essence.[23] The right of private property in Judaism is nearly absolute and can be restricted only in the most extreme circumstances. In accordance with man's role in the world, it is only through the protection of the individual's property that human beings are able to actualize the divine within them and act as full partners in creation.

Evidence of the high regard in which Judaism holds private property can be found in the punishments that are meted out in the Bible to those who undermine the social order through their flagrant disregard for it. Such, for example, is the attitude taken by the prophet Elijah against King Ahab for his mistreatment of Naboth the Jezreelite in the Book of Kings. Ahab is cited repeatedly in the text for his worship of the pagan gods Baal and Asherah, but his most important sin, for which he is stripped of his kingdom, is the murder of Naboth for the sake of stealing his vineyard. Here, the theft is seen as an atrocity, equal in weight to the murder itself: "And the word of the Eternal came to Elijah the Tishbi, saying: 'Arise, go down to meet Ahab King of Israel, who is in the Shomron, in the vineyard of Naboth, where he has gone to possess it. And you will speak to him, saying, "Thus says the Eternal: Have you murdered, and also taken possession?" And you shall speak to him, saying, "Thus says the Eternal: In the place where the dogs licked the blood of Naboth shall the dogs lick your blood, even yours." ' "[24]

The rabbinic tradition, as well, emphasized the gravity of acts that violate another's property, equating them with the destruction of the foundations of society. The flood in the time of Noah, for example, was depicted as punishment for the sins of his generation against the property of others: "Come and see how great is the power of thievery," the Talmud teaches, "for behold, the generation of the flood transgressed all, and yet they were not doomed until they stretched out their hands to steal."[25] Elsewhere, Talmudic sages equate theft and fraud with idolatry as the three worst sins.[26]

Property, understood as full dominion over an object, is a central pillar of Jewish law, and its protection is a recurring theme in the Bible and the rabbinic teachings. The significance with which the Torah invests the right of dominion over property is evident in the numerous prohibitions pertaining to the property of others. The commandment "You shall not remove your neighbor's boundary mark"[27] establishes the prohibition against stealing land. "You shall not have in your pocket different weights, large or small. You shall not have in your house different grain weights, large or small. . . . All who do such things . . . are an abomination to the Lord your God"[28] prohibits the acquisition of property through fraud. "You shall not see your brother's ox or his sheep go astray, and hide yourself from them, You shall surely bring them back to your brother"[29] prohibits the neglect of other people's property even when it is not in your care and obligates the return of lost items. By declaring criminal anything that results in the loss of other people's property, the Torah emphasizes the importance accorded to the institution of private property. This is expressed as a general principle in a number of verses in the Torah, such as "You shall not steal" and "You shall not defraud your neighbor, nor rob him."[30] The lengths to which the Torah goes to encourage a respect for private possessions, however, is demonstrated most severely in the Tenth Commandment: "You shall not covet your neighbor's house . . . or his ox, or his ass, or anything that belongs to your neighbor."[31] Here the prohibition goes beyond the unlawful acquisition of property to include even the "coveting" of another's possessions.[32]

Notice that when the Torah lists property crimes, it doesn't speak directly of property rights but of acts that damage someone's dominion over his property. The focus of these prohibitions is on the harm that is done against a person, on the different ways that the harm is executed, and not to his property. It is through these prohibitions that the Torah generates ownership or property rights. The way these rights are established is twofold. The first step is the establishment of prohibitions that limit freedom of action. Only after a community accepts it, the establishment of a right to dominion is generated, and thus the right to property as well. The commandments of the Torah are not meant just to obey the law, but to respect people's dominion.

But it is not only the violation of the law that teaches us the importance of dominion. We can realize the importance of dominion as the essence of property rights from the way Jewish law instructs us on how to transfer ownership. Apparently, transference of ownership is valid only when accompanied by an "act of acquisition" (ma'aseh kinyan), an expression of dominion. Similarly, expressions of dominion such as erecting a fence around a property or breaking down a surrounding fence are acts that signify the assumption of new ownership over the property (or at least of the previous owner's relinquishment of his claim.)[33]

An owner's dominion over his property is signified not only by his right to transfer, or to refuse to transfer, his assets to another, but also by his ability to do with his property what he wishes, even if that means its neglect or destruction. This is elaborated upon, for example, in a ruling of the Mishna, where it is written that if someone tells his friend, "Tear my garment!" or "Break my pitcher!," then the friend is liable for damages. But if the owner explicitly exempts his friend from damages, the exemption holds, because he is understood to be carrying out the owner's will.[34] While it is possible to debate the details of this ruling, it is clear that everything depends on the owner's will with regard to the object. Ownership, in other words, is understood to be so complete as to include even the right to destroy one's own property.[35]

As a result of such a theory, Jewish law establishes no ceiling on the ownership of property. Anyone should have the liberty to own as much as he wants or can. Ownership is a convention, and is generated spontaneously from competition over dominion on property, according to supply and demand. It is not given by society, nor is it created by society. Ownership is one of the most ancient institutions; its existence precedes the state. An owner may distribute his property to whomever needs it but he does so as an act of charity, not in response to a contending right.

Natural Resources

After defining ownership as a basic right, as a primordial norm in human society, independent of the vagaries of social distribution, I would like to suggest that perhaps that should be qualified in regard to the distribution of natural resources. A distinction between regular property and natural resources does not make sense from a theoretical point of view, but it may make sense if we consider the good of society. The fact that in the eyes of the public natural resources belong to everyone demands consideration. In a situation where social institutions already exist, natural resources are distributed one way or another, and it is important to inquire into the moral dimensions of the distribution. Unfortunately, the subject of the distribution of natural resources is a good example of a lacuna in Jewish law. Since Jewish law did not function as the law of a modern state in an authoritative way, political subjects of this kind have not been fully treated by it. Lately, because of the recent discovery of gas fields off the Israeli coast, the subject has started to provoke discussion among scholars of Jewish law in Israel. Unlike other economic topics based on private law and communal law, natural resources are a subject of state law. Precedents in Jewish law are lacking, and an original treatment is required. (This is an example of having to find principles and translate them into the contemporary context to treat a problem previously not envisioned by Jewish law.) Of course, there is the possibility that Jewish law has a libertarian, laissez-faire policy, and so doesn't have any limits on private ownership of natural resources. But the lacuna more likely results from the limits of scale of Jewish law in the past. I would like to attempt a new approach here.

I should start from the creation of human beings. Upon their very creation, God commanded Adam and Eve to "have dominion over the fish of the sea, and over the birds of the air."[36] Indeed, the Jewish tradition makes clear that human authority over all other creatures is unequivocal. Yet, at the same time, man is enjoined to act responsibly in the material realm. When God placed Adam and Eve in the Garden of Eden, he commanded them "to work it and to keep it"—to derive benefit from it, but also to protect it for future generations.[37] Thus, humanity had already undertaken such a responsibility before the rise of the community or state. This theological claim, however, may be a false start. For Adam had no competition from other human beings. Edenic existence does not provide a good analogy. It is not yet an economic existence.

A better beginning may be found in the Talmud. The Talmud raises the following discussion. When the land of Israel was divided between the tribes after being conquered, the tribe of Zebulun felt deprived. They complained to the Lord, that, unlike the other tribes, they did not receive flat, arable land. The Lord told them that instead of receiving land for agriculture, they would receive other resources and their benefits, specifically, snails in the sea for the production of religiously significant purple and blue dye and sand for the production of glass: "Lord of the world, to my brothers you gave fields and vineyards, and to me you gave mountains and hills. To my brothers you gave lands, and to me you gave lakes and rivers. The Lord answered him: they all need you for the snail, as it says 'For they draw from riches of the sea, And the hidden hoards of the sand'" (Numbers 33:19).[38]

Natural resources in the Land of Israel were given to the Israelites divided into tribes, and in this division there was an implicit norm (and an explicit demand) for equality. The tribes demanded to be equal, not only by size but also by the quality of natural resources. God attended to their demands. This source is the only one I have found regarding a just distribution of natural resources.

Thomas Aquinas justified private property with the claim that only when property is taken care of privately can one be assured that it will be well cared for.[39] The Talmudic sages had a similar argument: "A pot that is owned by two, is never hot or cold,"[40] meaning that whenever there are two people in charge, they neglect to take responsibility. The sages thus had much more hope for private responsibility than for communal undertaking. They even established rules for the defense of the communal interest, because they did not rely on the communal ability to protect its own rights sufficiently well. If that was their approach toward the community, it is likely that they would have thought similarly about the state. Therefore, it seems to me that the approach of the libertarians does fit the Jewish view of property rights.[41] Yet I must admit that the sources I try to rely on are few in number, and I hope that future discussions will add depth and breadth to this subject. The lack of sources, so far, doesn't supply me with an answer to the question regarding ceilings and floors for how much of a natural resource and its usufructs a private owner can ethically possess.

Products

Equal distribution presents a tension between values, an opposition of liberty and equality. Liberty entitles every person to decide to whom he wants to give, while according to the principle of equality, discrimination in distribution, unequal distribution, is immoral. That is why boycotting goods or preventing some members of society from benefiting from services is criticized and in many countries is legally forbidden. Jewish law does not forbid boycotting from a legal point of view, and not even on the basis of equality, but rather perceives it as a vice, as an immoral act.

Property rights as dominion are an expression of the value of liberty. But liberty never stands as a value in isolation. Every act should be judged with respect to a comprehensive evaluative framework. For instance, no one is permitted to inflict damage on his neighbor for the sake of his own liberty. Responsibility and charity toward one's neighbor are values that are no less important; neither is equality. The question of when property rights are limited depends on the place of these other values. Since each doctrine establishes its set of values according to its own scale of priorities, it is important to define the Jewish scale of priorities. As I mentioned above, property rights in Judaism entitle a person to exercise dominion over his property; a dominion that, although not absolute, entails a right to use, destroy, or sell one's property to whomever one wishes. I don't think that equality has an upper hand over liberty in that sense. In my opinion, the values that limit liberty are charity and caring for a fellow human being. Unequal distribution violates these values. As the Torah says, one must help his neighbor so he can continue to live by his side: "If your kinsman, being in straits, comes under your authority, and you hold him as though a resident alien, let him live by your side: do not exact from him advance or accrued interest, but fear your God. Let him live by your side as your kinsman."[42]

This obligation to help applies not only to your kinsman who is "in straits," but to every kinsman. Help is not only supporting the kinsman, but as the Torah defines it, letting him "live by your side as your kinsman." The Torah promotes an idea of community. Enabling one to live with his fellow human being in one community demands an obligation by each person to be charitable and generous to his neighbor. Boycotting is a grave obstacle to such communal life. The motto of the French Revolution— *liberté, égalité, fraternité*—would have to be shortened to capture the Jewish principle. It is not *égalité* but *fraternité* that is the basis of Jewish morality for equal distribution. So there should be a just distribution of products, but I don't think that Jewish law legislates a compulsory framework for this. Rather, it's a valuable ideal. It is appropriate for every community to make its own decisions that enable liberty, making it happen. Liberty is such an important value in the Jewish tradition that it comes before equality, even before equality of distribution of products.

Wealth

Religions do and should perceive wealth with suspicion. The main goal of a religious person is to be close to God, which is a spiritual path. Accumulation of wealth seems to contradict the right way to be closest to God. Yet in Judaism there is an ambivalence about wealth. There are sources that respect wealth. Worldly wealth, despite having no obvious spiritual content, is even said to contribute to receiving prophecy: "The Divine Presence rests only on one who is wise, strong, wealthy, and of great stature."[43] Of Rabbi Yehuda the Talmud says that he especially respected wealthy people.[44] On the other hand, the Talmud says that "Poverty is good for the Jews."[45] Indeed, wealth as a tangible achievement is not considered a value by all. The Talmudic sages argued about the question of who is considered "wealthy," and their answers vary from the most subjective to the most realistic, from the abstract "wealth" of human relationships to physical comfort.

> Our rabbis taught: Who is wealthy? He who has pleasure in his wealth: this is Rabbi Meir's view.[46] Rabbi Tarfon said: "He who possesses a hundred vineyards, a hundred fields and a hundred slaves working in them." Rabbi Akiba said: "He who has a wife comely in deeds." Rabbi Jose said: "He who has a privy near his table."[47]

This discussion about wealth is philosophical, but it doesn't avoid the practical implications of the various claims.

In answering the question "who is wealthy," the Talmudic sages begin to imply an ethics of wealth. Their different opinions regarding wealth express different attitudes toward economic ethics. Rabbi Meir, who understood wealth as a positive attitude toward life, said: "Who is wealthy? He who has pleasure in his wealth." For him, wealth in the sense of possession of physical property should not be considered a value, as something to live for. Rather, finding satisfaction in one's work, achievement, or condition—of which wealth is a sign—is what is most important. Rabbi Tarfon, on the other hand, had a much more practical attitude. He felt that there is nothing wrong in valuing economic wealth, and said: "He who possesses a hundred vineyards, a hundred fields and a hundred slaves working in them." Rabbi Akiba saw wealth in the interpersonal life and said: "He who has a wife comely in deeds." Rabbi Jose, who said: "He who has a privy near his table," saw wealth in the bare minimal of practical pleasure.

Judaism, in many sources, encourages the accumulation of wealth. Economic success is considered a worthy aim, so long as one achieves it through honest means. In the Jewish view, man's obligation to exercise dominion over the world, as a function of his having been created in God's image, grants him the right to affirm the wealth he has. Wealth that is gained through hard work and honest means is, in Judaism, a positive expression of man's efforts as a godly being. "One who benefits from his own labor is greater," says the Talmud, "than one who fears Heaven."[48] This stunning assertion is not meant to denigrate the fear of Heaven, but rather to affirm the principle that one who turns his talents into achievements is greater than one who neglects his own capacity to strive and create in the world. In the Jewish view, wealth that is derived from hard and honest work is considered a sign of virtue rather than vice. The Talmudic sages and their rabbinic successors teach that such wealth is the reward of the righteous.

But is it ethically permissible to use wealth in ways that diminish or extinguish the prospects of the non-wealthy when that outcome is an unintended by-product of other, morally benign effects? The Talmudic sages argue about the conflict between one person's use of his property and the competing good of another's very life. They decide that every person may tend, first and foremost, to his own life: "Two people were traveling, and [only] one of them had a canteen of water. [There was only enough water so that] if both of them drank they would both die, but if one of them drank [only] he would make it back to an inhabited area [and live]. Ben Petora publicly taught: 'Better both should drink and die than that one see his friend's death,' until Rabbi Akiba came and taught: 'Let him live by your side as your kinsman' (Leviticus 25:36)—your life takes precedence over the life of your friend's.' "[49]

In my opinion, we can conclude from Rabbi Akiba's teaching that the same idea is true about wealth: one person's life takes precedence over the life of his friend. No one is responsible to see his own life through the prism of his neighbor's. Competition is legitimate and even encouraged. A demand on the wealthy man to limit his capacity to increase his wealth, just because someone else is going to have less as a result, assumes that the "cake" is limited in size, and further that he is commanded to adopt a godly perspective on the world. But human beings are subjective creatures. The collective struggle of human beings to earn a livelihood is what, in fact, creates prosperity. An objective (God's eye) perspective limits the value of individual striving for wealth, and is not rated highly in Jewish thought. As it says in Song of Songs: "If a man would give all the substance of his house for love, he would utterly be condemned."[50]

Yet, by saying that accumulation of wealth is legitimate, I do not contend that it's a virtue that a person should strive for. The highest virtue is ethics and the knowledge of God, as Maimonides explained in the *Guide for the Perplexed*. According to his definition, possessions are "[T]he first and the most defective" of human perfection.[51] The true perfection is "acquisition of the rational virtues."[52]

Income

Jeremy Waldron claims that property rights are rights *to* property, rights to have property. He attributes this opinion to John Locke.[53] Such a claim connects property rights to human dignity. According to this opinion, it would seem logical that everyone should have an unconditional, justified claim to a basic level of income. Human dignity cannot be honored or maintained without such a basic level of income.

The Jewish idea of private property points us in a different direction, however. Human dignity does not entail having property, goods, or income as such, but the *capacity* to own them. Humans, unlike sub-rational animals, are bestowed with a bit of the divine within them. In the Jewish view, as mentioned above, property rights are not a right *to* property but a right *of* property. Man doesn't have to own property, but he gains it through his expression of his Godly portion, by using his wisdom, his interpersonal capabilities, and his practical and technological capabilities. (Of course, one can benefit from the fruits of labor of one's ancestors and inherit from them.) According to this view, income is just a commodity like any other commodity. Its true value is as an expression of man's dominion. The level of income depends on supply and demand, on the role income has in a market in which many human beings are expressing their own claims to dominion. Thus, income is not a reward or compensation for hard labor. It is the price that one is willing to pay for the supply of labor by his neighbor. The value of this price depends on how much one is willing to pay and the other is willing to work.

I do not claim that people have never tried to regulate income, subjecting it to considerations other than supply and demand. Economic history teaches about regulations on income, as well as about the regulation of prices of other goods. Regulations have their ups and downs. In Roman history, for instance, during the era of the Republic, the Romans had a laissez-faire policy in a market that was virtually a free market. But during the Empire, policy changed to a controlled and regulated market. The same attitudes were followed by the Jews of the time. As the Talmud teaches us, income and prices of goods were regulated or at least such regulations were accepted as legally binding.[54]

Since the Talmud set a precedent, setting regulations on income was considered legitimate. It was left to every Jewish community to decide whether regulations on income should be established or not. Enacting compulsory regulations on income by force, however, does not accurately reflect Jewish ethics. In my view, what the Talmud describes is a legal suggestion. From a theological-ethical point of view, income should be left to the rule of the free market.

The assumption of those who support setting floors and ceilings on income is that it is the more just policy. But their focus is on the employees. They neglect to concern themselves with the employers, who will be hurt if a policy of equality of income is applied. They will be hurt because they will not get the best employees, and their employees will not work as well as they would if they had to compete. Income has to play a role in the free market. Most people don't work for their own self-fulfillment. They need an incentive. Equality of income reduces competition, thus reducing an important incentive of the employees to work hard. Many employees who know that their income is guaranteed, that it will be the same whether they work with diligence or not, with creativity or not, will prefer not to be diligent and not to be creative.

What does deserve attention, perhaps even an active intervention, is the gap between maximum and minimum levels of income. Although slavery doesn't exist anymore in the developed world, employment can slip easily into conditions similar to slavery. One of the symptoms is too big a gap between maximum and minimum levels of income. When one employee gets a salary ten times higher than that of an employee who works under him, the relationship between them is hierarchical, and because of that liberty is diminished. The relationship will not literally be one of master and slave, but will virtually approximate that sort of relationship. That is why, for the sake of protection of liberty, I would urge the smallest gap possible.

Employment

The idea of a minimum wage has been gaining broad support as the social-welfare state becomes more and more popular around the world, although many free-market advocates are against it. I want to support the minimum wage from a Jewish point of view by distinguishing between justice and ethics in general. As I claimed previously, income is a commodity like any other commodity, and should be valued according to supply and demand. Income is not compensation for labor. But after saying that, I would like to claim that even though it is just to pay a low compensation, it is unethical, because labor can slip easily into slavery. Modern laws of labor are intended to protect workers from enslavement to their employer. The requirement of a minimum floor for income is a protection against such putative enslavement.

The Torah shows a sensitivity to liberty. The Israelites are reminded again and again about their past as slaves and are enjoined not to attempt the enslavement of others: "If a resident alien among you has prospered, and your kinsman being in straits, comes under his authority and gives himself over to the resident alien among you, or to an offshoot of an alien family, he shall have the right of redemption even after he has given himself over. One of his kinsmen shall redeem him . . . for it is to Me that the Israelites are servants: they are My servants, whom I freed from the land of Egypt, I the Lord your God."[55]

The Torah did not eliminate slavery, but it minimized it as much as was possible in a rural economy in an age when eliminating slavery seemed impossible.[56] It commanded the slaveowners to treat their slaves fairly. The value of liberty is expressed even more in the words of Jeremiah:

Thus said the Lord, the God of Israel: I made a covenant with your fathers when I brought them out of the land of Egypt, the house of bondage, saying: "In the seventh year each of you must let go any fellow Hebrew who may be sold to you, when he has served you six years, you must set him free." But your fathers would not obey Me or give ear. Lately you turned about and did what is proper in My sight, and each of you proclaimed a release to his countryman, and you made a covenant accordingly before Me in the House which bears My name. But now you have turned back and have profaned My name; each of you has brought back the men and women whom you had given their freedom, and forced them to be your slaves again. Assuredly, thus said the Lord: you would not obey Me and proclaim a release, each to his kinsman and countryman. Lo! I proclaim your release—declared the Lord—to the sword, to pestilence, and to famine; and I will make you a horror to all the kingdoms of the earth.[57]

The Talmudic sages developed this anti-slavery position and authorized a law that an employee may leave work and resign whenever he wants, and should get paid for the time he worked (as long as his resignation does not cause his previous employer excessive damage).[58]

Fixing a minimum wage was never an *obligation* under Jewish law. The Talmudic sages left it for each community to decide if they wanted to establish such a law or not, and, if so, what this minimum wage should be.[59] But I want to claim that the endorsement of ideas of equality and liberty demand an acceptance of the minimum wage. From a modern point of view, working below a minimum wage is slavery, and for a Jewish nation that must remember its past, enslavement of fellow men and women is morally unacceptable. Ignoring this development is a sin against the spirit of the Torah and the prophets.

But because we are not discussing here an absolute vice, I don't think that there should be a criterion of what this minimum wage should be. It should result from a social agreement and not from a theoretical idea of livelihood or dignity. Yet we should be aware that although boundaries should be made to protect the liberty of employees, we can't evade the rules of the free market. Bringing too many factors into the equation—such as gender, education, and age—may do these groups more harm than help. On the other hand, enabling workers to have a role in the economic decision-making of the companies that employ them is a very good suggestion, which not only will help to enhance their liberty but will also help to achieve greater economic progress.

Taxation

Taxation is an excellent indication of the change that Jewish law went through in regard to historic changes in the political and economic environment. In principle, we should bear in mind that taxation is dependent on the custom of the people, or on the law of the land, more than on some external legal principle. This is the view of Rabbi Meir of Rothenburg (1220–1293) in a *responsum* regarding a complaint about the levying of a tax in a certain community that seemingly contradicted Talmudic law. Rabbi Meir affirmed that custom, indeed, overruled Talmudic law: "Why do you ask me about taxation matters, which are principally [determined] by the laws of the land, when everything is determined by [local] custom, with each city set to follow its own customs?"[60]

Rabbi Meir did not mean to say that local custom in general and pertaining to taxation in particular is above the law, but rather that the people have a broad freedom in establishing their rules. I would like to describe the way Jewish law handled taxes historically in order to understand what can or should be done in the Jewish law of taxation in our time.

In antiquity, Jewish law defined taxes as a price for services. Tax was paid for security and water, and citizens paid according to the benefits they received. The tax was divided according to the number of citizens. Large families had to pay more than small families, simply because they benefited more from the city services. Their income didn't matter. Taxation was not progressive.[61]

This code of taxation was common practice in Jewish communities throughout history. It was followed in the European communities of the Middle Ages, where tax had to be paid to the ruler by each member of the society. But it was also followed internally, when a communal tax was collected to build communal institutions such as synagogues and the like. However, another consideration was added—the wealth of its members.[62] Wealth was not an entirely new parameter. It is mentioned in the Talmud, but in regard to a tax for security (paying the guardians, building walls, etc.), it was ruled out. It was only considered when the purpose of tax was education or care for the poor.[63] Later on, toward the nineteenth century, we find that communities followed a different approach that was much more progressive. A certain sum was fixed for every family, but social considerations were given for families that couldn't come up with the payment.[64] Nonetheless, taxes were levied differently by type, and community councils set a different parameter for each purpose. Security tax was still collected per capita, and the tax for protection of property was collected according to the value of property.[65]

In a modern state, where the state is a provider not only of security but also of education, justice, health, culture, and social purposes, taxation can no longer be divided according to its specific goals. Creating a system of taxation in accordance with that division would be unnecessarily complex, and would do more harm than good. That is why contemporary taxation assumes the form of a single payment, later to be divided according to the needs of the government. Now that charity has become a major consideration of the state (spending on justice, health, culture, and social purposes), it would be illogical to have different parameters for each goal. Taxation must have one policy. As I mentioned before, Rabbi Meir of Rothenburg ruled that the community, rather than the "law" in abstract, has the upper hand when it comes to setting the rules of taxation, and today it is the people who have decided on a progressive tax. It is not just a question of justice but a question of efficiency. Therefore, I think that a policy of progressive taxation is an accurate reflection of the spirit of Jewish law in our time.

Notes

1. See Joseph R. Strayer, *On the Medieval Origin of the Modern State* (Princeton, New Jersey: Princeton University Press, 1970).

2. Ronald Dworkin, *Taking Rights Seriously* (Cambridge, Massachusetts: Harvard University Press, 1977), 29–64.

3. Zeev Falk, *Erchei Mishpat Veyahadut: Likrat philosophia shel hahalacha,* Jerusalem, 1980, 117, 119; Chanoch Dagan, "Dinei Asiyat Osher: Bein yahadut leliberalism." *Mishpat Vehistoria,* Daniel Gottwin, Menachem Mautner, eds. (Jerusalem: The Zalman Shazar Center, 1999), 178–190; Shimon Federbush, *Mishpat Hamelucha Beyisrael* (Jerusalem: Mossad Harav Kook, 1952), 23–25, 126–128, 138–140; Rabbi Aharon Lichtenstein, "Leveirur 'Cofin al Midat Sedom,'" *Hagut Ivrit BeAmerica,* Menachem Zohari, Aryeh Tartakover, Chaim Ormian, eds. (Tel Aviv: Yavneh, 1972), 380–381; Meir Tamari, *With All Your Possessions* (New York: Jason Aronson, Inc., 1998), 36–38, 52–56, 210–211, 240, 242–243, 248–249, 277; Ephraim Frisch, *An Historical Survey of Jewish Philanthropy* (New York, New York: Macmillan, 1924), 77, 80; Michel Walzer, *Spheres of Justice: A Defense of Pluralism and Equality* (New York, New York: Basic Books, 1983), 3–6, 75–78, 92.

4. Tamari, *Possessions,* 37–38; Menachem Ben Shalom, *Hasids and Hasidism in the Periods of the Second Temple and the Mishna* (Tel Aviv: HaKibutz HaMeukhad, 1998), 52–53.

5. Lichtenstein, "Leveirur 'Cofin al Midat Sedom,'" 362–280; Dagan, "Dinei Asiyat Osher," 179.

6. Lichtenstein, "Leveirur 'Cofin al Midat Sedom,'" 380–281.

7. Federbush, *Mishpat Hamelucha Beyisrael,* 126–127.

8. Yitzhak Kister, "Dinei Tzedakah Beshimusham Bamishpat BeYisrael," *The Jewish Congress of Jewish Studies,* vol. 1 (1967), 173–169.

9. Frisch, *Jewish Philanthropy,* 77. Frisch was the first to point out the etymological connection between *tzedaka* (charity) and *tzadikut* (righteousness); according to him, it arises from the changing meanings between biblical and

Talmudic language. In the Bible, *tzedaka* means *tzadikut*—in other words, the characteristic of a righteous person—whereas in the language of the Talmudic sages, it means giving money to the needy. See also Tamari, *Possessions*, 36: "The Divine origin of wealth is the central principle of Jewish economic philosophy. All wealth belongs to God, who has given it temporarily to man, the basis of stewardship, for his physical wellbeing"; 52: "The 'haves' in Judaism have an obligation to share their property with the 'have nots,' since it was given to them by God partly for that purpose." See below, note 64.

10. Tamari, *Possessions*, 52: "Charity is not simply an act of kindness but rather the fulfillment of a legal obligation"; 240: "The community has a responsibility for the welfare of its members and a corresponding right to finance those needs through taxation over and above the individual's duty to contribute to charity." See also 277. Public responsibility does not allow the public to collect more than the amount that an individual is obligated in, since this is not a legal obligation. The community is allowed to oversee only the distribution (see more on this below). See also Dagan, "Dinei Asiyat Osher," 179: "The giving of charity in Jewish tradition is not a matter of mercy, kindness, generosity or personal conscience, but rather a matter of justice (thus explaining the linguistic affinity between *tzedaka* and *tzedek*). Giving charity is a fulfillment of a legal obligation: the realization of the community's rights and the rights of the unfortunates in the community, by way of the possessions of those who have." Dagan's main claim is based on a Talmudic discussion regarding a person who benefits from another's resources, while not depleting them in any way; in his opinion, this principle is a result of the ruling that a person is forced to give if it does not harm him ("coercion over the trait of Sodom"). The problem with this claim is that according to most medieval scholars—and their opinion was accepted as the common ruling—there is no connection between benefit without any obligation attached and the coercion over the trait of Sodom. Therefore, his assumption that it is possible to force a rich person to give of his possessions to the poor person is mistaken. According to Dagan, only some loss that the poor person causes the rich one can absolve the rich man from the legal obligation of benefitting the poor. But according to Jewish law, the virtual interactions that take place between the receiver and the giver who does not lose anything in the process are contractual, and based on the benefit. The minute the benefit causes loss, the virtual contract translates into a legal claim against the one who has benefitted. Only a benefit that does not cause loss does not create a contractual obligation and does not entail any claim for payment.

11. Walzer, *Spheres of Justice*, 3–6, 75–78, 92.

12. Maimonides, *Mishne Torah*, Matnot Aniyim 10:7.

13. http://www.betzedek.co.ilhttp://www.toraland.org.il

14. Mishna Pe'a, 8:8; BT Sota 21b; Maimonides, Matnot Aniyim, 9:13; R. Yoseph Karo, Shulkhan Arukh, Yore De'a, 253:1.

15. BT Ketubot 67b.

16. Maimonides, Matnot Aniyim, 7:3.

17. R. Shlomo b'r Adret, *Shut HaRashba*, 872; R. Yosef Karo, *Shulkhan Arukh*, Yore De'a, 253:2; R. Mordchai Ya'akov Breish, *Shut Khelkat Yaakov*, Yore De'a, 137.

18. BT Ketubot 67b.

19. Mishna Demai 3:1; Mishna Kidushin 4:5; Mishna Bava Kama 10:1; cf. Jerusalem Pe'a 1:1.

20. See, for example, the discussion of this question in Bava Batra 8b.

21. See Deuteronomy 15:4. "There shall be no needy among you." Rashi explains this phrase as a responsibility of every person on BT Baba Mezia 30b: "not to become needy." It is not the responsibility of the community but of the individual himself.

22. Job 31:2.

23. On man created in God's image, see Yair Lorberbaum, *In God's Image: Myth, Theology, and Law in Classical Judaism* (New York, New York, and Cambridge, Great Britain: Cambridge University Press, 2015).

24. I Kings 21:17–19.

25. BT Sanhedrin 108a.

26. BT Baba Metzia 59a.

27. Deuteronomy 19:14.

28. Deuteronomy 25:13–16.

29. Deuteronomy 22:1.

30. Leviticus 19:13.

31. Exodus 20:14.

32. According to the rabbinic tradition, "You shall not covet" does not apply to thought alone, but rather to the act of bringing unreasonable pressure to bear on one's neighbor in an effort to persuade him to hand over his property, even for monetary compensation. See, for example, Maimonides, *Mishneh Torah*, Laws of Robbery and Loss 1:9. However, even according to this interpretation, it is an extremely significant extension of the principle of private property.

33. Mishna Bava Batra 3:3. Some have attempted to define property on the basis of the discussion in Gitin 47b over whether "acquiring the fruits is like acquiring the body," viz., if someone who buys the produce of a field is comparable to the owners of the field itself. It was established that ownership of fruit is not the same as ownership of the object (see Maimonides, *Mishneh Torah*, Laws of the First Fruits 4:6). Some have deduced from this that, according to Jewish law, ownership is not determined solely by the right to make use of an object, since it is possible to draw up a contract by which one party is the owner of the object and the other of what it yields. Yet although this may be useful as a figurative example of ownership divorced from actual usage, it is a mistake to draw a parallel between objects and their yield, on the one hand, and possession and use, on the other. The owners of a field are still entitled to use it for purposes other than its produce. Moreover, ownership of the yield pertains not only to its

use, but also to the full possession of that yield.

34. Mishna Bava Kama 8:7.

35. On the strength of this law, Rashi offered an interpretation of the rule cited in Bava Kama 26b, which exempts a man from punishment if he uses a stick to break a vessel that someone has thrown from a roof, while it is still in flight. Rabbi Yosef Dov Halevi Soloveichik, author of *Beit Halevi*, explained: "As has previously been said, if someone threw a vessel from the roof and someone comes along and breaks it with a stick, he is not liable. Why so? He broke that which was already broken." Rashi adds on this case: "The owner of the vessel threw the vessel," he and no other. Rashi's insistence on this point is difficult to understand, since if the vessel is thrown by its owner from the top of the roof, then it must be considered to have been abandoned, and there is no liability for damaging an abandoned object. The most likely answer is that by throwing the vessel, the owner demonstrated his ownership by doing with it as he pleased. Ownership in this case is shown not by the use of the vessel but by its deliberate and willful destruction. Rabbi Yosef Dov Halevi Soloveichik, *Responsa of the Beit Halevi* (Vilna, Russia: Yosef Rubin, 1863), 1:24, 2:7. [Hebrew]

36. Genesis 1:28. This commandment was given to man while he was still in the Garden of Eden, and was not altered after he sinned. See also Yevamot 65b; Kidushin 35a.

37. Genesis 2:15.

38. BT Megila 6a.

39. Etienne Gilson, *The Christian Philosophy of St. Thomas Aquinas*, trans. by L. K. Shook (Notre Dame, Indiana: University of Notre Dame Press, 1956), 345–347.

40. BT Erubin 3a.

41. In his *Mishpat Hamelukha B'Israel* (The Law of Kingship in Israel, Hebrew) (Jerusalem: Mosad Harav Kook, 2005), 132–142, Shimon Federbush claims that although property rights in Jewish law are highly respected, regulations are necessary in order to protect ethical values. According to him, communal associations are recommended.

42. Leviticus 25:35–36.

43. BT Shabbat 92a.

44. BT Eruvin 86a.

45. BT Hagiga, 9b.

46. See Mishnah Aboth 4:1.

47. BT Shabbat 25b.

48. BT Brachot 8a.

49. BT Baba Metzia 62a.

50. Song of Songs 8:7.

51. Maimonides, *The Guide for the Perplexed*, III 54, trans. by Shlomo Pines (Chicago, Illinois: University of Chicago Press, 1963), 634.

52. Maimonides, *Perplexed*, 635.

53. Jeremy Waldron, *The Right to Private Property* (Oxford, Great Britain: Clarendon Press, 1990).

54. Baba Batra 8b and 89b–90b.

55. Leviticus 25:47–55.

56. See Moshe Weinfeld, *Social Justice in Ancient Israel and the Ancient Near East* (Jerusalem, Israel: Hebrew University Magnes Press, 1995), 231–247.

57. Jeremiah 34:13–17.

58. BT Baba Kama 116b, Maimonides Hilchot Schirut 9:4, R. Yoseph Karo, *Shulchan Aruch*, Choshen Mishpat, 333:3. See also David J. Schnall, *By the Sweat of Your Brow: Reflections on Work and the Workplace in Classic Jewish Thought* (New York, New York: The Michael Scharf Publication Trust of Yeshiva University Press, 2001), 103–126.

59. BT Baba Batra 8b.

60. *Rabbi Meirs von Rothenburg bisher unedirte Responsen* [MS Amsterdam II] (Berlin, Germany, 1891), #128.

61. BT Baba Batra 7b, R. Yoseph Karo, *Shulchan Aruch*, Choshen Mishpat 163:3.

62. See Yosef Karo, *Shulchan Aruch*, Orach Chayim, 55:21.

63. Rabenu Yerucham, Ntiv 29, Yosef Karo, *Shulchan Aruch*, Choshen Mishpat 163:2, Shulchan Aruch, Orach Chayim, 658:9.

64. See Yechiel Michel Epstein, *Aroch Hashulchan*, Orach Chayim, 150:2.

65. Choshen Mishpat, 163:4.

Islam

ISLAM, INEQUALITY, MORALITY, AND JUSTICE

MOHAMMAD H. FADEL

Introduction

Islamic thought on questions of property, income, equality, and justice is the product of numerous and diverse traditions that have interacted in different ways with the religious tradition of Islam. Prior to the nineteenth century, the most important philosophical tradition that influenced Muslim thinking would have been ancient Greek and Hellenistic philosophy, as interpreted by the Muslim philosophical tradition. Islamic thought over the last hundred and fifty years, however, has developed largely in response to classical liberal economic thought and Marxist economic thought, with leading figures of twentieth-century Islamism attempting to defend a particularly Islamic approach to questions of property, equality, income, and wealth that distinguishes it from both market capitalism and socialism.

Despite the different philosophical traditions that have influenced the way Muslims think about questions of economic justice throughout the long history of Muslim civilization, a constant has been the revealed sources of Islam—the Quran and the practice of the Prophet Muḥammad (the *Sunna*)—and how Muslim jurists interpreted those sources to produce legal rules that regulated economic life in a Muslim society. Revelation's teachings on property, wealth, and justice, however, were not free of tensions. Islam began in the seventh century, in the west Arabian town of Mecca, which hosted both the important religious shrine known as the Kaʿba—the House of God—and had become an important trading center. The Arabian tribe of Quraysh, which came to dominate Mecca, not only enjoyed the religious prestige of organizing the annual pan-Arabian pilgrimage to Mecca, but also grew wealthy by virtue of its ability to control biannual trading caravans that linked trade from Yemen in the south to Syria in the north. The earliest Quranic teachings reflected the increasingly stratified character of Meccan society as it came to be transformed by its connections to international trade, and so it vehemently condemned the cruelty, arrogance, and moral blindness of Meccan pagan society. In numerous early verses, it condemned the Meccans for their obsession with the accumulation of property, falsely assuming an equivalence between wealth and virtue, and their failure to recognize their true ends as servants of God.

Side by side with its denunciations of the vices associated with private property and the pursuit of wealth, revelation posited an alternative ethic of property based in generosity and solidarity. As a result, it regularly encouraged believers to give freely of their property to those in need and for the furtherance of other pious ends. Yet neither revelation's criticism of Mecca's economic structure nor its emphasis on a counter-ethic of generosity led it to adopt a categorical condemnation of private property or acquisitiveness. Other texts of revelation recognized and even protected private property. One verse, for example, criminalized theft,[1] and others explicitly affirmed the legitimacy of trade and commerce,[2] with the longest verse in the Quran devoted to setting out the procedures for recording commercial debt contracts. The tension between the Quran's polemic against property and acquisitiveness on the one hand, and its protection of private property and recognition of legitimate commerce on the other hand, alongside its promotion of an ethic of generosity, would combine to form an important and productive source of reflection in the development of Islamic law, morality, and ethics in subsequent generations in which Muslims sought to balance individual rights in private property and the right to pursue profit against a countervailing ethic of generosity and social solidarity.[3]

The most important site for considered reflection on these questions in the pre-modern period was the work of Muslim jurists, and although many of their teachings have been superseded, they still represent a common store of reflection that in practice remains an important baseline for even contemporary Muslim reflections on questions of economic justice. Accordingly, analysis of legal doctrines, in addition to the writings of modern Muslims, will provide most of the raw material for my discussion of the questions raised in this book. A careful consideration of the premodern tradition of reflection on these questions discloses, in broad outlines, a basic conception of economic justice as lying, primarily, in following fair processes of exchange, with little concern for the distributive outcome of these processes, except to ensure that all individuals enjoy a minimally adequate standard of living. In modernity, leading twentieth-century Islamist thinkers expressed greater skepticism toward the distributive outcomes produced by market exchange, and vigorously advocated greater state intervention in the economy to ensure what they deemed to be just distributive outcomes.

The editors of this volume have asked us to address a series of topics related to how Muslim thinkers have conceptualized the structure of the economy and the economy's relationship to questions of human equality, the kinds of property rights recognized in the economy, ownership and use of natural resources, whether justice demands that individuals in society have a claim to specific outputs of the economy, the place of wealth in the economy, distribution of the income produced by the economy, employment, and attitudes toward taxation. I have organized my essay to respond directly to each of the questions they posed to the Islamic tradition. I have endeavored to answer their questions using the predominant views in the Islamic tradition as I understand it. I have also provided, however, more recent views on these questions in those circumstances where prominent modern Muslim thinkers have offered distinct solutions or novel theories.

Many of the questions posed by the editors are quintessentially modern questions insofar as they are only meaningful in post-industrial-revolution societies that, more or less, have transcended Malthusian constraints and whose economies are organized largely around the principles of capitalism and market exchange. Most of the Islamic tradition, however, was produced in the context of pre-industrial economies, and although Muslims valorized market exchange, markets prior to the industrial revolution were of a radically different character, insofar as they lacked, among other factors, the complex layers of intermediation characteristic of the infinitely more developed division of labor present in modern market economies. When using the resources of the pre-modern Islamic tradition to discuss the questions posed by the editors, one is forced to search for conceptual analogues in the pre-modern tradition to what are quintessentially modern problems. Nevertheless, in many cases, I believe that the pre-modern tradition provides a principled basis from which modern Muslims can reason about these questions, provided that they update those pre-modern precedents in light of the radical differences between contemporary markets and pre-modern ones. The following sections present to the reader one Muslim's understanding of how the Muslim tradition would respond to the questions posed. After answering those questions, I give a conclusion that synthesizes the various strands of argument discussed in the essay to provide a general statement regarding an Islamic conception of the ethical issues involved in organizing and sustaining an economy.

Equality

The equality of human beings as servants of God is a core teaching of Islam, with the only morally relevant distinction among them being their righteousness. With respect to the economic sphere, however, human equality takes precedence over righteousness. This primitive equality manifests itself in juristic conceptions of the state of nature in which every person had an equal right to things of this earth as affirmed in the Quranic verse that states: "And He created for you, all of you, what is in the earth," without regard even to a natural principle of prior possession. Stable property entitlements, therefore, are a product of political community and not nature, where the only law is that of effective possession. In the primitive state of human equality, where a person could only enjoy possessory rights, there were natural limitations on the extent of property.

Within a polity, however, legal rights to property are recognized that enable accumulation beyond what any one individual could effectively possess. Within the context of an Islamic polity, Islamic law adopted both procedural and substantive doctrines that gave effect to different conceptions of equality. The most fundamental manifestation of equality is in the equal capacity of all persons to contract, whether male or female, Muslim or non-Muslim. In market exchange, then, perfect, abstract equality is the norm: market relations are imagined to take place between sellers and purchasers each of whom is equally capable of pursuing his self-interest effectively, and as a result, their agreements are just insofar as they are a manifestation of each trader's rational will. Accordingly, Islamic law did not adopt a theory of a "fair price" that existed outside of the parties' specific agreement; rather, the bargain struck between two equal persons, negotiating at arm's length, determined what was just.

It may seem odd that classical Islamic law did not adopt a "just price" theory or something akin to what modern lawyers would recognize as "unconscionability," i.e., contract terms so onerous that even if they were freely agreed to, the court cannot, in good faith, enforce those terms. The answer to this puzzle may lie in two sources. First, Islamic contract law expressly prohibited interest-bearing loans, as well as speculative contracts whose material terms were not specified from the time of contracting.[4] The second is that most trade, in fact, was in the cash market, and so contracts were not very complex. Islamic law certainly had no experience with the kinds of complex contracts of adhesion typical in modern consumer finance contracts that gave rise to the doctrine of unconscionability in the first place. In the modern world, however, as many of the formal barriers found in classical Islamic law have given way, modern Arab civil codes have recognized something akin to a just-price theory, insofar as they give judges the right to rescind a contract if the agreed-upon price was materially off-market (*ghabn fāḥish*).

The conception of procedural justice that structured market exchanges, however, was not applied across all economic sectors. For example, partnership law imposed certain substantive conceptions of equality based on fairness that transcended the parties' agreement to the contrary. Accordingly, for most Muslim jurists, a partnership was not just (and therefore was invalid as a matter of law) if profits and losses were not divided proportionally in conformity with the amount of capital each partner contributed to the venture. The notion that justice in cooperative ventures required proportional distributions of both gains and benefits was rejected by only one group of Muslim jurists, the Ḥanafīs, but they did not accept the principle of free contracting with respect to allocations of the costs and benefits of the firm. They permitted co-venturers to allocate the profits from their venture independently of each partner's respective capital contribution, but did not permit partners to allocate their losses except in accordance with their pro-rata ownership of the firm. The same obligation to share in risk underlies a fundamental Islamic principle of distributive justice: that the right to gain must be accompanied by the risk of loss.

Accordingly, one might say that in Islamic conceptions of equality, the formal equality of persons, which gives rise to contractual freedom, and the concomitant rejection of any kind of "just price" theory, is qualified by a substantive conception of equality that requires traders and joint-venturers to bear their fair share of risks. This mandatory principle of distributive justice seeks to prevent parties with greater economic power from using that strength to put losses, disproportionately, on their weaker counterparties. More generally, Muslim jurists endorsed the principle that "warding off harms is to be given priority to the attainment of unrealized goods" as a universal principle of distributive justice that they claimed was enshrined throughout various rules of Islamic law.

Modern Muslim thinkers, such as the Sunnī theorist Sayyid Quṭb, and the Shīʿī theorist, Muḥammad Bāqir al-Ṣadr, preserve elements of the classical tradition's attempt to balance formal equality and its respect for contractual freedom as determinative of outcome with substantive equality and its demand that individuals not use contract to evade their fair share of losses that arise from economic activity, albeit in language that goes beyond the legalism of the classical tradition. Contrary to Marxism, both Quṭb and Ṣadr reject any notion of distributive justice that would require strict equality of outcome as both practically impossible and normatively undesirable. They both point to the experience of the Soviet Union to argue that even in a Communist order, Marxists found it practically impossible to implement a substantive conception of economic equality. They also argue against substantive equality of outcome from a normative perspective: human beings, although they are generically equal, differ in numerous qualities that are economically relevant, in terms of talent, skill, and productivity, and so insisting on equality of outcome not only would be, according to Quṭb, unjust to exceptional individuals, it would also be harmful to society, which would be deprived of the benefits of their exceptional talents, skills, and productivity. For both Ṣadr and Quṭb, Islamic law provides the ideal balance between the formal equality of persons that underlies market relations, which is the condition for achieving the good of maximum possible economic growth, and substantive equality, by prohibiting substantively unjust agreements, such as usurious contracts (*ribā*) or contracts entailing excessive speculation (*gharar*)—or unlawful modes of doing business that are the natural result of market forces, such as monopolies. Islamic law's prohibition of otherwise consensual market exchanges and the end result of free-market competition, among other things, distinguishes the Islamic conception of equality, in their view, from both the Marxist conception and the liberal capitalist conception of equality.

Both classical Islamic conceptions of equality, as well as modern discussion of equality, agree on the necessity of giving a priority to reducing the economic inequality that results from market forces over the right of those who benefit from the market to retain their earnings to invest in new opportunities. The difference is the degree to which justice requires interference in the results produced by free exchange. The classical tradition was focused largely on ensuring that each person in an Islamic polity received minimally adequate resources to survive. Both Quṭb and Ṣadr, however, go beyond this minimum requirement and believe that greater equality in distribution, all things being equal, is Islamically desirable. For Quṭb, this is because excessive wealth undermines the moral integrity of both the wealthy and the impoverished. In the case of the rich, excessive wealth tends to produce in them the kind of moral vices that the Quran condemns, such as avarice and the unrestrained pursuit of sensual pleasure. In the case of the poor, their poverty drives them to lose their dignity and self-respect in their pursuit of wealth and honor by placing themselves in the service of the rich. Ṣadr argues that the state must do more than ensure that everyone enjoys the bare essentials with respect to food, clothing, and shelter; rather, it must also provide to everyone, in appropriate quantities and quality, those items which are consistent with prevailing conditions in an Islamic society. As the general level of prosperity increases in an Islamic society, justice therefore requires the state to intervene so that the poorest enjoy the general improvement in living conditions and are not continued to be confined to subsistence levels of consumption.[5]

Quṭb and Ṣadr can both be understood as responding to the increasing influence of socialism in Muslim societies. Some prominent religious leaders who were active in attempts to reform Muslim society, such as Jamal al-Din al-Afghānī, came to identify socialism—understood as an ethic of

sharing excess wealth—to be the epitome of revelation's teachings on economics and distributive justice. This, in turn, produced a line of thought
known as "Islamic socialism," which attempted to reconcile Islamic ideals
of generosity and equality with socialist ideals of common ownership of at
least the important means of production and a more egalitarian distribution of national income than market economics would allow.

For much of the twentieth century, one might say that "Islamic socialism" was the dominant economic paradigm in most of the Muslim world,
with Pakistan being the most important exception. The fact that Egypt
openly claimed to be adopting a path of Islamic socialism that made its experiment distinctive from either market capitalism or Soviet Communism
played an important role in lending prestige to the idea. Pakistan, however,
hewed a path closer to market capitalism, stressing classical Islam's ideals
of market exchange combined with a voluntary ethic of redistribution, not
state control of the economy, as the proper Islamic economic model. Despite the greater attractiveness of Islamic socialism to much of the Muslim
world in the mid-twentieth century, its appeal radically diminished as a
result of the palpable failures of socialist-inspired policies to produce either
egalitarian societies or prosperous ones, *and* the rise of the petroleum economy, which produced an enormous windfall for the previously marginal
states of the Arabian Peninsula. The conservatism of the Gulf Arab states,
in alliance with Pakistan, articulated a different Islamic conception of economic justice, one that catered to the need of states flush with cash to find
legitimate means to invest their windfall profitably. This model of Islamic
economic justice might be called "Islamic neo-liberalism." In contrast to
Islamic socialism, or the Islamic economics advocated by Ṣadr and Quṭb,
this conception of justice was deeply committed to the inherent fairness of
consensual market exchange, without regard to the social consequences,
i.e., negative externalities, of the market. As long as trade followed the
formal rules of Islamic law, and the wealthy fulfilled their Islamic obligation of charity to the less fortunate, this school of Islamic thought believed that distributive outcomes could not be criticized as unjust or un-
Islamic. This model, in turn, led to the development of Islamic finance,
which grew from very humble origins in the mid-1970s to becoming a
recognized niche in the world of international finance, with trillions of
dollars invested according to its own version of neo-liberal exchange. For
adherents of Islamic finance, the most important manifestation of equality

in the economic sphere is the formal equality individuals have to trade in the market and to pursue their own self-interest.

Property

Property, in Islamic law, comes into existence through a direct act of successful appropriation by a person through his own effort. The paradigmatic example of the creation of a property interest is hunting: the hunter attains a property right by virtue of his successful effort to subdue and control a wild animal. The property right arises when the hunter wounds the animal, not merely by pursuit, and it lapses if he fails to track down his prey in a diligent and timely fashion. On the assumption that his hunt is successful, however, the animal belongs to him, to do with as he pleases. A similar approach applies to land: a person becomes entitled to unused land (*mawāt*) by successfully appropriating it through acts such as irrigating it, building a permanent structure on it, planting trees, clearing trees, draining it of excess water, or plowing it with a view to farming. The same principles apply in general to appropriating water from a stream, grass from pasture, and wood from a forest. But the basic model of successful appropriation through the application of human labor only accounts for possessory rights in a state of nature, which are contingent on having the strength to defend possession against potential enemies. Within a polity, Islamic law structures not only the transfer of pre-political possessory rights (which through the creation of a common polity mature into property rights as against everyone else within that polity, even if not against the entire world), but the creation of property rights ab initio within the borders of that polity.

Within an Islamic polity, certain kinds of property—water, pasture, and firewood, for example—must be maintained as a common property. No one is permitted to convert common property into private property, although each person is permitted to take from the common what they reasonably require for their own needs, provided that it does not undermine the ability of others to avail themselves of the resources of the common. Accordingly, the right to extract resources from the common is subject to the ceiling of reasonable individual use consistent with the equal usage of others entitled to the common. With respect to outsiders, however, the common has aspects of exclusive collective property: while the residents of town A, for example, are co-tenants of town A's common and, therefore, cannot prevent each other from reasonable use of the common's resources, they are entitled to exclude residents from town B from benefitting from town A's common.

While the nature of common ownership places limits on the amount any co-owner may appropriate to his private property, no such limitation applies to unused land. Classical Islamic law recognized the right of individuals to become the owners of unused land through one or more positive acts of appropriation, such as clearing the land of trees, plowing it, draining it of water, etc. In contrast to the common that belongs to a town, classical Islamic law recognized no upward limit to the amount of unused land that a single person could own through recognized acts of appropriation. Likewise, the state could grant individuals licenses (*iqṭā'*) to develop particular tracts of land belonging to the state. Such licenses could only be granted on terms that furthered the public good, and the licensee was bound to abide by the terms of the grant in order to retain the property right. Other than the requirement that the terms of the license be consistent with the public good, however, there was no legal obstacle to amassing as many such grants as one could obtain from the government. On the other hand, however, it would clearly be a permissible exercise of state power to restrict eligibility for such licenses to individuals whose aggregate property holdings did not exceed a designated maximum, for example. And indeed, substantive Islamic principles of distributive justice provided that the state should use its powers to grant licenses over state land preferentially in favor of persons lacking land. Although classical Islamic law advised the state to give due concern to the landless, the state was under no obligation to do so.

One of the central demands of Islamic socialism in the twentieth century was to redistribute land from rich landlords to the cultivators. One of their primary arguments was a report attributed to the Prophet Muḥammad, in which he advised his followers who had land beyond their capacity to farm to give the surplus land to one of their landless brethren without demanding any compensation. To overcome classical Islamic arguments that were deployed against the legitimacy of such redistributionist schemes, various thinkers developed different theories to justify redistribution of land, the most sophisticated of which might be that of the aforementioned Ṣadr. Ṣadr, in a radical extension of Islamic theories identifying the origin of property in the affirmative act of appropriation, argued that Islam did not recognize absolute title in real property. Instead, Islam only recognized a right to use based on an original act of appropriation. The difference between privately owned land and public land, essentially, was that the "owner" of privately owned land could transfer his right to use to others without permission of the state, whereas the land owned by the state could never be transferred except in accordance with the rules established by the state for the use of that land. In both cases, however, the possessor of the land enjoyed his possession by virtue of the state's permission for possessor to maintain possession—provided, in each case, that the possessor is making good use of the land through his own labor.

Ṣadr goes so far as to take the remarkable position that labor is such a crucial factor in producing recognition of the entitlement in Islamic law that a usurper who wrongfully occupies another's land and then cultivates crops on that land is entitled to the output of the land by virtue of his labor. In such a case, the owner's recourse is limited to the fair rent of his land. He further develops his notion of labor as the only contribution to production that mandates recognition, to argue that the state can and should redistribute land in favor of the cultivators and against the interests of landlords. He also applies his labor theory of entitlement to industrial production to argue that the mere contribution of physical capital, such as machinery or animals or land, only entitles the capitalist to rent; the output of the venture belongs to the worker who produced the goods. Ṣadr's theory that only labor authorized the recognition of a property entitlement was no doubt intended to achieve a redistributive effect in favor of the working class and to the detriment of those in society whose only contribution to production was financial or physical capital.

Quṭb, by contrast, does not radically depart from accepted Islamic principles of property ownership, but instead argues that in a properly constituted Islamic society, the ethic of generosity should lead the wealthy to share their property with the poor so that they enjoy a sufficient amount of property to ensure their well-being. Moreover, it is crucial, according to Quṭb, that this sharing be, in an important sense, voluntary; otherwise, dependence on an unreasonable amount of coercion would suggest the absence of proper motivation and so would be worthless in promoting the kind of just society that Islam seeks to achieve.

Muslim theories of the origin of property bear an unmistakable resemblance to aspects of John Locke's theory regarding the origin of property. It is beyond the scope of this essay, however, to investigate whether there is any historical link between Islamic conceptions of the origin of property and Locke's theory. That possibility, however, is certainly worthy of further scholarly investigation. In any case, the presence of analogous concepts in Islamic thought and Lockean ideas provides a useful starting point for dialogue between liberal and Muslim theories of property holding.

Natural Resources

In classical Islamic law, natural resources were part of the commonly held property, in which case anyone had the right to appropriate for his personal use a reasonable amount of such resources while respecting the right of others to make use of the common for their needs as well. In such a case, the conversion from a common right to a private right found its justification in the human labor that manifested itself in the act of appropriation. As noted previously, the same logic applied to the right of individuals to hunt wild animals and fish in commonly owned bodies of water, e.g., rivers and lakes, or unowned bodies of water, e.g., the ocean. Individuals also owned natural resources that existed on the surface of their own property, such as a tree growing naturally on one's property. A wild animal that wandered onto one's property, however, did not give rise to an entitlement to that animal as against a hunter who had wounded that animal and was hot in pursuit. A person could also own water resources found on his land if, for example, he obtained that water by virtue of digging a well on his own land, in which case he could sell to others water that he did not need, or keep it for himself. A well dug in the countryside or the deserts, however, gave the person (or group of people) responsible for digging it only a right of first use, not ownership, and accordingly, they were obliged to permit others to use it after their herds were sated. Naturally flowing water, resulting from a flash flood or the like, could not be monopolized by those on higher ground to the detriment of those located at a lower elevation: those on higher ground were only entitled to keep a portion of the water and then were required to allow the remainder to flow down to those at lower elevations.

These cases provide examples of the legitimating role labor plays in transforming natural property held in common to private property belonging to a particular person with the right of exclusive use. As the example of a well dug in the countryside indicates, that use of labor can only provide a right of first use, but not exclusive ownership of the water that is found. Where water is extracted by effort from land that is already privately owned, however, the owner of the land also owns the water he finds on his property, which gives him the right not only to use it, but also to exclude others from using it except with his permission, including by means of sale.

With respect to mineral resources, classical Islamic law provided that mineral wealth, whether visible or underground, if located on state property, could not be privately owned. Rather, the state could grant licenses to specific individuals on specific terms to permit them to mine those resources for a defined period of time. Some jurists also concluded that underground mineral wealth, if discovered on private property, did not belong to the owner of the surface rights, but rather, belonged to the state, just like any other property that lacked an owner. In any case, the modern view of Muslim thinkers is that mineral wealth belongs to the public, wherever located, and can never be privately owned; rather, the state, in its capacity as owner of public resources, may authorize specific individuals to exploit those resources for the benefit of the public.

As classical Muslim doctrines concerning the common indicate, all persons had an inalienable right to access the common to satisfy their reasonable needs. At the same time, there was no place for the spirit of profit-maximization in the common. A person could only appropriate from the common that which was necessary for his needs, and were he to collect firewood from the common for the commercial purpose of sale to the townsfolk, presumably the fact that the common was the exclusive property of the town attached to it would limit the possible size of the market for products from that common in such a way that it would remain sustainable for its beneficiaries. Along these lines, Ṣadr argued in the twentieth century, more radically along the lines of his labor theory of entitlement, that the property rights that arise out of appropriation from the common are restricted to the person who does so directly. Accordingly, a person was not allowed to appoint another as his agent for gathering items from the common, and if he did, whatever goods were appropriated belonged to the appropriator, not the principal who retained him. Private persons were allowed, however, to exploit commercially natural resources found on their property, such as water, in circumstances where they made a productive investment, such as digging a well, to render that resource accessible to themselves. With respect to wells in the desert and the countryside, however, successful digging of a well only gave a right of first use, whereupon the "owner" of the well was obliged to allow others to water their animals from what remained of the water of his well. So, again, we see the same pattern confirmed: natural resources may be converted to private property, but only after reserving a certain portion of those resources for common use, and in the case of mineral wealth, it would be managed by the state for the public good, not the private benefit of the person exploiting the mine, although presumably he would be entitled to take a portion of the value of the extracted mineral in accordance with the terms of the license granted by the state.

Products

Classical Islamic legal doctrines also imposed certain distributive requirements with respect to the distribution of products of the economy in addition to guaranteeing equal access to the common and unowned land for purposes of reclamation. Specifically, through the institution of *zakat*, a scripturally mandated act of charity, classical Islamic law attempted to secure for every Muslim a sufficient amount of food to last him for a year. Aside from guaranteeing access to life's necessities, however, Islamic law generally allowed other products to be distributed through the market mechanism. Islamic law obviously distinguished between those products of the economy that are necessary to sustain human life and those that are not, and subjected only the former to a non-market scheme of distribution. This obligation arose out of the duty of solidarity that was an inherent part of the obligations arising out of being a Muslim. While non-Muslims were technically not eligible to receive *zakat* (they were also exempt from paying it), certainly by the late Middle Ages and the early modern period, if not earlier, large public endowments providing food to the urban poor without distinguishing between Muslim and non-Muslim had made their appearance in the Arab Middle East.

As mentioned above, classical Islamic law was largely indifferent to the distribution of products in society except to ensure that everyone had a sufficient supply of food to eat. While the *zakat* ensured, or sought to ensure, that the poor did not suffer from starvation at times of famine or other crisis, classical Islamic law also contemplated intervention in the distribution of food supplies to ensure an adequate supply of food for the urban population as a whole, not just the poor. Accordingly, in times of crisis, the state could take extraordinary anti-hoarding measures to intervene in the market by, for example, forcing local grain retail merchants to open their warehouses to the consuming public in the hope that increasing the supply of grain would drive down the price. Foreign merchants, or local merchants who imported grain to the city, however, would typically be exempt from such rules in the hope that increasing local prices would induce them to secure new sources of supply. When forcing local grain retailers to sell their inventory was insufficient to bring down prices, the state could also take further measures, such as setting maximum prices for grain or, in the most extreme case, displace the market mechanism entirely and set prices for retailers and consumers. As far as I know, however, such measures, which were always controversial, never extended to products other than staple foods; luxury goods and fruit and meat were never proper subjects of price restraints or controls in the eyes of the law.

Wealth

Islamic thought on wealth has been shaped by the conflicting messages of revelation regarding wealth. On the one hand, it ought not to be the end that organizes human life; but on the other hand, revelation respects the rights of property and even recognizes that if wealth is used for godly ends, consistent with its ethic of generosity, wealth can be a positive good. In classical Islamic law, a person was wealthy to the extent that he owned sufficient assets to oblige him to pay *zakat*. This minimum amount was calculated depending on the nature of the person's property holdings, but the rationale of the system, even if not always fully implemented through its positive rulings, was that a person was "rich," and therefore under the obligation to pay alms, if he could feed himself for a year. This minimum amount was known as *niṣāb*. Certainly, entitlement to the receipt of alms was also defined by reference to this amount, so that a person who did not own a year's worth of food was eligible to receive alms.

The most important legal justification for the accumulation of wealth was the extent to which it was gained through licit activities. To the extent that a person acquired a vast amount of wealth using licit means, there could be no ethical objection to the mere fact that a person had successfully acquired a vast amount of wealth. But there was also the element of luck, signified in the notion that God gives to and withholds His bounty from whom He wills without limit, not necessarily as a sign of favor or election, but rather as a test. Wealth and poverty, then, from the perspective of revelation, are both tests from God. To the extent a person is grateful for divine blessings, and is generous with the wealth God has bestowed upon him, he is blessed and may even expect that his worldly prosperity will only increase. Indeed, the early community is replete with stories of followers of the Prophet Muḥammad who sacrificed enormous amounts of their personal wealth for the support of his prophetic mission, and they subsequently provided models of the "engaged" wealthy, who use their wealth to further the good of the community. Institutionally, prior to the twentieth century, this resulted in the ubiquity of the pious endowment in Muslim societies. Such endowments were used for numerous purposes, both for the transmission of private wealth across generations and to fund religious and charitable organizations, such as hospitals, schools, poorhouses, or lodges for orphans and widows. In all cases, however, even endowments in favor of one's descendants had to have a residuary beneficiary that was charitable or religious. The impetus for the establishment of endowments was at least in part a response to a teaching of the Prophet Muḥammad that upon an individual's death, he loses all hope of earning additional merit before God except from three things: children of good character, who pray for him; a legacy of learning that is beneficial to others; or an act of ongoing charity. An endowment is precisely an act of ongoing charity, its income being dedicated to a charitable end in perpetuity, and therefore earning its founder merit from the time he established it to the end of time.

One historically controversial feature of Muslim laws of endowments was the fact that endowments for the benefit of the family were not legally distinguished from public endowments for the benefit of religion or charity, although both were perpetual. The British, in fact, tried to apply the rule against perpetuities to dissolve what they called family endowments in British India, which produced a great hue and cry by the Muslim population there. In classical Islamic thought, providing for one's descendants is itself understood to be a form of charity, in reliance on a prophetic teaching, in which he limited the testamentary disposition of one of his companions to one-third of his estate, saying "one-third is a lot" and that it is better to leave one's heirs prosperous than to give away one's wealth to needy strangers. Family endowments were structured in such a way then as to preserve an individual's wealth over generations until such time as the founder's lineal descendants died out, whereupon the endowed property would be applied to the charitable or pious cause the founder had specified.

Family endowments were often a preferred method for the intergenerational transfer of wealth because of its flexibility—the founder had almost unlimited freedom in allocating the income produced by the endowment property to the specific descendants he wished to benefit—and its ability to preserve intact real estate, whether agricultural or urban. The Muslim law of inheritance, by contrast, provided no flexibility to an owner of wealth, with precise rules determining the statutory share of each heir that could only be reallocated through the heirs' agreement at the time of the decedent's death. Islamic inheritance law, moreover, did not permit testamentary dispositions to exceed a third of the estate's value at the time of death, after the decedent's debts had been repaid, and in no case could the decedent, according to Sunni Muslims at least, make a testamentary disposition in favor of an heir. The final tool that was used to transfer wealth between generations was the inter vivos gift, which was an especially popular and religiously commendable mode of transfer of wealth to a daughter, usually at the time of her marriage.

A common criticism of the Muslim law of inheritance is that it made capital accumulation difficult because it allocated a mandatory share to every one of the decedent's children as well as a surviving spouse. It is beyond the scope of this paper to engage in the debate about whether such rules acted as an obstacle to economic development in the Muslim world relative to Europe and Great Britain, where different inheritance norms prevailed. From the perspective of this piece, however, the important point to emphasize is the egalitarian nature of Muslim inheritance law whereby each person in the family was given a predetermined share of the estate, albeit at the ratio of 2:1 in favor of male heirs to female heirs within the same class, e.g., brothers and sisters. Founders of family endowments typically followed the same pattern—although they were free to depart from it—in the terms of their endowment deeds so that the benefits of property holding would be distributed across subsequent generations in a manner that approached equality and tended to diminish concentrated holdings of property with the passage of time. But the broad sweep of Islamic inheritance law was not only intended to support an egalitarian distribution of wealth: it also was reinforced on the liabilities side, insofar as the kin that stood to benefit from mutual rights of inheritance were also under mutual duties of support. Accordingly, the kin was under a duty to support a family member who became impoverished, as well as under a duty to discharge liabilities arising out of a non-intentional tort committed by a member of their kin.

In the rules regarding the intergenerational transfer of familial wealth and the mutual duties of maintenance and of acting as insurers of family members' non-intentional torts, one sees another manifestation of the Islamic principle previously mentioned: that benefit comes only with responsibility for loss. This principle—that benefit must come with responsibility for loss—explains classical Islam's rejection of interest-bearing loans. Lending money at interest was deemed to violate this fundamental principle of Islamic commercial law because the debtor, insofar as it guaranteed the return of the principal, relieved the creditor of any risk of loss to his capital. Accordingly, the creditor had no legitimate claim to the profit that the borrower earned from his use of the capital. This is the basis for the common belief that Islam and commercial banking are incompatible. Indeed, the common belief that this is so has given rise to the creation of a niche sector in the financial market known as Islamic banking, a topic I will touch on below.

The prohibition against interest-bearing loans in classical Islam, however, did not result in an absolute prohibition against passive investment as a legitimate means of acquiring wealth. Rather, classical Islamic law authorized a passive investment vehicle—known as *muḍāraba* or *qirāḍ* in Arabic, and *commenda* in Latin—pursuant to which the investor would give a certain amount of money to an entrepreneur who invested it in a profit-generating venture. The investor and the entrepreneur would divide any realized profits from the venture in accordance with a pre-specified, pro-rata formula. Before the entrepreneur could realize any profits, however, he had first to return the investor's capital.

Unlike the case of a loan, which transfers title to the debtor, the capital of the *commenda* was understood to remain the property of the investor at all times. Accordingly, the entrepreneur did not guarantee the investor's capital, but the investor had a priority on the *commenda*'s assets until he recouped all his investment. Profits distributed to the entrepreneur are not understood to flow from a capital share in the venture, but rather understood to be compensation for the entrepreneur's labor. Classical Islam, therefore, permitted profit through financial intermediation—without a requirement that the investor engage directly in productive activities, but it did insist, following the universal principle that profit follows responsibility for loss, that the investor's capital be responsible for losses arising out of financial investments.

Modern Muslims, sympathetic with neo-liberal commitments to market exchange, have vastly expanded the opportunity for finance-driven profits divorced from productive activities in the real economy. Modern Islamic banking and finance, which some dismiss as *shari'a* arbitrage, is based on synthesizing conventional financial instruments, beginning with an interest-bearing loan, and going so far as to include various derivative instruments, such as options and swaps, using contractual forms borrowed from classical Islamic law. Two features of classical Islamic contract law lent itself to this modern appropriation.

First, classical Islamic contract law permitted implicit interest to the extent that the charge for credit was embedded in the price of a good offered for sale on credit. Accordingly, Muslim jurists recognized that the price of goods was determined in part by the element of time, so a credit sale (*al-bay' ilā ajal*) in which payment of the purchase price was deferred to the future justified a markup relative to the good's price if sold in the cash market. Likewise, a sale in which the purchase price was advanced to the seller prior to the date of delivery (*bay' al-salam*) justified a discount on the price relative to the good's price in the cash market.

Second, classical Islamic law had its own divisions between formalists and substantivists, with many jurists who would uphold a set of contracts—so long as each on its own was formally valid—even if, when viewed together, they produced a prohibited result. One common strategy to circumvent the classical prohibition against interest-bearing loans was to engage in back-to-back sales that would result in one party holding a certain sum of money against an obligation to return that sum plus some amount in excess of it, which would convert interest on a loan into a profit on a sale. For example, the lender would "purchase" object X from the borrower, for the sum of money that the borrower needed. The borrower would then re-purchase that object, or another object, at a price in excess of the price in the first sale, but with the obligation to pay on the second sale deferred to sometime in the future, such as a year. The object that is being bought and sold is irrelevant to the transaction except to hide the loan behind a veneer of sales.

Modern Islamic banking and finance systematically exploits similar strategies to avoid the form of interest-bearing loans while replicating them in substance. For example, conventional interest-bearing loans are synthesized using the fiction of a credit sale. The borrower approaches the bank, representing to it that it wishes to purchase a certain good. The bank agrees to acquire that good in the market, provided that the borrower/ purchaser agrees to enter into a contract to purchase that good from the bank once the bank acquires it. The bank will purchase the good in cash, and will sell it to the borrower/purchaser on credit terms, thereby earning for the bank a "profit" from the sale of the good rather than interest from the loan of money.

Finally, financial intermediation—which is the prerequisite for creating an opportunity to realize profits from financial activity unrelated to production—was achieved through the use of back-to-back *commenda* arrangements in which the "entrepreneur"—the Islamic bank—takes capital investments, i.e., depositors in a conventional bank, and uses the funds so collected to act as an investor in a second *commenda*, with an entrepreneur in the real economy, who is the functional equivalent of a borrower in conventional banking. Insofar as the money provided to the entrepreneur/ borrower is on terms that mimic conventional interest-bearing loans, the Islamic bank successfully replicates the practices of conventional banks, albeit using Islamic forms.

Modern Islamic finance also came to recognize the legitimacy of the limited-liability company, despite classical Islam's requirement that profit be commensurate with risk. This was justified largely on the theory that parties who choose to contract with limited-liability entities do so with the knowledge that their shareholders are not personally liable and, accordingly, are not injured by the limited liability of the entity.

Ṣadr, who wrote before the rise of organized Islamic banking, perhaps anticipated how Islamic forms could be wed to the ideals of market capitalism to justify a for-profit financial sector. Accordingly, he roundly condemned the back-to-back *commenda* structure, saying that if it occurs, the first "entrepreneur," i.e., the bank, would not be entitled to any profit that arises out of the second *commenda*, but rather whatever profits are realized should be divided between the second entrepreneur and the original investors. He based his argument on two points: the first is that the entrepreneur's return is based on his contribution of work, but in the back-to-back *commenda*, the bank does not perform any work; and, second, the capital of the first partnership belongs to the investors in the first *commenda*, and so the capital of the second partnership, unless the bank contributes its own capital, remains the exclusive property of those who funded the first *commenda*, not the property of the "bank" in its role as an investor in the second *commenda*. In this connection, he also rejected the classical Islamic maxim that profit follows responsibility for loss, at least insofar as it had been used to justify the structure of the back-to-back *commenda*. Rather than assumption of risk being the determinant of entitlement to profit, he argued that it was the presence of labor that justified profit. In the back-to-back *commenda*, the banker is not, in reality, contributing any labor and, accordingly, should not be entitled to any of the profits attained by the second *commenda*.

Income

The institution of *zakat* can reasonably be understood to represent a commitment to providing all Muslims a minimum income at least sufficient for subsistence. It was the most practical economic manifestation of intra-Muslim solidarity. Only Muslims were eligible to receive *zakat* funds, for the simple reason that it was considered a religious duty that applied only to Muslims. (The relevant doctrines of classical Islamic tax law will be discussed in greater detail below.) As mentioned previously, however, Islamic states provided other kinds of social welfare programs that distributed benefits to eligible members of the public on a non-sectarian basis, but eligibility would have been determined on a case-by-case basis in light of the terms of the specific endowment that established the benefit. It was only the *zakat* that provided an unconditional claim on the public treasury for a minimum income without requiring, for example, proof of poverty, or even an inability to provide for one's self through work.

While classical Islamic law was clearly concerned with providing a minimum subsistence level of income to Muslims, it did not show any concern with establishing a maximum ceiling of income—provided, of course, that income was obtained from licit sources, such as trade, investment, or labor. While there was no legally enforceable obligation to redistribute excess income from the well-off to those less well-off other than through the *zakat*, Islam established an ethic of generosity that was intended to counteract the spirit of acquisitiveness that it permitted, even as it did not fully embrace that spirit. This ethic of generosity generates supererogatory duties to share the benefits of one's good fortune with others, not so much out of a sense that one's good fortune is in itself unjust, but rather out of gratitude for the very fact that one is fortunate: a recognition of the role that luck plays in life's outcomes. Accordingly, the Quran declares: "If you show gratitude, I shall certainly increase you in abundance," an attitude that contradicts the smug, self-satisfied view toward wealth entertained by non-believers who believe their good fortune is theirs by virtue of their own merit and skill. The Quran personified this latter attitude in its recounting of the story of Qārūn, a wealthy Israelite at the time of the Hebrews' settlement in Egypt, whom the Quran described as having so much wealth that it would have taken a mighty band of men just to carry the keys to his treasure houses. When the learned of the Hebrews chastised him for his haughtiness, godlessness, and failure to share his good fortune with others, he dismissed them by claiming his wealth was his by virtue of his own effort and merit. He received his just deserts, however, when God brought down his palace upon him in an earthquake, reinforcing the lesson that all we have in this life is due to God's arbitrary plan for us, rather than our own personal qualities. The failure to recognize this fundamental fact literally leads to our own destruction, thus making imperative the duty to share as a manifestation of gratitude.

The idea that an Islamic society must maintain a distinction between compelled redistribution—practiced through the obligatory duty of *zakat*—and the supererogatory duties of generosity places important limits on the power of the state in the thought of an Islamist like Sayyid Qutb: it is crucial that an Islamic state produce subjectivities that are morally motivated to perform what are supererogatory duties, but not to compel them to do so, if it would undermine the possibility of creating the very ethical virtue of generosity and gratefulness that Islam seeks to cultivate in its followers.

Employment

Classical Islamic law recognized the validity of employment contracts, albeit with some conceptual difficulty. One formal problem of theorizing employment contracts is that classical Islamic contract law required the consideration to be present at the time of the contract in order for the contract to be binding. Because an employment contract was understood to be a sale of the laborer's labor power—itself a usufruct of the person of the laborer—this created a conceptual difficulty to the extent that the usufruct promised only came into existence during the future performance, and was not fully "present" at the time of the contract. The intangible nature of what the laborer sells, in turn, led jurists to stipulate additional prerequisites, relative to a contract for the sale of goods, to the validity of an employment contract. One way to understand their insistence on requiring strict conditions for the validity of an employment contract is their concern that the employment relationship is inherently exploitative and, therefore, degrading. Classical Muslim jurists were reluctant to recognize free contracting in the context of employment not because they held labor in contempt, but rather because they believed the employment contract violated the natural freedom of the laborer insofar as the employer "owned" the laborer's labor power and, accordingly, could compel him to work for the benefit of the employer. Thus, the usual remedy for an invalid employment contract was to give the worker a "fair wage" for work already performed, and transform the employment contract from a binding bilateral obligation to one that was terminable at will by the employee, thereby ensuring that the employee did not alienate, i.e., sell, his physical liberty by virtue of the employment relationship.

Classical Muslim jurists, as far as I know, neither required a minimum wage nor placed a maximum limit on wages, but rather enforced the terms of the parties' bargain, just as they did in the context of the sale of goods or other kinds of property. The most important limitation placed on wages was that a valid and binding bilateral employment contract could not come into existence unless the nature and quantity of the work was specified in reasonable detail, *and* the compensation for the contractual work was also defined, using a specific quantity of money or property that is not payable out of, and therefore contingent on, the worker's own output, e.g., paying a farmhand out of the sale of the oil that is pressed from the olives that he is hired to harvest. By converting such an arrangement to a unilateral contract, which gives the worker the option but not the obligation to perform, the worker is in an effective position, at least formally, to maximize the returns to his labor while not alienating his labor to the employer. From the perspective of law and economics, the classical rule of Islamic law invalidating bilateral labor contracts whose wage was dependent on the success of the venture can be understood as a response to the relative inability of the laborer—compared to an owner—to diversify firm-specific risk and, accordingly, would serve to limit the use of binding bilateral-wage contracts to those employers who had sufficient liquidity to pay their workers a determinate cash wage.

However, to the extent it recognized slavery, classical Islamic law legitimated a category of uncompensated labor, at least in the sense that the slave performed work for his master. In the case of slavery, the slave had a right not to wages from his employer but to reasonable maintenance in accordance with the means of the master. In addition, Islamic law, at least theoretically, placed limits on the amount of labor a master could extract from his slave by prohibiting the master from imposing excessive burdens on the slave. According to some jurists, if a master abused his slave, for example, by inflicting excessive and disproportionate punishments, the slave would, by operation of law, be mandatorily manumitted from his master. Labor in the household was also exempt from the monetary economy and, accordingly, gave rise to no claim for wages. On the other hand, classical Muslim jurists were divided regarding the extent to which a wife, for example, was under a *legal* obligation to perform household tasks. One school of jurisprudence rooted such an obligation in social custom, but limited it to the extent that she would engage in household work for her own benefit, i.e., that she is obliged to sweep and clean if that is something customary for a woman of her station in life, but only to the extent that she would do so for herself, not to the standards of another, e.g., her husband. Any task that was customarily procured in the market, on the other hand, if the wife discharged it, in theory could serve as grounds for a claim to compensation, and the Mālikī school in particular recognized a doctrine of "toil and striving (*kadd wa si'āya*)," pursuant to which a woman could claim property belonging to her deceased husband as a creditor, and not an heir, based on her contributions to the husband's business. Modern Moroccan family law jurisprudence has relied on this notion to justify redistribution of family property legally owned by the husband to the wife.

Modern Muslim thought does not problematize the employment relationship in the same way that classical Islamic thought did, and instead of seeing it as an inherently exploitative or even degrading relationship (insofar as it compromises the laborer's autonomy), they come to see having access to a job as a right that must be guaranteed by the government. I have already mentioned that, in accordance with Ṣadr's labor theory of ownership, labor is entitled to appropriate the products of the workplace. So far from being concerned that compensating laborers out of the fruits of their labor exposes them unfairly to the firm's commercial risks, Ṣadr's theory of labor seeks to invert the traditional hierarchy of property rights, vesting ownership of the products in the laborers, and giving capital only a rent for the use of the machines and other factors of production they contribute. For modern Muslim thinkers, regardless of the nature of their economic theory, it is crucial that able-bodied persons have access to work appropriate to their circumstances and training, and that they receive wages for their work that allows them to live a dignified life. Within such a scheme, however, they reject the idea of a perfectly egalitarian system of compensation, generally agreeing that the more highly skilled the labor, the higher returns it is entitled to claim. They implicitly deny, therefore, that wages are set by the relative supply-demand curves for specific kinds of labor, and instead assume that wages should be set on what they must believe are the objective considerations of the employee's relative merit.

Taxation

Classical Islamic law took an extremely narrow view of taxation, with Muslim jurists generally concluding that the imposition of taxes, other than those imposed by revelation, was illegal. The judgment that taxation, as a general rule, was illegal derived from the Muslim jurists' conception of the sacrosanct nature of private rights—in particular, the right to property. Taxation, insofar as it threatened the very existence of a person's property, was viewed as contradicting the very essence of a property right, namely, the right of an owner to the exclusive benefit of his own property and his right to exclude others from it, save with his own freely granted consent. Accordingly, only revealed laws could trump this foundational premise of Islamic property law. The two principal taxes that revelation explicitly endorsed are the aforementioned *zakat* and the land tax, *kharāj*. The obligation of *zakat* is mentioned repeatedly in the Quran, while the revelatory basis of the land tax is established through the normative practice of the Prophet Muḥammad.

The Quran not only repeatedly demanded that Muslims pay *zakat* as a manifestation of their obedience to God, it also described it as a right of the poor, and implied that the wealthy could be compelled to pay it. The Quran specified eight classes of persons eligible to receive the *zakat*: the needy, the weak, those who collect it, those whose hearts are to be reconciled to Islam, to purchase the freedom of slaves, debt relief, the path of God, and the stranger. It did not, however, specify the kinds of properties that were subject to the *zakat,* nor the minimum amount of property required before *zakat* became obligatory, nor the applicable rate at which it would be calculated. Muslim jurists developed detailed rules covering the types of property that were subject to *zakat*, the minimum amount of each that triggered liability, and the applicable rate based on the practice of the early community and interpretation of historical precedent.

While the *zakat* clearly is a redistributive tax, the public authorities had greater discretion in deciding how to allocate revenues obtained from the land tax. Even here, however, the Quran, when it discussed the status of land surrendered by the enemy, stated that it should only be used to achieve public goods or to benefit "the orphaned, the weak, and the stranger, so that it does not circulate exclusively in the hands of the wealthy among you." Public revenues, therefore, could either be spent to support public works, such as roads, hospitals, schools, defense, etc., or be given directly to the less fortunate of the community to relieve their burdens. This priority toward the needy is another reflection of the principle of Islamic jurisprudence mentioned above, "warding off harms is to be given priority to the attainment of unrealized goods." When applied to questions of public spending, classical Islamic conceptions of distributive justice meant giving priority to the needy over those less so.

At the same time, because of the normative aversion to non-scriptural taxes, prior to the nineteenth century, Muslim states often resorted to ad hoc measures to raise money that were not necessarily reflective of a well-thought-out theory of taxation. Indeed, in many cases, Muslim states raised revenue through the imposition of user fees that could be justified on the grounds of payment for a service provided by the state to the public and hence would take the guise of a consensual transaction. It is likely, however, that such user fees were highly regressive and worked at cross-purposes with the redistributivist bent found in the *zakat* and in the principles governing public expenditures.

Modern Muslims have largely come to accept the legitimacy of the state's power to tax for the purpose of raising revenue to pursue the public good, and not just to further the ends of distributive justice, although it is not unusual to come across religious figures continuing to teach that all taxation, other than that expressly provided in revelation, amounts to an unjust taking of property, a position that no doubt has inhibited the efficiency of tax collection in many post-colonial Muslim states. The acceptance of the legitimacy of general powers of taxation, however, has had the unintended effect of stalling efforts at reinterpreting the doctrine of *zakat*, with the result that in the modern age, it has taken on more of a purely ritual function than an effective tool of redistribution. This is because the rules that were developed by Muslim jurists to operationalize the obligation of *zakat* were developed in agrarian societies in which animal husbandry and agriculture—rather than financial capital—were the chief sources of wealth. While there have been halting attempts by some contemporary Muslim jurists to rationalize the historical rules of *zakat* in light of the realities of modern economies and our increased understanding of finance, the fact that the obligation of *zakat* has become almost entirely privatized means that efforts at a broad reinterpretation of the principles of *zakat* have fallen largely on deaf ears, and as a result, from a modern perspective, it appears, at first glance at least, to be an irrational system of revenue generation.

Conclusion

Given the nature and space limitations of this essay, my analysis is necessarily high-level and a simplification of the kinds of answers Muslims have given and may yet give to the questions posed by this book. Nevertheless, there are important strands of thought that provide a certain coherence to the various views of Muslims as expressed over the centuries. The first is the commitment to the sanctity of private property and respect for consensual trade as the primary means of distribution. At the same time, Islamic ethical teachings are intended to inculcate in Muslims a general disdain for the impulse to acquire, at least if that is a goal in itself. One can say then that economic growth, in Muslim economic thought, cannot be understood to be a goal in itself. It is a good if it leads to better outcomes for humanity, but whether growth in any particular society does, in fact, lead to better outcomes for humanity depends more on the political economy of the state in which the economic growth is taking place than on the mere fact of growth as such. If growth is taking place in such a way that it does not foster unbridled acquisitiveness, its benefits are shared with the most vulnerable in society, it preserves a reasonably equal opportunity for all to live a decent life, and it preserves earth's resources for future generations, then we can conclude that economic growth is good. But if growth comes at the expense of these larger ends, then it is either a matter of indifference or even evil if it actively works in opposition to the achievement of these goals.

At the same time, a good society is one that is not only concerned with distributive justice in the aggregate, but also in the individual case. Therefore, distributive justice cannot be achieved at the expense of individual rights, or at least the arbitrary violation of individual rights, including the right to own property and trade on one's God-given talents in an attempt to enhance one's own position in the world. It is here that the Quranic ethic of gratitude in Muslim thought is supposed to do its work: instead of taking success as a sign of divine entitlement, a Muslim is supposed to reflect on the fortuitous nature of worldly success and be spurred to acts of generosity that countermand the worst impulses of a market economy. Distributive justice, throughout Muslim thinking, therefore, cannot be thought of independently of the justice of the individuals who make up society. Religion is supposed to motivate us, as individuals, to live just lives as individuals and as a collective.

Notes

1. *Al-Mā'ida*, 5:38 (providing for the amputation of the hand of a thief).

2. See, for example, *al-Muzzammil*, 73:20 (describing believers journeying on long-distance trading ventures), and *al-Nisā*, 4:29 (prohibiting appropriation of other's property unless the exchange was based on mutual consent in the course of commerce).

3. The reader interested in various Quranic teachings that mention property (*māl*) might consult the following verses: *al-Baqara*, 2:177, 2:247, 2:264; *Āl 'Imrān*, 3:14; *al-An'ām*, 6:152; *Hūd*, 11:29; *al-Isrā'*, 17:34; *al-Kahf*, 18:34, 18:39, 18:46; *Maryam*, 19:77; *al-Mu'minūn*, 23:55; *al-Nūr*, 24:33; *al-Shu'arā'*, 26:88; *al-Naml*, 27:36; *al-Qalam*, 68:14; *al-Ḥāqqa*, 69:28; *Nūh*, 71:21; *al-Muddaththir*, 74:12; *al-Fajr*, 89:20; *al-Balad*, 90:6; *al-Layl*, 92:11, 92:18; *al-Humaza*, 104:2, 104:3; *al-Masad*, 111:2. The word *amwāl*, the plural of *māl* (property), appears in the Quran fifty-five more times. Numerous other verses condemn the human tendency to conflate worldly prosperity with spiritual success, see, e.g., *al-Kahf*, 18:32–40, while others condemn acquisitiveness, e.g., *al-Takāthur*, 102:1–8 and *al-Humaza*, 104:1–3. Others warn humans that their wealth will not save them from divine punishment if they otherwise deserve punishment, see, e.g., *Āl 'Imrān*, 3:10 and *Saba'*, 34:37. For two of the many Quran verses encouraging generosity, see, e.g., *al-Baqara*, 2:261 and 2:177.

4. These are the doctrines of *ribā* and *gharar*, respectively. *Ribā* is often translated as "interest," but the doctrine is, in fact, much broader than economic interest. *Gharar* is often translated as "speculation," but it also covers doctrines of indefiniteness and indeterminacy of the consideration as well. The best common-law analogue to *gharar* is the concept of aleatory contracts.

5. Muḥammad Bāqir al-Ṣadr, *The Islamic Economic Doctrine*, trans. by Kadom Jawad Shubber (London, Great Britain: MECI Ltd., 2010), 386.

Confucianism

CONFUCIAN PERSPECTIVES ON THE MORALITY OF ECONOMIC INEQUALITY

STEPHEN C. ANGLE

Introduction

Confucianism prides itself on being a this-worldly tradition; for 2,500 years, its leading thinkers have been concerned with questions related to social, political, and economic equality and inequality, among other topics. Confucians have argued about systems of land tenure and taxation policy right alongside their more abstract thoughts on human nature, our place in the broader cosmos, and the shapes of good human lives. It is thus natural to ask what Confucians have to say about the morality of economic inequality. We will see that in most respects they are not egalitarians, but neither will they countenance extreme inequality: their goal is a harmony that is good for each and for all.

The tradition of thought and practice that we generally refer to in English as Confucianism can usefully be divided into three main periods of creative growth. During its classical era—roughly the fifth century BCE through the second century CE—influential thinkers articulated values, concepts, and *problematiques* in response to the many challenges of their time; the ideas and the texts in which they were expressed are foundational for the tradition. The second important period is the era of neo-Confucianism, a sophisticated revival of Confucianism in the very different political, social, and intellectual context of the eleventh through eighteenth centuries CE. Confucianism has faced new challenges and new opportunities, finally, in the twentieth and twenty-first centuries CE, which has often been labeled the era of new Confucianism. My objective in this essay is to explore topics related to economic inequality from a contemporary Confucian standpoint, but for two reasons we will be unable to leave behind the prior two-and-a-half millennia of Confucianism. First, throughout its various incarnations, Confucianism has emphasized continuity with and learning from the past—especially the lives and words of past exemplars. Second, contemporary Confucianism is far from settled or unified. The enormous disruptions to Chinese state and society that occurred at the beginning of the twentieth century (collapse of the last dynasty and imperial system; rise of nationalist and Communist revolutionary parties) undermined most of the institutions that had undergirded Confucianism, at least as an explicit body of thought and practice. As we will see, precisely what it means to be a Confucian today, and what Confucians should say about issues of inequality, is very much open to debate.

This is not to imply that Confucianism is completely up for grabs. In the remainder of this introductory section, I spell out five ideas that collectively should shape any Confucian discussion of the morality of economic inequality: care for one and all, relational appropriateness, moral and material well-being, cultivated harmony, and the problem of selfishness. These concerns are central to classical and neo-Confucianism, though expressed in different ways at different times. As we will see later in the essay, a modern Confucianism that is thoroughly informed by these ideas will adopt distinctive positions on many of the issues related to economic inequality under consideration in this volume.

There is general agreement that the most important concept in Confucian philosophy is *ren*, sometimes translated as "benevolence" but in most contexts better rendered with the more general term "humaneness." The *Analects* record Confucius's succinct definition of humaneness as "loving others," but also give us the early Confucian Youzi's statement that filial devotion is the "root" of humaneness.[1] In a variety of ways, the subsequent tradition develops these twin thoughts: humaneness is broadly inclusive caring, but it is based in, and appropriately sensitive to, special relationships. Mencius can therefore say both that it is definitive of humanity to feel alarm and commiseration—which he says is the initial "sprout" of humaneness—upon seeing a baby about to fall into a well, no matter whether the baby is related to one or not; and also that there is nothing wrong with a high-status leader having more wealth than a commoner, so long as the leader sees to it, out of his concern for them, that the commoners, too, have sufficient means.[2] That is, he can care more for those close to himself, but must also care for others. The neo-Confucian Zhang Zai gives us one of the most famous elaborations of what came to be called "graded caring," again in terms of a familial model: "Heaven is my father and earth is my mother, and even such a small creature as myself finds an intimate place in their midst. Therefore, that which fills the cosmos I regard as my body and that which directs the cosmos I regard as my nature. All people are my brothers and sisters, and all things are my companions."[3]

Zhang goes on to discuss the different kinds of care apt for different inhabitants of the cosmos, from the emperor to the elderly to the orphaned and weak. Both the family analogy and the body analogy make the same basic point: one cares for all, even if one appropriately cares more for some (e.g., one's head or one's parent) than for others (e.g., one's toe or one's distant cousin).

A second key concept is *yi*, often translated as "righteousness" and sometimes even as "justice," but better understood as "appropriateness." *Yi* is concerned with appropriate behavior in the context of some kind of relationship with another. As Sor-hoon Tan has emphasized, "actions conform to *yi* norms in terms of their effect on the existing or potential relationships among the people involved."[4] Since relationships are complex and evolving, it makes no sense to think of appropriateness in terms of static principles. We can formulate norms of appropriateness as general rules that apply to a given type of situation (say, eating when one's elders are present), but these norms are always rules of thumb rather than absolute principles, and need to be adjusted in accord with the evolving situation. The primacy of relations has immediate significance for how to think about a topic like distributive justice. As Tan puts it, "even in distributive situations in which conditions of scarcity cause competition and conflicts, . . . the actions of *yi* are not so much acts *dividing* benefits or burdens as they are parts of interactions *relating* persons to one another."[5] Not only does the Confucian language of appropriateness resist formulation in terms of principles, that is, it also fits poorly with the individualistic ontology of most Western discussions of distributive justice. I will explore the consequences of this for discussions of inequality as the essay proceeds.

Third, Confucian understandings of flourishing privilege ethical development but also recognize the necessity of material well-being. This comes out, for example, in *Mencius* 7B:24:

> Mencius said, "The mouth in relation to flavors, the eyes in relation to sights, the ears in relation to notes, the nose in relation to odors, the four limbs in relation to comfort—these are matters of human nature (*xing*), but they are also fated (*ming*). Nonetheless, the superior person does not refer to them as 'human nature.'
>
> "Humaneness between father and son, appropriateness between ruler and minister, propriety between guest and host, wisdom in relation to the worthy, the sage in relation to the way of heaven— these are fated, but they also involve human nature. Nonetheless, the superior person does not refer to them as 'fated.'"[6]

In this passage, "human nature (*xing*)" represents the ideal for creatures such as us; "fate (*ming*)" is that which we cannot avoid. The lesson is that while preferences for the satisfaction of physical desires and for virtuous relationships are both innate (the latter usually starting out only as subtle promptings, mere "sprouts") *and* are both aspects of our ideal selves, we must focus on the cultivation of virtuous reactions rather than physical desires. The physical desires will take care of themselves even without our attention, whereas without conscious attention, the virtues are easily swamped by desires. Later neo-Confucians discuss the same issue when they recommend that we "preserve Cosmic Pattern and rid ourselves of human desire." Here, "human desire" is a technical term for physical desires that go too far, demanding more than is situationally apt. Admittedly, the neo-Confucians' language almost invites misunderstanding, and they had their share of critics who thought they were advocating the wholesale disregard for material well-being. A careful reading makes clear that this is not the case, though: they, too, saw that material well-being is necessary for ethical flourishing.[7]

The fourth issue to consider is the Confucian socio-political vision, which can be called cultivated harmony. "Harmony" refers to the way that different elements can fit together, mutually complementing one another; "cultivated" recognizes that this harmony is not spontaneous but neither is it coerced. More specifically, Confucians reason further that people are different from one another, having different strengths and weaknesses. Mencius famously argues for a division of labor based on the idea that "things are inherently unequal"; the neo-Confucian Wang Yang-ming bases his conception of social harmony on the differences in people's "capacities (*caineng*)."[8] However, Confucians also note that different elements can nonetheless complement one another, forming smoothly into a whole. The *Analects* attribute to Confucius the sentiment that "the superior person is harmonious but not uniform; the petty person is uniform but not harmonious."[9] This valuing of harmony over sameness runs throughout Confucian thinking, from the most mundane of metaphors (the distinct but balanced flavors in a soup) to the heights of neo-Confucian metaphysics ("cosmic Pattern" is precisely the most all-encompassing harmony).[10] Still, these valuable harmonies cannot be relied upon to emerge spontaneously. Some texts suggest that spontaneous, uncultivated harmony did once exist, although others see the age before human civilization made the conscious cultivation of harmony possible as full only of chaos and suffering.[11] Harmony, therefore, requires human intervention. Confucians advocate the cultivation of harmony through ritual and education rather than coercive law and punishments, both because they are convinced of the efficacy of the former and because they worry about the inevitable failures of the latter.[12]

A fifth and final consideration that shapes Confucian views of inequality is their criticism of selfish concern for personal profit. In the *Analects*, we read that "those who act with a view to their own personal advantage will arouse much resentment"; "personal advantage" is *li*, which can also be translated as "benefit" or "profit."[13] The *Mencius* also famously inveighs against focusing on personal benefit: the text opens with Mencius criticizing a ruler who asks for advice on "profiting (*li*)" his state. Mencius responds that if the ruler focuses on personal profit (of his state, as against that of other states), his example will lead his ministers, nobles, and commoners to each look to their own personal profit, with the result that they vie against one another and undermine the stability and well-being of the state. Instead, Mencius says, the ruler and his people should focus their attention on humaneness and appropriateness.[14] This does not mean that Mencius ignores the effects of one's material well-being on one's behavior or moral development. He recognizes that most people cannot be relied upon to act morally if they are impoverished and worried about their family starving to death. Similarly, Confucius prioritizes "enriching" the people over "teaching" them.[15] Still, the tradition tends to denigrate the conscious seeking of material advantage for oneself, which in neo-Confucianism is labeled with the arch-vice of "selfishness." Selfishness means to ignore the relevant interests and perspectives of others, and neo-Confucians develop insightful explanations of the ways that a whole host of personal and social problems can be traced back to selfishness. There is a possible tension, though, between wanting to avoid talking about profit—because of the ways in which this can prompt selfishness—and yet wanting to see that everyone has their needs met. After all, we can expect that some public policies will be more effective than others at producing or distributing the goods needed to meet everyone's needs, but adjudicating among these policies may require thinking explicitly about which ones are likely to be most profitable or advantageous. This tension underlays some important debates in the neo-Confucian era about the proper means and objectives of public policy.[16]

Equality

Taken together, the five factors I have just discussed—humaneness, relational appropriateness, moral and/versus material well-being, cultivated harmony, and the opposition to selfish profit—shape Confucian thinking about economic inequality, both traditionally and into the present moment. I will draw on these considerations as I develop Confucian views on the practical questions of inequality that will occupy the later sections of this essay. First, though, we need to canvas several topics concerning the ways that equality and economic justice have been conceptualized by Confucians.

Fifty years ago, Donald Munro wrote in his *Concept of Man in Early China* about the commitment of Confucians to what he called "natural equality," in repudiation of earlier ideas of hereditary privilege.[17] Natural equality, Munro explained, was a descriptive thesis about the common capacities of all people, based on the belief that all people share a nature that gives them the ability to make moral evaluations and develop a virtuous character. Natural equality supported a further commitment to the moral development of all, but it did not lead to a belief in political or social, much less economic, equality. Hierarchies abounded in Confucian theory and practice, but Confucians sought to square natural equality with sociopolitical hierarchy via the idea of meritocracy. Not only was it fair for those whose virtue was more developed to have superior positions; having virtuous superiors was also thought to offer the less virtuous their best chance to improve their own characters. Although the exact terms in which these ideas were expressed changed over the centuries—for example, with neo-Confucianism relying on a more metaphysical idea of the shared nature—the dual endorsement of equality and hierarchy remained largely stable.

With this background in mind, the contemporary scholar Chenyang Li has put forward three theses. The first is that equality is not an intrinsic value for Confucianism. Sometimes it is a descriptive fact about the world—such as the fact that all people are equal in the sense of being born with a certain moral potential—and sometimes it is instrumentally valuable for further ends, as we will see. But it is not automatically valuable, and neither is inequality automatically to be avoided. Second, Li notes that Confucians sometimes speak about what Aristotle called "numerical equality," which means "treating people indiscriminately without consideration to individual circumstances." He gives Munro's idea of "natural equality" as an example. Third, Li states that Confucians pay much more attention to what Aristotle calls "proportional equality," which means "treating all relevant persons in relation to their due in relevant aspects." Aristotle defines it as "to each according to his desert."[18] However, Li notes:

A person's due is what he deserves or what is appropriately accorded to him; it is not based solely on what he has contributed or earned. We may say, for example, that in a good society a physically disabled person is to be duly provided with special facilities even though he may have not done anything to earn it. Understood this way, proportional equality demands that society provide special facilities to the disabled, but not to people who are not disabled. This apparently unequal treatment is nevertheless equality in the proportional sense.[19]

It seems fair to ask, though, how much work is really being done here by any sense of "equality." When one's due is closely tied to an amount one has produced, as in Aristotle's notion of desert, then this is readily understood as a kind of (proportional) equality: your ratio of output to desert may be the same as mine, even if you produce (and receive) more than I do. In the case of the disabled person whom Li imagines, though, how are we to conceptualize this as an equality? I believe that the farther we move away from a pure notion of desert, the less helpful "proportional equality" is. Instead, we might look elsewhere to understand what sorts of inequality are acceptable.[20]

The most influential recent account of Confucian economic or distributive justice is that of Hong Kong–based political theorist Joseph Chan, who, in a series of articles and an important book, has articulated three principles that he believes collectively capture Confucian thinking on these topics. He summarizes the principles as follows:

1. *Sufficiency for all*: Each household should have an amount of resources sufficient to live a materially secure and ethical life.

2. *Priority to the badly off*: People who fall below the threshold of sufficiency—those who have special needs or are badly off—should have priority in being taken care of.

3. *Merit and contribution*: Offices and emolument should be distributed according to an individual's merits and contributions; any subsequent inequality of income is not illegitimate.[21]

Chan makes clear that these principles are his reconstruction; they make explicit what he takes to be lying behind the disparate statements related to economic justice found in the early Confucian classics. He also emphasizes that the basic orientation of the principles is perfectionist: that is, above all they are aimed at enabling people to become better people and live good lives. The Confucian conception of what makes for good people and good lives, in turn, is rooted in particular understandings of human nature and human possibility. It is this idea of perfectionism, rather than any version of equality, that drives the Confucian account of economic justice.

Still, there are a few ways that ideas of equality and inequality figure into Chan's principles. To begin with, the standard of sufficiency is meant to apply equally to all households. As Chan notes, exactly what it means will be relative to the level of development of a given society, but he emphasizes that both Mencius and Xunzi put considerable weight on the idea that each household be accorded an equal amount of land. Mencius's famous version of this idea is the "well-field system," so named because the Chinese character for "well," 井 (pronounced *jing*), resembles a grid dividing a square piece of land into nine smaller squares. Mencius says that this system was used in ancient times, with each of eight families being given equal plots, and all eight families having responsibility to tend the central plot, the produce from which would go to the state.[22] Chan's explanation of the well-field idea in terms of "sufficiency" for material and ethical well-being is very plausible, and, in fact, some similar ideas are made explicit during the neo-Confucian era, when the idea of a well-field-like division of land is revived and debated. Many neo-Confucians felt that a literal re-imposition of well-field landholding patterns was impractical, and some were opposed to land redistribution for other reasons. But the idea behind the well-field came through clearly in the writings of its advocates, such as Zhang Zai. Zhang says that the well-field system is necessary to ensure that the people are "nurtured," otherwise it does not matter how much they are taught or how strict the criminal laws may be.[23] Without their equal portions of land to ensure material well-being, people will act badly, just as Mencius argued long ago. Again, the "equal" nature of the land does not seem important in itself, but rather is a means to ensuring a given amount of land goes to each household.

Chan's third principle contains another, more controversial role for equality and inequality. He says that so long as sufficiency has been assured and that excess is apportioned in keeping with individual merit and contribution, then "any subsequent inequality of income is not illegitimate." Now, some of the third principle is clearly in keeping with the consensus within Confucianism, which accepted legitimate differences of income, land-holding, and wealth. This is very clear in Xunzi's writings, as well as in various later Confucians, though I find some of the attempts to read approval of differential income into the *Mencius* and *Analects* to be a bit forced.[24] The issue I want to focus on, though, is whether there are no limits to legitimate economic inequality, so long as sufficiency is assured for all, as Chan maintains. Li believes that there are limits, in keeping with his endorsement of proportional equality, and he thus reads a passage from the *Analects* in which Confucius praises "even distribution (*jun*)" as "opposing a big gap between the rich and the poor, rather than advocating egalitarianism."[25]

The interpretation of Confucian views of equality that offer the strongest rejection of unlimited economic inequality, though, belongs to the final scholar whose views I will canvass in this section, Sor-hoon Tan.[26] Although Tan's view overlaps with those of Li and Chan in certain ways, her fundamental understanding of how Confucianism approaches distributive issues is quite different. She writes that a close scrutiny of the texts shows

> . . . no concern about whether those involved receive or deserve equal shares, or arguments about whether someone should have more or less of something, or something proportional to some kind of merit. Instead, the concern is overwhelmingly about the effect of actions on specific interpersonal relationships, actual or potential.[27]

This reorientation of our approach to distribution has four salient consequences. First, by orienting us toward the appropriateness (*yi*) of specific actions in the context of specific relationships, Tan suggests that general principles (such as Chan's three principles) are the wrong way to operationalize Confucianism. She elaborates:

> Principles of justice treat opportunities, resources, and goods that are supposed to be distributed as possessions or potential possessions of individuals always competing for resources and goods. Confucians treat them *not as objects to be possessed* by one and denied to others, but as *facilitators of personal cultivation* effecting appropriate interpersonal relationships constituting harmonious communities.[28]

I will say more in a moment about how we can discuss economic inequality if distributive "principles" are the wrong way to go. But let us next notice Tan's second point, which is that instead of focusing on possession, Confucian concern for humaneness and relational appropriateness leads them to emphasize sharing. As she says:

> Approaches to distributive justice that develop formulae for right divisions of benefits and burdens tend to deepen the sense of sep-

arateness and even encourage self-centredness if, as often happens, distribution problems are viewed as zero-sum competitions for quantifiable resources or opportunities and each sees herself constantly pitted against others in such competitions.[29]

Recall, for example, the well-field ideal. Why, Tan asks, is it designed in such a way that each household's contribution to the state comes by way of communal labor on the central plot of land, when taxation could have been designed in any number of other ways? Tan says that this is because it "educates the people to give priority to what is shared over what is privately owned; and working together on the public land also nurtures relationships of cooperation and mutual help."[30] Tan clearly agrees with Chan that Confucians are perfectionists, but sees that the very way in which distribution is conceived—rather than merely the way that it is arranged—can have effects on individuals' moral development.

Tan's third point is to agree with much of what Chan has to say about the importance of sufficiency and the priority of the badly off, but rather than thinking of them as specific principles, she argues that they can be integrated into a situation-specific, "needs-based" conception of socioeconomic justice. Tan acknowledges that pre-modern Confucians did not typically use a vocabulary of "needs," and thus that her needs-based theory is a modern reconstruction, but she offers good evidence not only that "sufficiency" and "the priority of the badly off" are better understood with a vocabulary of needs than via talk of desires or happiness, but also that needs works better than "merit" or "desert" to explain why office-holders should receive their emoluments. "The meritorious do not *deserve* office because of merit," she says, and their remunerations are not reward for their merit; instead, those with merit are expected to shoulder commensurate responsibilities, and what they receive in return is intended to provide "what is needed for them to efficiently discharge the responsibilities of their position, to contribute to the state and the people's well-being."[31] I will return to this idea below.

The idea that remuneration should match whatever is needed to perform one's role certainly puts limits on how much inequality can be legitimate, in something like the same way as Li's use of proportional equality (albeit not, in Tan's case, via the idea of desert). Only if a high official needs an elaborate carriage in order to play his ritual role in the social hierarchy, for example, should he have one; rich commoners with fancy conveyances would not pass the standard of "relational appropriateness," and thus even if sufficiency had been achieved by one and all, such an imbalance in wealth would be illegitimate. This brings me, finally, to the fourth point that we can gain from Tan. She argues that another reason to criticize dramatic economic inequality is that it will result in exploitation of the poor and weak by the rich and powerful, and such exploitation is "inherently divisive and alienating," resulting in the destruction of relationships and social harmony.[32]

Tan concludes one of her essays by noting that even from her "relational" perspective, some principles of just distribution can be useful, so long as they are understood as rules of thumb rather than one-size-fits-all solutions to every case. As I move toward the latter sections of this essay, in which we face questions about specific kinds of inequality, Chan's first and second principle will indeed be useful as ways of summing up critical issues to which a Confucian will necessarily attend. However, I also want to emphasize Tan's further suggestion, which is that if we take seriously the "dissonances" between Confucian perspectives and familiar, individual- and ownership-centered perspectives on economic justice, we may come to see "radically critical perspectives with which to interrogate contemporary experience."[33]

Property

As I now turn to a series of specific contexts in which to discuss the morality of economic inequality, there are three ways in which I can proceed: I can report the views of modern Confucians, to the extent that they have addressed these questions; I can extrapolate from the institutions of traditional China; or I can construct Confucian perspectives based on the values I have articulated in the first part of the essay. For the most part I will follow this third path, because in the first two approaches, it is often difficult to extricate Confucian theory from the contingent historical circumstances in which the theorists lived. This is particularly relevant for modern Confucians: for many of them, the defining event of their lifetime was the successful Communist revolution in China, and in some cases their views of issues like private property or income distribution may be determined more by their support for—or opposition to—the People's Republic of China than their Confucian commitments. Or at least this is a concern that we need to bear in mind: I will still bring their voices into the conversation as seems appropriate.

Let us begin with the issue of how Confucians should think about inequality and property. An obvious first question is: who owns land and other means of production? Historically, Chinese rulers periodically made claims to own all the land in their realms, and for at least one sustained period (Sui and early Tang dynasties, late-sixth through early-eighth centuries) managed to partly implement an "equitable fields system" that regulated the amount of land distributed to each rural household.[34] In most other eras, a *de facto* or *de jure* system of private landholding prevailed, though the resulting inequalities of landholding were regular targets of Confucian criticism.[35] The twentieth century saw dramatic and often bloody movements for land reform, and under the People's Republic of China, all land is state-owned, though there is an evolving system of private land-use rights. Confucians in the twentieth century varied on their views of state socialism, with some quite supportive and others arguing for private property.[36]

Based on the arguments outlined earlier in the essay, we know that Confucians should oppose dramatic inequality of landholding, and we have now seen that historically, this was the case. On the other hand, neither Confucian values nor the historical record supports a radical egalitarianism. Perhaps the most we can say with confidence is that either a softer socialism or a welfare-state capitalism with significant checks on wealth inequality (see below) each seem like a plausible candidate for a modern Confucian approach to property.

Natural Resources

Historically, Confucians have been poor stewards of the environment and of natural resources.[37] For two reasons this is somewhat surprising. First, Confucianism advocates harmony and, especially when we get to neo-Confucianism, explicitly puts value on all things. Many of the essays in the 1998 volume *Confucianism and Ecology* indicate plausible directions for future Confucian environmentalism, thoroughly based in classical and neo-Confucian texts.[38] Second, many neo-Confucians found time spent outdoors, in nature, to not just be enjoyable but actually critical to their moral development, and some went so far as to embrace the "wild" state of the outdoors.³⁹ Nonetheless, Confucians rarely advocated public policies aimed at preserving the environment. One plausible explanation for this failure has to do with the difficulty that a philosophy rooted in particular relationships has in seeing broad structural problems. The early neo-Confucian Zhou Dunyi famously refused to cut the grass outside his rural studio, which was meaningful for himself, his family, and his students, but had no effect on deforestation taking place elsewhere. As I will have more opportunities to discuss later in the essay, the move from small-scale, relational ethics to large-scale policies often proved challenging.

This does not have to be the case, however; as I have argued in another context, once the nature of this blind spot becomes clear, modern Confucians can think systematically about what is needed for moral growth and large-scale, sustainable harmony—as indeed they sometimes did, historically, for example, in the case of the well-field property system just discussed.⁴⁰ Because a vibrant awareness of the dynamic and yet fragile processes of life in our cosmos is important to moral growth, modern Confucians would seek to ensure access for all to nature, through a system of public parks and protected wilderness areas. Mindful of the long-term effects that human exploitation of natural resources can have, and motivated in part by a "humane" care for all things in the cosmos, Confucians today should also carefully regulate who is allowed to make use of resources like fossil fuels, how they can access such resources, and so on. In keeping with what I have said above, these resources will be located on or in state land, and so approved permits for extracting them will be based on our best current understanding of how an ecosystem of which we are only one part can be sustained. Finally, there is no reason why these Confucian concerns about shared access to and stewardship of natural resources should end at national borders. Through appropriate international means, Confucians will seek to see that these ideas of shared access and stewardship are extended to all people and all natural resources around the globe (and beyond, as that becomes relevant).

Products

In most modern capitalist societies, the distribution of products is primarily determined by their prices, coupled with the amount of money that a given individual is willing and able to pay for the product. There are, of course, some restrictions: some products are illegal for health-related reasons, like cocaine, or in order to protect an endangered animal species, like carved ivory. Other products are subject to special taxes, often because their use entails special expenses for the state or because the state wants to discourage their use (cigarettes and automobiles, for example, may be taxed for both reasons). Liberal societies tend to employ such restrictions sparingly, though, out of a desire to avoid restricting individual freedom: restrictions suggest a kind of paternalism, whereby the state substitutes its judgment for the individual's, thus infringing on the individual's agency. Given that one of the earliest metaphors for leadership in the Confucian tradition is serving as a "parent to the people," we might expect Confucians to direct the state to play a greater role in the distribution of goods. And, indeed, some of the considerations raised in the first sections of this essay also push toward some degree of paternalism, such as Tan's emphasis on providing for "needs." Tan envisions a role for "needs experts," who will assist in the crafting of policies, though she adds that these experts must conceive of their role as "servant," who determines needs based on individual situations and wants, rather than as "master," prescribing needs based on their own judgment of what the individual ought to want.[41] Admittedly, this is a complex area, but especially given the large body of empirical data showing that people are often poor decision-makers concerning their own well-being, it seems clear that Confucians will favor some degree of paternalism regarding products.[42]

Wealth

Earlier in the essay I discussed a debate about whether Confucians would endorse arbitrarily large inequalities of resources, so long as sufficiency was observed. I will return to that subject below, particularly regarding the idea that remuneration should match need, when I discuss income. Here, let us recall that a second reason noted above for opposing dramatic inequality of resources is the possibility—or even likelihood—that the rich will exploit the poor under such circumstances. This is more a matter of wealth than income, because it depends on ongoing differences between rich and poor, differences that are magnified by the compounded effects of differential income over years or even generations. Why should we suppose, though, that such exploitation will occur, given that we are assuming that "sufficiency" has been met? And second, if indeed Confucians would oppose dramatic differences of wealth, how might they recommend responding to such differences in the contemporary world?

Here are three reasons to be concerned about dramatic inequality of wealth. First, even if sufficiency has been met according to some standard—Chan suggests "a decent material life"—it may be that critical opportunities for moral growth are reserved for those with much more wealth. Perhaps one can only realistically run for political office if one has significant family wealth, or perhaps the ability to learn more about other peoples and cultures that comes with travel is limited to the wealthy. (Perhaps this is true of some contemporary societies, and perhaps not; the key thing is that either of these is easy to imagine.) In such cases, notwithstanding the best intentions on the part of the wealthy, the poor are systematically disadvantaged. A second reason has already been suggested by Tan. Given our natural tendencies toward selfishness, in a world of limited resources and competition over interests, dramatic inequality is likely to result in divisive exploitation. It is just too easy, too tempting, for a wealthy person to use her extra resources to allow her to win out over her much-poorer competitor. As this happens repeatedly, the cultivated social harmony that Confucians seek will be undermined. Even setting aside selfishness and competition, a third reason for concern is that sufficient differences in wealth make it difficult for wealthy and poor individuals to understand each other's challenges: their perspectives become mutually opaque. But the exercise of Confucian virtues like humaneness and appropriateness, and the ability to arrive at harmonies, depend on synthesizing multiple perspectives.[43]

A partial response to these concerns is available: as Jiang Qing and Daniel Bell have argued, the mutual participation in rituals by rich and poor, bosses and employees, can help to mitigate some of the harsh differences that might otherwise attend great inequality.[44] But absent further argument, it is hard to see how this response justifies unlimited inequalities of wealth. Confucianism is certainly prepared to countenance some differences, and shared rituals can—if well designed and taken seriously—be positive factors in these cases. But when the differences in wealth become too extreme, it seems inevitable that the positive effects of rituals will be swamped by the overwhelming differences between wealthy and poor, who might as well be living in different worlds.

What, finally, would Confucians have us do about existing inequalities of wealth? Assuming that Confucians have charge of state policies regarding income, on which see below, this is principally an issue of differential accrual of wealth over generations, and so it makes sense to tackle it through some version of inheritance tax.[45] Above a certain amount, passing on wealth to one's descendants would be difficult. Given both the history of charitable practices by local Confucian gentry in late-Imperial Chinese society, and the Confucian goal of cultivating our moral selves, it makes sense to arrange things so that much of the disposal of excess wealth will take place via support for charitable causes.

Income

Earlier in the essay, I looked at whether there should be any limits on income inequality (assuming that sufficiency for all is met), and if so, whether it should be via a "merit" criterion or a "need" criterion. As I now turn to the specific question of what Confucians would say about dealing with income inequality, let me add two observations. First, given that "merit" is most readily determined in the contemporary world by the market value for one's services, it seems that a merit criterion would put no limit at all on income inequality. Assuming a well-functioning labor market, one's income should correspond precisely to one's merit. This, though, runs against the idea that Confucians should resist dramatic inequalities, and thus provides another reason to prefer the need criterion. Admittedly, one might try to construct a measure of merit distinct from the labor market, and thus avoid the conclusion that CEOs are three hundred times more meritorious than the average worker in their firms. But it is difficult to see how such a measure could be constructed in a non-arbitrary way.

Second, we need to think more about the idea, clearly accepted by many historical Confucians, that different societal roles might correspond to greater need and thus greater income. This is not the idea that a disabled person might need more than someone without disabilities, which is plausible enough, but rather the very different thought that someone with more seniority, or perhaps with a leadership position, might need more than a junior subordinate. As far as I can tell, there are two different arguments that Confucians have put forward to justify such an arrangement. On the one hand, it may be that elaborate clothes, jewelry, transportation, housing, and so on are necessary for someone to play his or her appropriate role in a social hierarchy, and that differential incomes can serve as a proxy that enables such differences in material accoutrements. Xunzi is the most explicit of traditional Confucians on this score, writing, for example, of the ways in which the cushions, bells, and pennant with which the chariot of the Son of Heaven is adorned serves to nurture both his own and, in a corresponding way, the people's dispositions.[46] Even in our own, more egalitarian and less ritualized world, most of us see little wrong with the U.S. president occupying the White House and using silver and china when dining with foreign dignitaries, all wearing elaborate (and expensive) finery.

On the other hand, it may also be that these perquisites of office are necessary in order to convince qualified individuals to take on these onerous roles. Confucian texts regularly speak of the difficulties of serving the people as ruler; the well-known neo-Confucian Huang Zongxi (1610–1695) notes that in early times, "some men worthy of ruling, after considering it, refused to become princes. . . . Others undertook it and then quit."[47] This is because, Huang notes, it runs against our natures to do that which promotes only the benefit of others and not of ourselves. Here we see, in a different form, the age-old Confucian recognition that material well-being is crucial to us, even if it can be problematic to focus ("selfishly") on one's own benefit. Huang then goes on to lament the fact that latter-day rulers have primarily aimed to serve themselves rather than the people, amassing huge estates and thinking of the people as working for them. Huang's mixed feelings—and lack of a simple solution to the conundrum he identifies—is typical of the Confucian tradition, which sees value in hierarchies that are marked by material differences, but is also worried about excessive inequalities, for all the reasons I have already canvassed.

How might these strands be brought together into a workable approach to income inequality? The first step is to emphasize something that I have mostly been taking for granted, but which is far from assured in our contemporary world: the provision of means sufficient to one's needs. Confucians will see this as a non-negotiable baseline within their own nations, and will work internationally—and contribute their own country's resources—to see that it is achieved around the globe. The question of what degree of inequality is appropriate in light of differing roles in society is more controversial, and too complex to solve in the limited space I have left. Suffice it to say that Confucians will generally see it as apt that more senior (chronologically or otherwise) individuals have more, although they are also acutely conscious of the dangers of selfishness (and of exploitation, discussed above, concerning wealth), and so the inequalities should be distinctly limited.

Jobs

What land was to early Confucians in their agricultural society, employment is to modern Confucians. Rather than ensuring that each household has an amount of land sufficient to meet its needs, therefore, Confucians today will emphasize the availability of jobs. In fast-changing modern economies, there are often mismatches between the skills needed by employers and those available in the workforce: Confucians will emphasize the importance of flexible primary-through-tertiary education, whose graduates can readily adapt to change; as well as of job-training programs with enough financial support to make them accessible to those who need them. The social ideal of "cultivated harmony" takes it for granted that people have different levels of talent and drive, just as modern families and societies have many different needs, and thus many different kinds of roles that must be fulfilled. In particular, Confucians see childcare (and especially early childcare) as vitally important.[48] Individual families will determine how to balance the fulfillment of their needs, but modern Confucians will not expect women to play any less important roles within the family and the broader economy than men.[49]

Taxation

Taxation serves two complementary roles: raising funds for necessary public programs and regulating the level of inequality in the society. Confucian support for assisting the poorly off and the physically or mentally disabled, for education and job training, and for international assistance all mean that the government must have funds. Confucian rejection of dramatic inequality without insisting on complete equality makes a progressive taxation scheme apt for both funding and redistribution. I have already discussed the need for an aggressive system of estate taxes, and in that section mentioned the desirability of arranging the taxation system so as to encourage charitable giving. I agree with authors like Chan, who stress that Confucians prefer bottom-up, voluntary solutions to social needs rather than top-down impositions by the government.[50] The details of balancing government programs, government and privately funded non-profit organizations, and primarily volunteer organizations, will be complex and depend on local circumstances, but one consideration to keep in mind will be that the broader the involvement of the populace in caring for one another, the more we are likely to approach the Confucians' goals of individual and societal moral improvement.

Conclusion

The Confucian societal vision underlying the various specific economic issues I have just reviewed is simple and inspiring: a community of individuals with diverse capabilities and interests, developing themselves, their loved ones, and ultimately the whole community through a balance of individual effort and mutual support. This kind of harmony takes collective effort to achieve, and the fellowship on which it depends can be undermined in many ways, including the absence of realistic opportunities to live good lives and the presence of extreme inequality—two ills that often go hand in hand. Modern Confucians accept differences and some degree of inequality, though they will resist inflexible hierarchies that put any one group permanently above another. Confucians believe that we all have the capacity to become good people and live good lives—we are equal in this way—but realizing these capacities takes effort on each person's part and support from those around one: it is not easy, and success will inevitably vary. As this chapter has argued, and as our present world makes clear, though, dramatic social divides and dramatic economic inequality are enormous barriers to our jointly achieving good lives.

Notes

1. *Analects* 12:22 and 1:2, respectively. All translations from Chinese are my own unless otherwise indicated.

2. *Mencius* 2A:6 and 1B:5.

3. Zhang Zai, "The Western Inscription," in Wing-tsit Chan, *A Sourcebook in Chinese Philosophy* (Princeton, New Jersey: Princeton University Press, 1963), 497, slightly modified. When referring to individuals' names, I will follow the Chinese practice of putting surname first (as in the case of Zhang Zai) unless that person's own practice is to put his or her surname last in Anglophone contexts (such as Wing-tsit Chan and several other contemporary scholars referenced below).

4. Sor-hoon Tan, "The Concept of *Yi* (义) in the *Mencius* and Problems of Distributive Justice," *Australasian Journal of Philosophy* 92, no. 3 (2014), 494. Tan's essay contains considerable evidence for this reading of *yi*.

5. Tan, "The Concept of *Yi*," 494, emphasis in original.

6. *Mengzi: With Selections From Traditional Commentaries*, trans. by Bryan Van Norden (Cambridge, Massachusetts: Hackett Publishing Company, 2008), 189, slightly modified.

7. For further discussion, see Stephen C. Angle, *Human Rights and Chinese Thought: A Cross-Cultural Inquiry* (New York, New York: Cambridge University Press, 2002), 75–83.

8. *Mencius* 3A:4; Wang, Yangming, *Instructions for Practical Living*, trans. by Wing-tsit Chan (New York, New York: Columbia University Press, 1963), 119.

9. *Analects* 12:23.

10. See Stephen C. Angle, *Sagehood: The Contemporary Significance of Neo-Confucian Philosophy* (New York, New York: Oxford University Press, 2009), 61–74; and Chenyang Li, *The Confucian Philosophy of Harmony* (New York, New York: Routledge, 2013).

11. Michael Ing's discussion of the spontaneous harmony described in the "Liji's 'Li Yun'" chapter as the "age of great unity" is particularly insightful; see Michael Ing, *The Dysfunction of Ritual in Early Confucianism* (New York, New York: Oxford University Press, 2012). Among others, Xunzi sees pre-civilizational times as chaotic; see the opening of *Xunzi* 19.

12. The most famous statement of these twin views is *Analects* 2:3: "The Master said, 'Lead them with government and regulate them with punishments, and the people will evade them with no sense of shame. Lead them with virtue and regulate them by ritual, and they will acquire a sense of shame and moreover, they will be orderly.'" Translation from E. Bruce Brooks and A. Taeko Brooks, *The Original Analects: Sayings of Confucius and His Successors* (New York, New York: Columbia University Press, 1998), 110. Some Confucians worried that even the best system of rituals could periodically fail, resulting in what Michael Ing has called a "tragic theory of ritual"; see Ing, *Dysfunction*.

13. *Analects* 4:12; translation from Brooks and Brooks, *Original Analects*, 15.

14. *Mencius* 1A:1.

15. *Mencius* 1A:7 and *Analects* 13:9.

16. See Julia Ching, "Neo-Confucian Utopian Theories and Political Ethics," *Monumenta Serica* 30 (1972), 1–56.

17. Donald Munro, *The Concept of Man in Ancient China* (Stanford, California: Stanford University Press, 1969).

18. Chenyang Li, "Equality and Inequality in Confucianism," *Dao: A Journal of Comparative Philosophy* 11 (2012), 295–297.

19. Li, "Equality," 297.

20. Li's essay looks at economic, moral, and political equality and inequality. It is arguable that "proportional equality" may be more apt to the moral and political cases than it is to the economic one.

21. Joseph Chan, *Confucian Perfectionism: A Political Philosophy for Modern Times* (Princeton, New Jersey: Princeton University Press, 2014), 175–176.

22. See *Mencius* 3A:3, and Chan, *Confucian Perfectionism*, 170–171.

23. Zhang Zai,《张载集》 [*Collected Works of Zhang Zai*] (Beijing, China: Zhonghua Shuju, 1978), 297.

24. Both Chan and Li cite relevant passages from Xunzi, and Li adds the following from the influential Han-dynasty Confucian Dong Zhongshu: "Let the rich be rich enough to show their wealth yet not be pretentious; let the poor have enough to take care of their lives without becoming worried" (Li, "Equality," 303). As for forced readings, the only *Mencius* passages Chan cites on this topic are 3B.4 and 7B.32. I agree with him that these passages endorse the idea that nonlandholding government advisers can be paid for their contributions, but it is less clear that they support Chan's statement, in the next paragraph, that "Mencius . . . [does] not object to economic inequalities" (Chan, *Confucian Perfectionism*, 175).

25. Li, "Equality," 303; the passage is *Analects* 16:1.

26. Sungmoon Kim, *Confucian Democracy in East Asia: Theory and Practice* (Cambridge, Great Britain, and New York, New York: Cambridge University Press, 2014), ch. 6, also argues against unregulated inequality with the "sufficiency" threshold, and puts forward "Confucian democratic welfarism" as an alternative, which is similar in several ways to the views I will develop below.

27. Sor-hoon Tan, "Justice and Social Change," in *Comparative Philosophy Without Borders*, Arindam Chakabarfti and Ralph Weber, eds. (London, Great Britain: Bloomsbury, 2016), 207.

28. Tan, "The Concept of *Yi*," 489, emphasis added.

29. Tan, "The Concept of *Yi*," 504.

30. Tan, "The Concept of *Yi*," 503.

31. Tan, "Justice and Social Change," 213. Tan also argues that passages in the early classics show a "prioritization of need over merit."

32. Tan, "The Concept of *Yi*," 502–503. Jiang Qing and Daniel Bell have

both argued that rituals shared by low- and high-status individuals can help to mitigate the oppositions that might otherwise be generated by status differences. See Jiang Qing 蒋庆,《蒋庆. 政治儒学：当代儒学的转向、特质与发展》 [*Political Confucianism: The Changing Direction, Particularities, and Development of Contemporary Confucianism*] (Beijing, China: Sanlian Shudian [Harvard-Yenching Academic Series], 2003), 322; and Daniel A. Bell, "Hierarchical Rituals for Egalitarian Societies," in *China's New Confucianism: Politics and Everyday Life in a Changing Society* (Princeton, New Jersey: Princeton University Press, 2008), 38–55.

33. Tan, "Justice and Social Change," 219.

34. Joseph P. McDermott and Shiba Yoshinobu, "Economic Change in China, 960–1279," in *The Cambridge History of China: Volume 5, Part 2: Sung China, 960–1279,* John W. Chaffee and Denis Twitchett, eds. (Cambridge, Great Britain: Cambridge University Press, 2015), 321–322.

35. See Nishijima Sadao, "The Economic and Social History of Former Han," in *The Cambridge History of China: Volume 1: The Ch'in and Han Empires, 221 B.C.–A.D. 220*, Denis Twitchett and Michael Loewe, eds. (Cambridge, Great Britain: Cambridge University Press, 1986), 557–558, for Confucian criticisms of unequal landholding in the Han dynasty; and Hoyt Cleveland Tillman, "The Rise of the *Tao-Hsüeh* Confucian Fellowship in Southern Sung," in *The Cambridge History of China: Volume 5, Part 2,* 765, for Zhu Xi's concerns. Zhang Zai's advocacy of the well-field system, mentioned earlier, is also related to his concerns about unequal land tenure.

36. See Stephen C. Angle, "Confucianism: Contemporary Expressions," in *The Wiley-Blackwell Companion to Religion and Social Justice*, Michael D. Palmer and Stanley M. Burgess, eds. (New York, New York: Wiley-Blackwell, 2012). Influential Confucian Mou Zongsan (1909–1995) was initially rather friendly to socialism, but later argued that private property "is the defense line of the human individual and protects the dignity of the human being" (Angle, "Confucianism: Contemporary Expressions," 98). Mou's argument for this conclusion depends on his distinctive idea of "self-restriction," on which see Stephen C. Angle, *Contemporary Confucian Political Philosophy: Toward Progressive Confucianism* (Cambridge, Great Britain: Polity Press, 2012). Fan Ruiping has also argued that Confucianism grounds a right to private property, though there are reasons to be skeptical about his approach; see Fan Ruiping, *Reconstructionist Confucianism: Rethinking Morality After the West* (Dordrecht, The Netherlands: Springer, 2010); and Stephen C. Angle, "A Reply to Fan Ruiping," *Dao: A Journal of Comparative Philosophy* 9, no. 4 (2010), 463–464.

37. Mark Elvin, *The Retreat of the Elephants: An Environmental History of China* (New Haven, Connecticut: Yale University Press, 2004).

38. Mary Evelyn Tucker and John Berthrong, eds. *Confucianism and Ecology: The Interrelation of Heaven, Earth, and Humans* (Cambridge, Great Britain: Center for the Study of World Religions, 1998).

39. There is a lot packed into this sentence that is beyond the scope of the present essay to spell out, but to begin with, we should keep in mind the very consciously cultivated balance between human and natural environments that characterizes Chinese scholars' gardens. Again, see Tucker and Berthrong, eds. *Confucianism and Ecology.*

40. I develop a related argument to support modern Confucian opposition to oppression in Angle, *Contemporary Confucian Political Philosophy*, ch. 7.

41. Tan, "Justice and Social Change," 215.

42. See Richard H. Thaler and Cass R. Sunstein, *Nudge: Improving Decisions and Health, Wealth, and Happiness* (New Haven, Connecticut: Yale University Press, 2008), for a discussion of our limited decision-making capabilities and for a range of plausible paternalist proposals that take our limits into account. Sungmoon Kim, *Public Reason Confucianism: Democratic Perfectionism and Constitutionalism in East Asia* (New York, New York: Cambridge University Press, 2016), 63–65, argues that Confucians should limit themselves to paternalism concerning our physical well-being and avoid "moral paternalism."

43. Both the second and third reasons resonate with Sungmoon Kim's argument that too much inequality will erode the familial-civic bonds and trust on which a modern Confucian polity—especially a modern Confucian democratic polity—rests. Kim, *Confucian Democracy*, 177.

44. See Jiang, *Political Confucianism*, 322; and Bell, "Hierarchical Rituals."

45. Historically, many neo-Confucians were resistant to state-led plans to redistribute land or wealth. In some cases, this was because of a deeper skepticism about the ideal of harmony that informed such redistributionist plans—see, for example, Chang Woei Ong, "The Principles Are Many: Wang Tingxiang and Intellectual Transition in Mid-Ming China," *Harvard Journal of Asiatic Studies* 66, no. 2 (2006), 461–493, on the Ming Dynasty Confucian Wang Tingxiang—but most were concerned about the levels of coercion involved, or simple impracticability.

46. *Xunzi,* 19.

47. Huang Zongxi, *Waiting for the Dawn*, trans. by Wm. Theodore de Bary (New York, New York: Columbia University Press, 1993), 91.

48. See Erin M. Cline, *Families of Virtue: Confucian and Western Views on Childhood Development* (New York, New York: Columbia University Press, 2015).

49. See Li-Hsiang Lisa Rosenlee, *Confucianism and Women: A Philosophical Interpretation* (Albany, New York: State University of New York Press, 2006), ch. 7.

50. See Chan, *Confucian Perfectionism*, 184–189.

Buddhism

ECONOMIC JUSTICE IN THE BUDDHIST TRADITION

CHRISTOPHER S. QUEEN

Introduction

Buddhism is widely associated with progressive teachings and exemplary models of economic life. The idea of "Buddhist economics" was paired with the slogan "small is beautiful" by economist E. F. Schumacher in a book of that title in 1973. Voluntary simplicity and renunciation are salient themes in the legend of Gotama, a prince who exchanged his palace for homelessness and promoted monastic life as a direct road to happiness and liberation. The teaching of a middle path between self-indulgence and self-denial, the opening words of the Buddha's first sermon, is offered as a key to sustainable levels of acquisition and consumption in modern times of increasing income inequality and consumerism. Right livelihood, another early teaching, denotes occupations that avoid harm to animals, workers, and the public. Schumacher concludes that these Buddhist teachings amount to an "economics as if people mattered" that may provide a basis for societies of opportunity and prosperity for all.[1]

As Buddhism evolved over two millennia in Asia and the West, however, we see patterns of economic life that diverge from the simple picture of "wandering and intellectually schooled mendicant monks" that the sociologist Max Weber envisioned in his account of the earliest Buddhists. In the Buddhist communities that sprang up in Northeast India in the fifth century BCE, and their successors in Southeast Asia, China, and Japan, we encounter a larger canvas that includes the patronage by moneyed classes, hereditary nobility, and citizens of modest and moderate means, as religious giving became the central pillar of salvation for the laity. Offering food, robes, and property to the monks, and building Buddhist shrines, stupas, viharas, pagodas, wats, temples, *gompas*, and zendos earned the donors spiritual merit and favorable rebirths in the future. In return, the monks offered ritual blessings and religious instruction to members of society in search of comfort and direction. Chief among the lay supporters of the *sangha*, or religious order, was the king himself, who, in addition to spiritual merit, sought religious legitimation for the power of the state.

Underlying these relationships were four attitudes toward material prosperity. First, wealth is good, insofar as it provides for the satisfaction of material needs and opportunities for religious giving. Poverty is never praised in Buddhism. Second, wealth gained without greed or harm to others—"right livelihood" that avoids trade in arms, meat, alcohol, or living beings—is regarded as a sign of virtue. The virtuous wealthy are the most honored members of lay society. Third, the prestige of the wealthy is further measured by the ways in which they spend their wealth. Generosity (*dāna*), particularly toward the monastic community, earns the donor spiritual merit, a favorable rebirth, and opportunities to acquire more wealth. The more respected the recipient—a senior monk, for example—the greater the merit earned. Fourth, and most important, material wealth and poverty are regarded as ultimately inconsequential in the quest for salvation. For traditional Buddhists, both lay and ordained, the achievement of spiritual liberation, *nirvāṇa* (Pali *nibbāna*), and not worldly prosperity, is the ultimate goal of life. Material wealth was considered to be morally neutral compared to generosity, a spirit of nonattachment, and service to others. Personal virtue and contentment in life represent the true wealth, the Buddha taught, differentiating those who are rich from those who are poor.[2]

In light of these principles, modern notions of equality, human rights, and distributive justice, particularly as they relate to economic opportunity and prosperity, do not find direct parallels in early Buddhism. "A just arrangement for the distribution of wealth"—one definition of economics "as if people mattered" today—was never the object of classical Buddhist teaching. Indeed, generosity toward the poor is rarely mentioned, except as a desirable policy of the state. The names of wealthy donors are recorded in early narratives and lithic inscriptions for their gifts to the sangha, not the lay community, however needy. Even gifts to the monks are discretionary and would not be expected to precede spending on oneself, family, friends, and employees (ideally, one-quarter of one's income); saving for contingencies in the future (one-quarter); and, most important, reinvesting in enterprises that produce more wealth (one-half).[3] With the rise of Mahayana Buddhism in the common era, voluntary giving by laypersons to the poor is praised as a way "to eliminate the causes of suffering and to increase blessings and virtues," while giving to the sangha remains the surest way to a higher goal, "to repay kindness, to increase the causes of happiness, and to increase wisdom and forsake afflictions."[4]

For ancient Buddhists, Hindus, Jains, and other traditionalists in South and East Asia, disparities of wealth and poverty, like differences of physical strength, mental health, and social status, are believed to be dictated by the operation of *karma*, literally "action," as it is manifested in the laws of nature and moral conduct in the human sphere. The outcome, or fruit (*phala*), of an action may appear immediately, or it may remain latent until it ripens later in this life or the next. Belief in the transmission of moral effects over many lifetimes, governed by the law of karma, shapes common attitudes toward social and economic justice. Thus, a person's economic standing, whether rich or poor, reflects his or her ethical conduct in the past. A popular example is the story of King Vessantara, who demonstrates his virtue by giving away his riches, his throne, and even his children in acts of spontaneous generosity. Immediately after he makes his final gift—his grief-stricken wife—his vast merit, earned by making these gifts, results in the sudden restoration of his wealth, his kingdom, and his family. The accumulation of the king's karma, earned in this life and in countless previous and later lives, elevates Vessantara to the status of a *bodhisattva*, one who selflessly helps others. The cost to his family—the children were cruelly abused by their new master, for example—as well as the extremes of privilege and deprivation that form the backdrop of the story, are subordinated in the minds of hearers to the conviction that acts of generosity will eventually benefit the donor and those around him. The family lives happily thereafter and the king himself is later reborn as Shakyamuni Buddha.[5]

As we survey the evolution of Buddhist economics and its implications for questions of equality, property, natural resources, products, wealth, income, jobs, and taxation, we encounter both continuity and transformation. The value of material comfort remains secondary to spiritual advancement, for example, at the same time that monastic institutions become increasingly rich as a result of lay benefaction. The relationship between sangha and state becomes both codependent and adversarial as philanthropy flows to the pagoda at the expense of the palace and is then confiscated in lieu of taxes by the government. In medieval China and Japan, the vast economic holdings of monastic institutions are buttressed by their rising political power, as Buddhist monks, armed and trained in traditional martial arts, engage in insurrections and internecine warfare. Finally, in the post-colonial period of the nineteenth and twentieth centuries, ideologies of popular dissent from elite power support the rise of Buddhist liberation movements committed to universal human rights, democratic institutions, and economic justice. Such "socially engaged" Buddhism combines elements of traditional teaching with new conceptions borrowed from a globalizing, transnational culture.

Core religious values of Buddhism—the *dharma* in its widest sense—appear, evolve, and reappear throughout these epochs. They may be grouped around the categories of Discipline, Virtue, Altruism, and Engagement for purposes of analysis.[6] In the early scriptures, the ethics of *Discipline*—the avoidance of harm to oneself and others—is reflected in the Five Precepts (*pancasila*) against injury, dishonesty, theft, sexual misconduct, and intoxication; and the hundreds of restrictions of monastic conduct inscribed in the *Vinaya* codes for monks and nuns. Complementing these proscriptions in the earliest writings, an ethics of *Virtue* was introduced to include such lists as the Divine Abodes (*brahmavihāras*) of kindness, compassion, joy at the well-being of others, and impartiality; and the Perfections (*paramitas*) of generosity, morality, courage, patience, mindfulness, and wisdom. The ethics of *Altruism* refers to the vocation of the bodhisattva, the hybrid hero of the Mahayana reforms, who may be ordained or lay, human or divine, male or female. Motivated by the thought of future enlightenment (*bodhicitta*) and great compassion for others (*mahā karuṇā*), the bodhisattva vows to save all sentient beings through tireless skillful means, deferring his or her own reward until all others are fully liberated. Finally, the ethics of *Engagement*, a complex of beliefs and practices that emerged in the modern period in Asia and the West, recognizes the collective, systemic, and institutional causes of human suffering—political oppression, corporate greed and exploitation, and ecological disturbances that disproportionately impact the most vulnerable populations—and formulates social strategies to combat them.

Each section that follows touches on features of Buddhist economics as they appear in (1) the Theravada cultures of South and Southeast Asia, as reflected in the Pali literatures associated with the Buddha's early teaching; (2) the Mahayana cultures that originated in India and flourished in China, Tibet, and East Asia, including Chan/Zen, Pure Land, Nichiren, and Vajrayana traditions; and (3) the modern period, marked by the rise of Engaged Buddhism in Asia and the West. Each phase of this evolution may be seen to point to distinctive practices and teachings in the economic sphere.

Equality

Buddhism first appeared in the fifth century BCE, a time of rapid economic and social change in Northeast India. The development of iron technology made possible the clearing of forests, the expansion of agricultural lands, surplus food production, and growing populations. The traditional organization of society into tribal confederations was supplanted by the rise of monarchies and the consolidation of economic and political power. Cities and the occupations they supported—manufacture, trading, accounting, and financial services—became the setting for the career of the Buddha, who was raised in a royal household of wealth and privilege. Among his followers, the Buddha counted bankers, kings, women of financial means, and *gahapatis*—high-status agricultural entrepreneurs with large land holdings, workforces, and produce markets that extended along the teeming river- and land-based trade routes. Of the 1,009 passages in the Pali records that name a place of the Buddha's activity, 83 percent (842) cite one of five cities: Sāvatthī, Rajagaha, Kapīlavatthu, Vesali, and Kosambi.[7] As a result of generous land donations to the growing sangha, these references suggest that the congregation of monks frequently spent the rain-retreat season in the environs of these cities, and that the Buddha's message was directed to the social, economic, and spiritual challenges faced by rapidly growing urban populations.

These challenges differed from the concerns of the Brahmanical priesthood in traditional agricultural society. Rather than offering Sanskrit incantations for the ending of drought or the prosperity of newlyweds, the Buddha spoke of the ethical and psychological stresses created by changing social relationships and marketplace politics. In his dialogues with petitioners from all walks of life, he insisted

> that a person be judged by his individual virtue rather than his familial, class or social origins. This was precisely the demand of the new urban social classes who . . . were not much interested in speculative metaphysics, for their emphasis was on practical and everyday concerns of making good in this world and assuring one's welfare in the next.[8]

These concerns were met by the Buddha's warnings of the danger of harming others, lying, stealing, sexual abuse, and intoxication, which would damage relationship and reputation in business and social circles; and his affirmation of the values of friendliness, compassion, joy in the success of others, and impartiality, which foster harmony in the family and enhance professional connection and customer service in the workplace. In this way, the core ethical teachings of the Five Precepts and Divine Abodes resonated with a rising managerial class no longer attracted to Vedic ritualism, theology, and magic.

Social and economic equality were neither a reality nor an ideal in the Buddha's time. The division of society into four hereditary castes (*varṇa*) was first described in the *Puruṣa-Sukta* of the Rig Veda, in which the Brahmin priesthood emerged from the mouth of the "cosmic man," the Kshatriya nobility from his torso, the Vaishya merchants from his hips, and the Shudra laborers from his legs. This mythic picture was parodied in the Buddha's story of creation, the *Aggañña Sutta*, where the nobility is elevated to top rank in a society, and where status is acquired by virtuous action, not social location. While acknowledging the existence of caste inequality in his time, the Buddha came to be known for disregarding these distinctions, ordaining aspirants from all backgrounds into the company

of monks and nuns. In this respect, the primitive sangha was a countercul-
ture founded on a new vision of equality and opportunity. The goal was
spiritual liberation, however, not social, economic, or political advancement. Devotion to the Buddha's Middle Path promised a better life in this
world and the next.[9]

By the turn of the Common Era, the social patterns described in the
earliest Buddhist records were supplemented and, in some cases, replaced
by a new social vision embodied in the figure of the bodhisattva. Portrayed as a heroic devotee of the Buddha's way, the bodhisattva reflects a
broadening definition of spiritual equality: bodhisattvas might be lay or
ordained, divine or human, male or female. This Mahayana ("great vehicle") movement might also be expected to reflect a broadening of access
to the practice of Buddhism for persons of all social and economic strata
and a continuation of the Buddha's redefinition of elite-ness along ethical lines. Yet bodhisattvas were not portrayed as poor or low-caste. The
wealthy merchant Vimalakirti and the brilliant Queen Srimala are rem-
iniscent of prominent lay figures in the early period in their commitment
to the spread of the dharma. Yet we miss references to the figures of lowly
background or personal tragedy that we had met in tales of the Buddha's
previous lives (*Jatakas*), conversion stories of the monks and nuns (*Therag-
atha, Therigatha*), and the Buddha's dialogues with the population at large
(*Suttapitaka*). Srimala teaches the universal presence of Buddha-nature
(*tathāgatagarbha*) in all beings while at the same time appealing primarily to
Indian royal patronesses and court ladies in China and Japan. Her story,
and those of the other new savior-figures, is preserved in Sanskrit, the elite
language of Brahmins and pandits.[10]

The importation and adaptation of Buddhist teachings to China offered new opportunities to promote social and economic equality. Two
examples will suggest the opening of new life-options for spiritual seekers.
The biography of the fourth-century nun, An-ling Hsu, reflects the transmission of sexual equality from India to East Asia via Buddhist teachings.
As a bookish girl in a middle-class family, An-ling resisted her parents'
pressure to marry. Her father, a mid-level government official, consulted
the Buddhist missionary, Fo-t'u-teng, who foretold An-ling's future emi-
nence by conjuring a magic vision of her previous life as a "śramana in
the midst of a large gathering, preaching the dharma . . . helping living
creatures." By allowing An-ling to renounce marriage and family life, her

father freed her to achieve success and to bring wealth and honor to his family. Hsu became a scholar and founder of nunneries for like-minded girls, as her father was promoted to the high office of prefect by his prince.[11]

Perhaps the most-cited text in Chinese Buddhist history is the Platform Sutra of the Sixth Patriarch, composed over several centuries and memorializing the teachings of Huineng, a humble employee in a large Chan (Zen) monastery. The paradox of the work is its attribution to an illiterate servant, who nevertheless defeated the erudite heir-apparent of the retiring abbot by dictating a teaching verse of great subtlety. This feat might be taken as evidence that medieval Chinese Buddhism honored the contributions of the culturally disadvantaged, yet the final versions of the sutra comprise a compendium of commentaries on nine philosophical-devotional texts, unlikely to be comprehended by a single unlettered monk. The message is rather that the dharma, like *Buddha-nature* itself, is the birthright of all sentient beings.[12]

Among the socially engaged Buddhisms of the twentieth century, none has placed equality of human dignity and opportunity higher on its agenda than the Buddhist conversion of India's "untouchables"—called *dalits* (oppressed) or *bahujans* (common folk)—in the decades following their initiation in 1956. Embracing the European slogans "Liberty, Equality, Fraternity" and "Educate, Agitate, Organize," which the movement's leader, Dr. B. R. Ambedkar, brought back from his graduate studies in New York and London, the "New Vehicle" (*Navayana*) or Ambedkar Buddhists have made the overthrow of the Indian caste system their primary objective. If the Buddha's teaching was directed to the relief of human suffering, and if membership in his order was offered freely to persons from all backgrounds of caste, class, and wealth, the Ambedkar Buddhists argue, then their own religious practice must focus every effort on the realization of equality—social, political, economic, and spiritual—for all members of society. Ambedkar Buddhists number in the millions in India today.[13]

Property

Just as religions are embodied in ritual and morality, they are also grounded in sacred space and holy shrines. Religions "make homes and cross boundaries" at the same time, according to one theorist.[14] But they are not, for that reason, defined primarily by their acquisition of "property"—land, buildings, furnishings—which in most cases accumulate over time as a byproduct of their success. In India, religious seekers and devotees were known more for voluntary homelessness than for their construction of ornate temples. Called *sadhus* (holy men), *śramaṇas* (ascetics), *sannyāsis* (renunciants), and *munis* (silent ones, in the Vedic tradition), Indian religious wanderers even came to the attention of Alexander the Great, who called them *gymnosophists* (naked philosophers). In this tradition, we have seen the ease with which King Vessantara renounced his kingdom to practice the moral purity of total generosity.

Prince Siddhartha's renunciation of his royal palace and position in favor of the wandering life stands as the primary symbol of Buddhism's material asceticism. His followers came to be called *bhikkhus* (mendicants) or *paribbajakas* (those who have gone forth). But life in the jungle and at the margins of settled society—the mark of the traditional sadhu—never caught on as the goal of the dharma. The reality of summer monsoons in South Asia quickly overtook any possibility of permanent wandering for the Buddha (the "Awakened One") and his followers. Monks, like householders, need shelter during the inclement months, and increasing numbers of devotees of the Buddha's teachings were eager to provide a nearby place for the sangha to settle and teach. Donations of property became an early mark of the popularity of the movement, particularly among the landed and moneyed classes. Among the most celebrated gifts of property were those of the banker Anāthapiṇḍika and the patroness Visākhā, who donated monasteries at opposite ends of the city of Sāvatthī. As the third rainy season approached, Anāthapiṇḍika requested permission to provide shelter for the monks, who had been staying in caves, ravines, and graveyards. With the Buddha's consent, the banker built the Jetavana Monastery, eventually comprising sixty dormitories, with meeting halls for public lectures, rituals, and training. Some years later, Visākhā, renowned for her generous gifts of food and robes to the sangha, sold her jewelry and built a second monastery on prime land near the city gate, the Pubbārāma or "Eastern Park." Many of the Buddha's recorded teachings are situated on these sumptuous grounds.

By the fourth century CE, the Buddhist monastic establishment in Sri Lanka had become the largest landholder on the island. Temples, paddy lands, and coconut gardens provided not only for the religious activities of sanghas throughout the year, but also for their economic and political support.

> On the one hand, land ensures the continuity of the monkhood: for as long as monks have land, they need not worry about their livelihood. And as long as the monkhood survives, the *dharma* survives. On the other hand, the king's protection of the *sangha*'s wealth and virtue demonstrates his right to rule. Landed wealth thus serves as the mediating vehicle by which the *sangha* and the state share political power and moral legitimacy.[15]

A similar pattern of triangulation between wealthy donors; Buddhist capital accumulation, including landholding; and state oversight evolved in China, posing unprecedented challenges. The dominance of Confucian values, such as respect for traditional family and official authority, as we saw in the story of An-ling Hsu, was threatened by the growing wealth and political influence of Buddhist temples and monasteries. One expression of this tension was the invention of the "merit-cloister" during the Tang dynasty (618–906), whereby land was placed under monastic control as a tax shelter. The donor ceded ownership of the land while retaining management rights over its use. This and other features of a growing Buddhist commercial presence in China resulted in periodic retaliation by the state in the form of confiscation of monastic lands, the forceful laicization of monks, and the imposition of quotas on the establishment of new temples and monasteries. Major persecutions, as they came to be known, occurred in the years 446, 574, and 845.[16]

In the Aggañña Sutta's account of the evolution of society, boundaries for private property are first drawn when greedy neighbors begin to hoard naturally growing rice. The division of land into private plots leads to social strife and the election of the first king, who is charged with enforcing civil order and, along with holy men, setting standards of righteous conduct. Paradoxically, the holy men of the Buddhist order quickly assumed the role of property holder and faced inevitable challenges associated with wealth and political power. Cases of what might be called "corporate Buddhism" in South Asia and China were replicated in medieval Korea, Japan, and Tibet. Not until the modern period do we see a generalized rejection of these tendencies in the humanistic and socialist writings of twentieth-century reformers such as the Chinese Taixu, the Thai Buddha-dasa, the Japanese Daisaku Ikeda, and the Taiwanese Xingyun.[17]

Natural Resources

Just as the Aggañña Sutta pictured a primordial paradise where food grew freely for human consumption, many early records of the Buddhist movement suggest harmonious perspectives on man's relation to the natural environment. In the Jataka tales of the early Pali literature, the future Buddha is personified as a wild animal who sacrifices himself for others: antelope, elephant, deer, yak, lion, rhinoceros, tiger, panther, bear, hyena, otter, and more. In addition to illustrating core Buddhist virtues, the literature celebrates forests, rivers, flowers, herbs, and landscapes that anticipate the magical "Buddha-realms" in the *Sukhavati* or "pure land" literature of the later Mahayana. The early tradition emphasizes the sacredness of trees in the legend of the Buddha, who was born and died under flowering shala trees (*Shorea robusta*) and enlightened under a giant fig tree (*Ficus religiosa*), which came to be called the *bodhi* or "awakening" tree. The *Sutta-Nipata* has the Buddha say,

> Know ye the grasses and the trees. . . . Then know ye the worms and the moths, and the different sorts of ants . . . . Know ye also the four-footed animals small and great, the serpents, the fish which range in the water, the birds that are borne along on wings and move through the air . . . Know ye the marks that constitute species are theirs, and their species are manifold.[18]

The Vinaya monastic code forbids the cutting of trees and the contamination of water with food or other waste. Monks are instructed to build toilets and wells to protect water-born creatures and to provide pure water for drinking and bathing. "Those who destroy or contaminate water resources do so at great karmic peril," observes scholar Chatsumarn Kabilsingh. "This illustrates early awareness of the need to preserve natural resources."[19]

The Buddhist king Aśoka Maurya (ca. 274–232 BCE), a midlife convert to Buddhism, included among his Rock and Pillar Edicts a record of policies designed to serve his subjects while protecting the natural environment.

Medicinal herbs, suitable for men and animals, have been imported and planted wherever they were not previously available. Where roots and fruits were lacking, they have been imported and planted. Wells have been dug and trees planted along the roads for the use of men and animals.

Significantly, these measures are not enacted or announced to bring credit to the king or his government, but rather "in order that the people may follow the path of Dharma with faith and devotion." The implication is that the path of the Buddha encompasses humans, plants, and animals in a holistic vision of well-being.[20]

Buddhism's record of environmental protection was never perfect, however. In the medieval Japanese ritual of *Hōjō-e*, for example, the annual release of animals to teach compassion for living creatures and moderation in the use of natural resources, large temples routinely discount the death of thousands of birds and fish in order to have sufficient stocks for an impressive public ceremony. For these prestigious Buddhist institutions, "the release of animals . . . was more often a matter of displaying political power or appeasing various deities."[21]

In the twentieth century, the rise of environmental movements on a global scale have provided a platform for the resurgence of Buddhist teachings on reverence for nature. Traditional notions of dependent origination, the non-harming of living beings, moderation in the consumption of natural resources, and humility, compassion, and mindfulness in interactions with other beings have all been applied to specific challenges of environmental protection. A flood of anthologies detailing the teachings of "green Buddhism" and "eco-Buddhism" have appeared in recent years, and engaged Buddhist groups have mounted many forms of social activism to combat environmental degradation. The "ecology monks" of Thailand, who "ordain" trees to halt the cutting of forests; and the Buddhist Peace Fellowship, which committed civil disobedience to stop nuclear weapons testing at a U.S. government test site in Nevada in 1993, are but two examples of the global response of engaged Buddhists to the environmental crisis.[22]

Products

What constitutes a product in Buddhism? Certainly, religious teachings may be considered cultural products or intellectual property. The activities of the sangha, such as the offering of teachings, advice, and counseling may likewise be considered educational and pastoral services, products of sorts. But from the earliest times, we also encounter what might be more narrowly considered economic products and services, as they grow out of and interact with the economic system. An example of the commodification of the Buddha is suggested by his deathbed instructions to his attendant Ananda that worship of his remains (*sarīra-pūja*) should be left to nobles, Brahmins, and landowners so that the monks may focus on their spiritual duties (*Mahāparinibbāna-sutta* V.10). By the first century CE, the commercial value of this teaching was disclosed in donor inscriptions and physical portraits carved in the stone entrances to cave temples and reliquary monuments (*stupas*), where the remains—or relics (*sarīra*)—of the Buddha or his chief disciples are interred.[23]

In Chinese Buddhism we find a wide range of products and services marketed by large temples, including "grain milling, oil seed pressing, money lending, pawnshops, loans of grain to peasants (with interest), mutual financing associations, hotels and hostelries, and rental of temple lands to farmers in exchange for some percentage of the crop."[24] Some of these businesses were imported from India, in violation of regulations in the monastic code, but others appeared for the first time in China. These include the buying and selling of monk ordination certificates, formerly issued and sold by the state, but later manufactured and traded by monasteries as a source of income. The certificates could be used to obtain tax exemptions and to back lending at monastic rates, which the borrower regarded as a form of spiritual merit-making. The accumulation of "inexhaustible treasuries" of land, money, and goods acted as endowments to ensure future wealth and prosperity, while lay investment in monastic "merit cloisters" offered the donor a tax shelter while allowing continued profits from management of the donated land or goods. Ornatowski calls these financial products "the best examples of 'capitalist' innovations in China originating from Buddhist practices."[25]

By modern times, the cult of relics and amulets had been fully institutionalized in Thailand. Tambiah describes the annual *Kathin,* or robe-donation ceremony, in the remote mountain hermitage of a renowned forest monk, Acharn Čūan. Sponsored by the Bangkok Bank of Commerce, the ceremony provided the bank's elite clients—aristocrats, royalists, politicians, high-end merchants, and Chinese financiers—an opportunity to make merit while meeting and cultivating old and new business partners. In preparation for the three-day event in 1978, for example, the bank minted forty thousand bronze amulets depicting a meditating Acharn Čūan on one side and the bank's seal and the inscription "Kathin, 1976, Wat Phūthaung, Čangwat Naungkhāi" on the other. During the rain retreat that preceded the ceremony, Acharn Čūan had ritually blessed each of the amulets with a traditional mantra. Four thousand amulets were donated to the monastery for sale—at about $1 each—while the rest were retained by the bank as premium gifts to selected depositors. Following the ceremony, in which 175,000 *baht* ($8,750) were donated, along with robes and other domestic articles, the distinguished supporters, who had been bused in from Bangkok and other cities, were invited to shop in the hermitage gift shop. Typical items at monastic gift shops in rural Thailand include a selection of amulets in common or precious metals, and lockets, rings, statuettes, and bumper stickers bearing the senior monk's image and the branding of the secular sponsor.[26]

Wealth

The first major recorded donation to the Buddhist sangha was the pleasure garden of the Maghadan king Bimbisara, which he provided for the itinerant monks to shelter during the rains and to meet with supporters, outside the hustle and bustle of the city. Unlike traditional donations of land to the Brahmin priesthood by the nobility, which were given to individual priests for agricultural cultivation and the staging of fee-based sacrifices, the gift of parklands, residences, and temples to the Buddhist sangha were made to the sangha as a whole. Indeed, the *bhikkhu*-sangha has been called the first confederate institution in the history of religions, and the receipt and sharing of wealth by members of the Buddhist order may be considered a primitive form of economic socialism. Outside observers remarked on the high degree of due process and collective harmony instituted by the Vinaya monastic code, which was the first body of teachings committed to memory by the primitive community.[27]

Lay supporters of the ancient sangha were given a virtual menu of opportunities to practice virtue and altruism in exchange for merit, prosperity, and the prospect of a better rebirth. These included the offering of daily food and drink to the monks, the annual provision of robes, medicines, bedding, lights, and vehicles, and the ultimate gifts of land, shelter, and reliquary monuments. One wealthy donor admitted to the Buddha, "Lord, I had these sixty dwelling-places built because I need merit, because I need heaven," while commoners were observed to be overjoyed when first permitted to donate robes to the monks, proclaiming "now we will give *dāna*, now we will gain *puññya*." The Buddha was quick to encourage these motivations, assuring donors that they would enjoy fame, beauty, confidence, happiness, honor, longevity, and a superior rebirth.[28]

In few of these contexts do the early records recommend free offering of material support to the poor. As Ornatowski observes,

> There is little clear evidence in Theravāda Buddhism supporting redistribution of wealth, except for the idea of *dāna*, which implied redistribution of wealth *to the sangha* and not necessarily to the poor, and the idea of *karuṇā*, which implied more individually-based acts of compassion toward one's fellow sentient beings rather than an overall program for social change.[29]

Here again, "the law of *kamma* [karma], with its all-encompassing explanation of existing inequalities, tends to do away with Buddhist perplexity over the plight of the poor."[30]

These Indian patterns of religious giving, wealth accumulation, and attitudes toward the rich, the poor, and the state, are carried with few changes to East Asia following the arrival of Buddhism in China in the early Common Era. A modern manifestation of these values may be seen today in the Foguangshan (Buddha's Light Mountain), a Taiwanese Pure Land sect of Mahayana Buddhism. Its founder, Master Xingyun, "sees nothing wrong with making money or becoming rich, as long as one has done so in a moral way and shares the benefits of one's prosperity with others." This perspective is a fair distillation of the values that first appeared in the early Buddhist records: diligence, frugality, and morality; selfless giving to the sangha; a recognition that life is short and that self-cultivation, including the acquisition of wealth, is virtuous; and a conviction that inequalities of wealth and privilege in society manifest the karma of past behavior. Based on these conceptions, the Foguangshan Buddhists have achieved great wealth and global reach, which they have invested in a growing network of temples, hospitals, schools, universities, and social service projects throughout Taiwan and abroad.[31]

While this prosperous Buddhism has been interpreted as an expression of the Confucian-inspired capitalism of the "four dragons" of East Asia—Hong Kong, South Korea, Singapore, and Taiwan—we must not presume that all contemporary Buddhism has hitched its fortunes to capitalism. Modern Asian Buddhist reformers have argued that the values of socialism and humanism, as defined and manifested in the West, may offer a better match for the traditional collectivism of the ancient Buddhist sangha. The Chinese modernist Taixu advocated a "democratic socialism" that would counter the predatory commercialism of the modern West, while the Thai reformer Buddhadāsa Bhikkhu proposed a "dharmic socialism" to counter both the individualism and greed of modern capitalism and the violence and depersonalization of Marxism and Communism. Many other thinkers and movement leaders associated with Engaged Buddhism, including the Dalai Lama ("universal responsibility"), the Thai activist Sulak Sivaraksa ("small-b buddhism"), and Soka Gakkai International president and preceptor, Daisaku Ikeda ("humanistic socialism"), have identified the ways in which the traditional mental poisons of hatred, greed, and delusion are reflected in unbridled modern capitalism.[32]

In the West, scores of Buddhist writers and movement leaders have written about the spiritual and material suffering caused by an economics of perpetual growth, which the advertising and marketing industries fuel by creating unquenchable thirst for new products and services. In these studies, we may see the aptness of the term "thirst" itself, which evolved from the ancient Buddhist term for the inexhaustible craving that causes spiritual disorientation and despair: *tṛṣṇā* (Sanskrit) and *tanha* (Pali). Anthologies such as *Mindfulness in the Marketplace: Compassionate Responses to Consumerism,* edited by Allan Hunt Badiner, and *Hooked!! Buddhist Writings on Greed, Desire, and the Urge to Consume,* edited by Stephanie Kaza, serve as antidotes to the excesses of Buddhist wealth and commercialism in Asia and the West.[33]

Income

Commentators on Buddhist economics have devoted considerable effort to refuting the claims of the German sociologist Max Weber that early Buddhism was limited to the otherworldly asceticism of the monastic community. The sangha and its supporters, according to Weber, lacked the "this-worldly asceticism" of diligence, thrift, and the sense of a religious vocation he found in early Protestant communities. Lacking these characteristics, the "religious technology of wandering and intellectually schooled mendicant monks" placed the Buddhist movement outside the economic life of society and robbed it of the proto-capitalistic potential he found in reformist Christianity. While critics have not attempted to show that early Buddhism was attuned to Weber's "spirit of capitalism," they have noted the keen attention of the ancient records to the economic life of monks and laypersons. The salient place of right livelihood (*sammā-ājīva*) among the core guidelines of the Eightfold Path, along with its elaboration in several discourses for lay practice, gives us an insight into the ways in which income was considered on the path to Buddhist liberation.[34]

Buddhist ethics exemplify elements of discipline, virtue, altruism, and engagement, as we have noted. Right livelihood is described in the Buddha's discourses as the avoidance of occupations that harm others (discipline) and the pursuit of occupations that sustain and liberate others (virtue and altruism). Modern commentators have expanded these teachings to include an analysis of the collective harm or benefit caused by modern organizations and industries, and the means of subverting or supporting them (engagement). The classical summation of occupations to be avoided include trade in weapons, living beings (livestock farming), meat (hunter, fisherman, butcher, meat wholesaler), and intoxicants and poisons (alcoholic drink). Such occupations, utterly forbidden to monks and discouraged for laypersons, will surely result in a lower rebirth, if not in immediate misfortune. Peter Harvey cites modern writers who extrapolate the early warnings to present-day applications, such as scientific experimentation on animals, manufacturing pesticides, and "working in advertising, to the extent that this is seen as encouraging greed, hatred and delusion, or perverting the truth."[35]

Among contemporary Buddhist thinkers, Sulak Sivaraksa, the Thai dissident and founder of the International Network of Engaged Buddhists, has reflected systematically on the sociological meaning of the Five Moral Precepts (*pañca sīla*), the Buddha's central ethical teaching. Each of them offers guidance in the matter of right livelihood. The first precept, "I vow to abstain from taking life" (*ahimsa* or "non-harming," a universal teaching in world religions), is considered in terms of vegetarianism, the logging industry, and the manufacture and global marketing of armaments and pesticides. The second precept, "I vow to abstain from stealing," is interpreted affirmatively as the responsibility to create an economic system in which decent jobs are provided to all, where "decent" implies both the inherent morality of the work and the equity of its compensation. Poverty results when governments fail in their obligation to regulate the economy, and "stealing" by neighbors and corporations is the result. "It is not enough to live a life of voluntary simplicity without also working to overturn the structures that force so many people to live in involuntary poverty."[36]

Sulak's reading of the third precept, "I vow to abstain from sexual misconduct," is directed to the universality of patriarchal domination of women in the family, industry, and the public sphere. (The multibillion-dollar industries of human trafficking, pornography, and prostitution—mainstays of the Thai tourist industry—are not mentioned in Sulak's analysis, but are surely worth considering.) The fourth precept, "I vow to abstain from false speech," is focused on the role of mass media, education, and "patterns of information that condition our understanding of the world." The rise of social media addiction and "false news," as it has impacted mental health and the direction of national elections, for example, may be taken as pressing concerns of Buddhists, for whom "purify the mind" shares equal standing with "do good" and "avoid evil" in the traditional formula. Finally, Sulak sees the fifth precept, "I vow to abstain from intoxicants that cloud the mind," as a window onto the global trade in heroin, coca, coffee, tobacco, and alcohol. "Equally serious," as the full-scale wars that have been fought by governments and drug cartels over markets and supply chains, according to Sulak, "is the economic violence of forcing peasants to plant export crops of coffee or tea and the unloading of surplus cigarette production onto Third World consumers through intensive advertising campaigns."[37]

Jobs

In contrast to the Buddhist aversion to "wrong livelihood," as outlined above, we may turn to its approval of jobs and vocations that support social harmony and the path to liberation. Right livelihood encompasses a set of attitudes about how employees should be treated and how they should conduct themselves in return. According to the *Sigālovāda Sutta*, sometimes called the "lay Vinaya," or social code, employers should respect workers and servants

> by arranging their work according to their strengths, by supplying them with food and wages, by looking after them when they are ill, by sharing delicacies with them and by letting them off work at the right time.[38]

They should avoid overworking employees or forcing them to do degrading work. In his Rock Edict XI, King Aśoka includes slaves and servants in a list of those who should be treated respectfully, along with parents, friends, acquaintances, relatives, priests, ascetics, and animals. Meanwhile, according to an early Mahayana text, employees should be trustworthy, hard-working, and mindful of their employer's reputation.[39] These guidelines, which grew out of the urban work environments of Iron Age society, may be thought of as an economics of virtue and altruism, supplementing the economics of discipline we discussed in the last section.

As Buddhism took root in China and East Asia, traditional restrictions on monastic labor dissolved and new forms of work appeared within growing temple complexes. Agricultural labor, commercial activities, and forms of banking and usury became commonplace. According to Ornatowski, this loosening of traditional Vinaya restrictions was justified "as long as it was for the benefit of the Three Treasures":

> [T]he practice of monk labor in many Zen monasteries led to the famous saying ... "one day no work, one day no food." [The eighth-century Ch'an monk] Huai-hai used the term *p'u-ch'ing*, meaning collective participation, to refer to monk labor, with the idea that this implied "all monks in the sangha would work together on a basis of equality to achieve a common goal."[40]

These developments helped to dampen criticisms in China that the burgeoning Buddhist institutions were parasites on society, absorbing vast wealth in the form of pious lay donations, while contributing nothing to the economy.

In contemporary Buddhism, a virtual explosion of new occupations and corresponding attitudes toward labor and economic development have accompanied the rise of socially engaged Buddhism.[41] Among the earliest innovators in this field was Dr. A. T. Ariyaratna, founder of the Sri Lankan village development organization, Sarvodaya Shramadana. Founded in the 1950s as a program of rural work-camps for urban students, Sarvodaya grew by the 1980s to a network of economic-development activities in over twelve thousand villages across the island. Students worked hand-in-hand with local monks, townspeople, and government officials to build and repair infrastructure—roads, bridges, wells, septic systems—and to found training camps and schools that teach Buddhist economics and social transformation. With international funding and tens of thousands of volunteers, Sarvodaya incorporated Theravada Buddhist principles of collective liberation (*sarva-udāya*, "social uplift") with Gandhian principles of voluntary service (*shrama-dāna*, "work-gift").[42]

In 1982, the Brooklyn-born Zen master Bernard Tetsugen Glassman Roshi, known to his followers simply as "Bernie," opened the Greyston Bakery in New York City. After founding the Zen Community of New York on an estate donated by a wealthy businessman, Glassman sold the property and moved the community to an impoverished neighborhood in Southwest Yonkers, north of the city. Here he offered employment opportunities to local residents regardless of education and training, work history, or past social barriers, such as incarceration, homelessness, or drug use. The business took off when Ben & Jerry's contracted with Greyston for the brownies for their Chocolate Fudge Brownie ice cream. With the success of the bakery, Glassman rehabilitated decaying apartment buildings to offer affordable housing to his workers, and over the thirty years that followed, opened a childcare center, a medical clinic, a hospice to serve employees and neighbors suffering from HIV/AIDS, and a workforce development center to provide skills training to hard-to-employ individuals. In his book *Instructions to the Cook: A Zen Master's Lessons in Living a Life That Matters*, Glassman invites readers to cook "the supreme meal," that is, to transform the ingredients of their lives into forms of service that may be offered widely and lovingly to others. In terms of his business model, which was analyzed and praised in the *Wall Street Journal* and other national media, Bernie explained, "We don't hire people to bake brownies, we bake brownies to hire people."[43]

Taxation

At the birth of Prince Siddhartha, his father consulted wise men to predict the direction of the child's career. All agreed that the boy would be a great wheel-turner (*chakravartin*), but they disagreed on whether this ancient term meant a righteous king (*dhamma-rāja*) or a spiritual teacher (*sadhu*). As a young man troubled by the suffering of the commoners he met outside the palace, the prince abandoned his family and embarked on years of study and contemplation, finally awakening to the possibility of a state of being free from suffering. The newly Awakened One preached his first sermon, which came to be called the Turning of the Wheel of Law (*dhamma-chakka-pavattana*). In the years that followed, the community of "world renouncers," founded by the Buddha on the spiritual dharma of morality and mindfulness, developed a complex relationship to the "world conquerors," who moved the levers of government, guided by the secular dharma of public administration and politics. Modern scholars thus speak of the "Two Wheels of Dhamma" in appraising the relationship of the ancient Buddhist sangha to the emerging royal states of the time.[44]

As we have seen, the interaction of sangha and state has taken many forms, both complementary and adversarial in the course of Buddhism's evolution in South and East Asia. In the Theravada lands of South and Southeast Asia, the cordial relationship between the Buddha Gotama and his royal patrons, King Bimbisara of Magadha and King Pasenadi of Kosala, resonated through the centuries in countries like Sri Lanka, Burma, and Thailand, where the sangha operated free of taxation in exchange for its legitimation of the policies of the state. The lay supporters of the sangha—large landowners and bankers—were also the primary taxpayers and underwriters of state power.[45] And the sangha and state played complementary roles in creating a social safety net for less fortunate members of society. Kings like Aśoka and Udayi, the subject of Nagarjuna's "garland of royal council," are enjoined to protect "the blind, the sick, the lowly, the protectorless, the wretched and the crippled equally, to attain food and drink without interruption." Meanwhile, religious giving to the sangha has sometimes had what Harvey calls a "redistributive effect," as the monks redirect surplus donations to support those who seek refuge in the monasteries: the destitute, orphans, and lay students of the dharma.[46]

These patterns of peaceful "adjustment, accommodation, and amelioration" between sangha and state continued in China and East Asia until such times as the sangha became bloated by the competitive donations of a merit-seeking laity and the ballooning income from their own enterprises. The state lost tax revenues as increasing amounts of land came under monastic control, and the pool of draftees for military service and corvée labor for public-works projects shrank as tens of thousands of peasants left the land to serve as monks. Monastic wealth was conspicuously lavished on religious festivals, feasts, and the construction of temples, reliquaries, and monuments. The results were disastrous:

> Urged on by Confucians and Taoists who decried these trends as leading to the impoverishment of the empire, the state engaged in periodic persecutions of Buddhism by forced laicization of monks, seizure of monastery wealth (especially gold, silver, and copper) and placing limits on the number of monasteries and temples.[47]

Similar dynamics of collaboration and competition for loyalties and material resources may be documented in the medieval histories of Korea, Japan, and Taiwan.

In the modern period, the tax-exempt status of Buddhist institutions continues throughout Asia and wherever traditional temples and monasteries have been transplanted and legally registered in the West. At the same time, the popularity of lay sanghas and householder lifestyles in the West have supplanted the locus of authority and tradition held by the ordained sangha in Asia. Consequently, the role of Buddhists and their institutions vis-à-vis the state has changed, as unordained "Buddhist sympathizers" practice in rural retreat centers, urban storefronts, or private homes. The numbers are too small to threaten—or legitimate—the state, and the style of socially engaged Buddhism, which originated in Asia with mass movements for the end of the Vietnam War, the autonomy of Tibet, or the human rights of the Untouchables, is filtered through non-government organizations such as the Buddhist Peace Fellowship in Berkeley, California; the Zen Peacemakers of Montague, Massachusetts; or the International Network of Engaged Buddhists, headquartered in Thailand. In these times, taxation is a negligible matter compared to the idealistic and ambitious missions of these organizations—to oppose social violence and materialism and to relieve the sufferings of populations caught in institutional webs of hatred, greed, and delusion.

Notes

1. E. F. Schumacher, *Small Is Beautiful* (London, Great Britain: Blond & Briggs, 1973), 53–75.

2. Gregory K. Ornatowski, "Continuity and Change in the Economic Ethics of Buddhism: Evidence from the History of Buddhism in India, China and Japan," *Journal of Buddhist Ethics*, vol. 3 (1996), 200–202.

3. *Sigālovāda Sutta, Digha Nikāya III*, cited by Ornatowski, "Continuity and Change," 207.

4. Peter Harvey, *Introduction to Buddhist Ethics* (Cambridge, Great Britain: Cambridge University Press, 2000), 192–195.

5. John S. Strong, "Rich Man, Poor Man, Bhikkhu, King: Quinquennial Festival and the Nature of Dāna," in Russell F. Sizemore and Donald K. Swearer, eds., *Ethics, Wealth, and Salvation: A Study in Buddhist Social Ethics* (Columbia, South Carolina: University of South Carolina Press, 1990), 107–108.

6. For a discussion of these categories, see "Introduction: A New Buddhism" in Christopher S. Queen, *Engaged Buddhism in the West* (Boston, Massachusetts: Wisdom Publications, 2000), 12–17.

7. Balkrishna Govind Gokhale, "Early Buddhism and the Urban Revolution," *Journal of the International Association of Buddhist Studies*, vol. 5, no. 2 (1982), 7–23. Uma Chakravarti, *The Social Dimensions of Early Buddhism* (New Delhi, India: Munchiram Manoharlal Publishers, 1996).

8. Gokhale, "Early Buddhism," 19.

9. For analysis of the Buddhist myth of creation and the rise of social distinctions, including caste, kingship, and renunciation, see Stanley J. Tambiah's discussion of the *Aggañña Sutta* in *World Conqueror and World Renouncer: A Study of Buddhism and Polity in Thailand Against a Historical Background* (Cambridge, Great Britain: Cambridge University Press, 1976), 9–18.

10. Diana Y. Paul, *Women in Buddhism: Images of the Feminine in the Mahāyāna Tradition* (Berkeley, California: University of California Press, 1979), 289–292.

11. Arthur F. Wright, *Studies in Chinese Buddhism* (New Haven, Connecticut: Yale University Press, 1990), 69–72.

12. John R. McRae, "The Story of Early Ch'an," in Kenneth Kraft, ed., *Zen: Tradition and Transition* (New York, New York: Grove Press, 1988), 125–139.

13. Christopher S. Queen, "Dr. Ambedkar and the Hermeneutics of Buddhist Liberation," in Christopher S. Queen and Sallie B. King, eds., *Engaged Buddhism: Buddhist Liberation Movements in Asia* (Albany, New York: State University of New York Press, 1996), 45–72.

14. See Thomas Tweed's definition of religions as "confluences of organic-cultural flows that intensify joy and confront suffering by drawing on human and suprahuman forces to make homes and cross boundaries." *Crossing and Dwelling: A Theory of Religion* (Cambridge, Massachusetts: Harvard University Press, 2006), 54ff.

15. Steven Kemper, "Wealth and Reformation in Sinhalese Buddhist Monasticism," in Sizemore and Swearer, eds., *Ethics, Wealth, and Salvation*, 159.

16. Ornatowski, "Continuity and Change," 214–220.

17. Stuart Chandler, *Establishing a Pure Land on Earth: The Foguang Buddhist Perspective on Modernization and Globalization* (Honolulu, Hawaii: University of Hawaii Press, 2004), 94–95.

18. Cited by Chatsumarn Kabilsingh, "Early Buddhist Views on Nature," in *Dharmagaya: A Harvest of Essays in Buddhism and Ecology* (Berkeley, California: Parallax Press, 1990), 8–9.

19. Kabilsingh, "Early Buddhist Views on Nature," 11.

20. Aśoka, Rock Edict II and Pillar Edict VII, in *The Edicts of Asoka*, trans. by N. A. Nikam and Richard McKeon, eds. (Chicago, Illinois: University of Chicago Press, 1959), 64–65.

21. Duncan Ryūken Williams, "Animal Liberation, Death, and the State: Rites to Release Animals in Medieval Japan," in *Buddhism and Ecology: The Interconnection of Dharma and Deeds* (Cambridge, Massachusetts: Harvard University Press, 1997), 154.

22. Stephanie Kaza, "To Save All Beings: Buddhist Environmental Activism," in Christopher S. Queen, ed., *Engaged Buddhism in the West* (Boston, Massachusetts: Wisdom Publications, 2000), 159–183.

23. Gregory Schopen, "Monks and the Relic Cult in the Mahāparinibbāna-sutta," in *Bones, Stones, and Buddhist Monks: Collected Papers on the Archaeology, Epigraphy, and Texts of Monastic Buddhism in India* (Honolulu, Hawaii: University of Hawaii Press, 1997), 99ff. For an image of wealthy donors memorialized at the entrance of the Karli cave temple near Mumbai, see Hugo Munsterberg, *Art of India and Southeast Asia* (New York, New York: Harry N. Abrams, 1979), 53.

24. Ornatowski, "Continuity and Change," 216.

25. Ornatowski, "Continuity and Change," 218–220.

26. Stanley Jeyaraja Tambiah, *The Buddhist Saints of the Forest and the Cult of Amulets* (Cambridge, Great Britain: Cambridge University Press, 1984), 374–389.

27. Chakravarti, *Social Dimensions*, 55–57.

28. Chakravarti, *Social Dimensions*, 58–59.

29. Ornatowski, "Continuity and Change," 210.

30. Sizemore and Swearer, eds., *Ethics, Wealth, and Salvation*, 58.

31. Stuart Chandler, *Establishing a Pure Land on Earth: The Foguang Buddhist Perspective on Modernization and Globalization* (Honolulu, Hawaii: University of Hawaii Press, 2004), 95. For a comparison of the political economy of this Taiwanese Buddhist sect with that of two others, see Richard Madsen, *Democracy's Dharma: Religious Renaissance and Political Development in Taiwan* (Berkeley, California: University of California Press, 2007).

32. See Queen and King, eds., *Engaged Buddhism*, for chapters on each of these figures.

33. Allan Hunt Badiner, ed., *Mindfulness in the Marketplace: Compassionate Responses to Consumerism* (Berkeley, California: Parallax Press, 2002); Stephanie Kaza, ed., *Hooked!: Buddhist Writings on Greed, Desire, and the Urge to Consume* (Boston, Massachusetts: Shambhala Publications, 2005).

34. Max Weber, *The Religion of India: The Sociology of Hinduism and Buddhism* (New York, New York: The Free Press, 1958), 206; Max Weber, *The Protestant Ethic and the Spirit of Capitalism* (New York, New York: Charles Scribner's Sons, 1958).

35. Harvey, *Introduction to Buddhist Ethics*, 187–188.

36. Sulak Sivaraksa, *Seeds of Peace: A Buddhist Vision for Renewing Society* (Berkeley, California: Parallax Press, 1992), 73–75.

37. Sulak, *Seeds of Peace*, 76–79.

38. *Sigālovāda Sutta (Digha Nikāya 3.191)*, cited by Harvey, *Introduction to Buddhist Ethics*, 188.

39. Cited by Harvey, *Introduction to Buddhist Ethics*, 188–189.

40. Ornatowski, "Continuity and Change," 220.

41. See Martin Baumann, "Work as Dharma Practice: Right Livelihood Cooperatives of the FWBO," and related chapters in Queen, ed., *Engaged Buddhism in the West*; and Claude Whitmyer, *Mindfulness and Meaningful Work: Exploration in Right Livelihood* (Berkeley, California: Parallax Press, 1994).

42. George D. Bond, *Buddhism at Work: Community Development, Social Empowerment, and the Sarvodaya Movement* (Bloomfield, Connecticut: Kumarian Press, 2004); and Joanna Macy, *Dharma and Development: Religion as Resource in the Sarvodaya Self-Help Movement* (West Hartford, Connecticut: Kumarian Press, 1983).

43. Bernard Glassman and Rick Fields, *Instructions to the Cook: A Zen Master's Lessons in Living a Life That Matters* (New York, New York: Bell Tower, 1996).

44. Frank Reynolds, "The Two Wheels of Dhamma: A Study of Early Buddhism," in *The Two Wheels of Dhamma: Essays in the Theravada Tradition in India and Ceylon* (Chambersberg, Pennsylvania: AAR Studies in Religion, 1972), 6–30; and S. J. Tambiah, *World Conqueror and World Renouncer: A Study of Buddhism and Polity in Thailand Against a Historical Background* (Cambridge, Great Britain: Cambridge University Press, 1976).

45. Chakravarti, *Social Dimensions*, 70.

46. Harvey, *Introduction to Buddhist Ethics*, 194–199.

47. Ornatowski, "Continuity and Change," 217.

Overview

ECONOMIC INEQUALITY ACROSS TRADITIONS

STEPHEN R. MUNZER

In reading the chapters of this book, one should keep in mind the question "Inequality of what?" The contributors discuss the inequality of wealth, income, property, natural resources, and products. They also consider the relations between these forms of inequality on the one hand and employment and taxation on the other. The inquiry threatens to become jagged if different traditions do not all have positions on some of these matters. For that reason, it makes sense, after this introduction, to begin with the central forms of economic inequality—income, wealth, and property—and later take up satellite issues of natural resources, products, employment, and taxation.

It is evident that one can compare the views of various traditions on economic inequality along a number of dimensions. Here are at least some of these dimensions.

Principles and sociocultural institutions. Relatively abstract principles or positions, such as how to provide for the poor, at some point have to make contact with the societies in which they play an important role. Classical Confucianism, for example, arose in a hierarchical society. It might seem to have difficulty in putting hierarchy and equality together. But, in fact, there is no conflict, because the hierarchy that concerns Confucians is moral rather than economic. The scholar atop the moral hierarchy often would have less money than the wealthy merchant, who was at the bottom of the moral hierarchy. Modern Confucians, while not economic egalitarians, resist putting any group of wealthy persons permanently above other groups.

Canonical texts. It helps to separate canonical texts that lay down laws—pertaining, say, to charging interest on a loan—from those that do not. The Torah, the Talmud, and centuries of rabbinic commentary undergird Jewish law. The Quran and the sayings of the Prophet Muḥammad, along with an extensive tradition of juristic reasoning, serve as the basis of Islamic law. A key issue for very old religious texts that generate a system of laws is whether one can adapt these laws to contemporary circumstances without betraying the canonical texts. Other religions have canonical texts without creating laws. For instance, the Christian tradition considers the Bible a canonical text. But most strands within that tradition do not recognize a Christian body of "law" that is on a par with Jewish or Islamic law. The canon law of the Roman Catholic Church may be an exception. Once one turns to secular traditions, the contrast is even sharper. Unlike the Hebrew Bible or the Quran, John Locke's *Two Treatises of Government* (1690) and Karl Marx's *Das Kapital* (1867) are not "canonical" texts of liberalism and Marxism. The former is not a fount of laws, and the latter is not a source of normative laws, even if it contains some economic "laws" in the sense of tendencies in capitalist economies to operate in certain ways (e.g., the tendency toward growing concentration and centralization of capital). Nevertheless, these books are very important texts in the history of liberalism and Marxism.

Traditions, religious and non-religious. Religious traditions, which include Buddhism as well as those mentioned earlier, consist of both theistic and non-theistic religions. In origin, they are typically older than most non-religious traditions, such as liberalism and feminism. Consider the matter of income inequality. A Buddhist approach stresses not so much grossly disproportionate incomes as whether a person is earning income from an occupation that does not harm living creatures. Some liberals are apt to favor a minimum basic income or earned-income tax credits to offset widely disproportionate incomes. Feminists are likelier to focus on a government cash transfer for those who do unpaid work at home and on equal pay for the same work, whether done by women or men. Religious and non-religious traditions sometimes differ on the scope of their normative recommendations. Non-religious traditions, such as liberalism, generally offer universal prescriptions, even if they are sometimes adjusted for different societies and cultures. But Jewish law, for example, concentrates on economic justice among Jews and to a lesser extent between Jews and non-Jews. Unequal incomes in societies composed of non-Jews is not a topic on which Jewish law has much to say. A most interesting intermediate tradition is natural law theory. Natural law rests on reason and its application to human beings and the organization of society. Some Jews, some Christians, and some Muslims have worked out their religious views partly in terms of natural law. Which religious tradition extends a welcoming hand to natural law theory often shapes the details of what natural law is said to require, permit, or prohibit.

Cross-tradition dialogue. Think about a salient issue of economic inequality: whether a society should redistribute wealth so that the rich have somewhat less than they currently do and the less well-off, though not poor, have somewhat more than they currently do. Can traditions converse productively with each other on this issue? The answer depends on which combinations of traditions one has in mind. It seems unlikely that much useful dialogue would take place between Jewish law and the Buddhist tradition on this matter, because their foundations, concerns, and worldviews differ so sharply. To judge from Joseph Isaac Lifshitz's chapter, it would appear that Jewish law shows concern for the poor not out of justice but rather as an act of individual mercy and communal obligation. Jewish law allows for progressive taxation but not taxation to redistribute wealth (as distinct from income). The Buddhist tradition is well aware of wide differences in wealth. Yet it concentrates on avoiding the spiritual ills caused by capitalism and an appetite for material goods, not on shifting wealth around. By contrast, fruitful dialogue seems likely in the case of different visions of natural law: Jewish, Christian, Islamic, and secular. Still, one need not have closely shared assumptions to make intellectual exchange fruitful. Spirited exchanges between some feminists and some liberals have benefited both groups. At least in the last half-century, contestation between some Marxists and some liberal analytical philosophers who detect a theory of economic justice in Marx's corpus has been interesting. Some Marxists hold that Marx has no theory of justice at all. Some liberal analytic philosophers maintain that, despite Marx's dismissive observations about justice and other "juridical" concepts, he does have some views on economic justice in capitalist societies. Analytic philosophers generally concede, though, that Marx thinks that in a post-capitalist society, concepts like justice would be largely obsolete.

East and West. There must be very few scholars who are intimately familiar with the approaches to economic inequality taken by all of the traditions represented in this book. For most of the rest of us, a sharp contrast between East and West catches the eye immediately. To those versed in at least some of the traditions in the West, the worldviews underlying Confucianism and Buddhism seem remarkably different. Of course, these worldviews exhibit concern for the poor and those who live from paycheck to paycheck. These worldviews also reach deeply into human ills associated with economic inequality. Confucianism seeks, among other things, social harmony and overcoming selfishness. Early Buddhism exhibits a range of attitudes toward material goods, though it does not see departures from economic equality as inherently unjust. Instead, the ultimate goal is to achieve emancipation from everything that holds one back from right action. As will become apparent, modern Buddhists have a more complicated attitude to monastic values, desire for wealth, and capitalism.

So much for a handful of dimensions in which one might expect to see contrasts between assorted traditions. It is now time, after defining terms, to plunge into the details of the traditions represented in this collection.

Wealth, Income, and Property

Here are some mildly stipulative definitions that jibe pretty well with ordinary language. *Wealth* is an accumulation of things that have a monetary value. The amount of wealth a particular person has is often measured by that person's assets minus her liabilities at a given time. A person's wealth can increase or decrease over time even if there are no new assets or liabilities, because of unrealized capital gains or losses. To illustrate, if someone owns a hundred shares of stock worth $1,000 at time t_1, and if the value per share increases by half at time t_2, then she will have $1,500 worth of stock at t_2. What goes up can go down. *Income* is a benefit—usually measured by money and derived from either labor or capital or both—that generally arrives in a recurring period of time, such as a month or a year. One might think of wealth as congealed, unspent income. *Property* is a tangible or intangible thing that has a monetary value and carries with it rights and duties. Tangible things include land, houses, automobiles, and cash. Intangible things include copyrights, patents, trademarks, stocks and bonds, and a wavelength on the electromagnetic spectrum. Usually a person who owns property has rights to exclude others, to use it, and to give it away or sell it as well as duties not to use it to harm others and sometimes, especially in the case of land, to pay taxes on it. There is also a literature on self-ownership and the possibility of property rights in body parts. Economists, lawyers, philosophers, and some contributors to this volume might prefer to define these terms somewhat differently, but the foregoing definitions should do for immediate purposes.

Confucianism might seem to be an ethic rather than a religion or a political theory, but it has aspects of all three. Stephen C. Angle shows that texts and ideas from the classical period (fifth century BCE to second century CE) have implications for economic inequality. Key Confucian ideas include *yi* (appropriateness), care for everyone, overcoming selfishness, and prizing relations across all persons in society. Harmony and moral and material well-being serve as foundations for society. Donald Munro understands Confucian "natural equality" as an endorsement of both equality and hierarchy. Yet it is not clear how modifying the noun "equality" by the adjective "natural" leads to a compelling account, for the tension between equality and hierarchy might make for unsteady foundations. Perhaps one can dissolve the tension by building on the work of Joseph Chan. He suggests that it is ideas "of perfectionism, rather than any version of equality, that drives the Confucian account of economic justice." Chan offers three principles concerning what one might call economic justice: sufficiency for all; giving priority to those who are badly off; and contribution and merit.

There is some disagreement within the Confucian tradition. For instance, Sor-hoon Tan, who has a "relational" interpretation of Confucianism, argues that Confucian texts are not especially concerned with whether some persons have more or less than others, or merit or deserve equal shares of economic goods. "Instead, the concern is overwhelmingly about the effect of actions on specific interpersonal relationships, actual or potential." Tan makes a special point about *yi*, or appropriateness, in regard to property: material goods ought not to be assigned to some persons and withheld from others. Rather, the various forms of property are "*facilitators of personal cultivation* effecting appropriate interpersonal relationships constituting harmonious communities." The relational and sometimes abstract vision exemplified by Tan has, unsurprisingly, been handled roughly by the upheaval in China over much of the twentieth century. Some Confucians argue for various forms of socialism while others make a case for private property. If one had to distill a common position, it might lie in "a softer socialism or a welfare-state capitalism."

Between and sometimes within religious traditions, there is no uniform answer to the question of how much inequality of wealth, income, or property is permissible. Buddhism, a non-theistic tradition dating back more than two millennia, has distinctive perspectives on economic justice. Though Buddhism began with Gotama Buddha and a group of mendicant monks, in time it favored a middle path between self-denial and self-indulgence. Four attitudes toward material prosperity, writes Christopher S. Queen in his chapter, are characteristic of Buddhism. First, wealth is good insofar as it satisfies material needs and opportunities for religious giving. Second, only without greed or harming others is it permissible to acquire wealth. Third, the wealthy gain merit and prestige by giving, especially to monastic communities. Fourth, the ultimate good in life, for both rich and poor, is to attain *nirvāṇa* (spiritual liberation).

So far as wealth is concerned, early Buddhism does not much emphasize distributive justice or economic equality. However, reincarnation and multiple lifetimes operate under a regime of *karma*. In the case of a person who is rich today, his or her wealth reflects right action in previous lives. It is just the opposite with the poor of today. Queen puts it this way: The law of *karma*, in the view of some scholars, "with its all-encompassing explanation of existing inequalities, tends to do away with Buddhist perplexity over the plight of the poor."[1]

And yet, many modern Buddhist reformers, in Asia and in the West, regard humanism and socialism as values better suited to the traditional collectivism of the *sangha* (religious order). Asian examples include the democratic socialism of Taixu in China, the dharmic socialism of Buddhadāsa Bhikkhu in Thailand, and the Engaged Buddhism of the Dalai Lama. These figures oppose the individualism and avarice of capitalism without descending into what they see as the depersonalization and violence of Marxism and Communism. In the West, Buddhist thinkers frequently criticize an unending thirst for wealth, which brings with it material suffering for the poor and spiritual despair for the rich. This spiritual sadness and material suffering have their roots, many of these thinkers believe, in an economics of everlasting growth.

Buddhist views on income tend to focus more on how one gains income than widely disparate incomes. The root of these views lies in the concept of *sammā-ājīva,* or right livelihood. A Buddhist should avoid lines of work that harm others and instead should take up occupations that free others and enrich their lives. The Thai Buddhist Sulak Sivaraksa interprets the traditional moral precept, "I vow to abstain from stealing," broadly. He believes everyone is responsible for constructing an economic system in which all occupations are inherently moral and compensation for work is equitable.

As for the main monotheistic religions, D. Stephen Long finds no single Christian perspective on the inequality of wealth, income, or property. Certainly that was true prior to the arrival of modern economies. Yet Protestant thinkers of the nineteenth and twentieth centuries, such as Ernst Troeltsch and Karl Barth, attended to Christian social teachings and theological ethics, respectively. And Pope Leo XIII's influential encyclical *Rerum novarum* (1891) launched a Catholic social ethic in which economic inequalities are open to serious question. If *Rerum novarum* is an updated scholastic natural-law approach to economic inequality, the liberation theologies of the 1960s and 1970s militate against inequality by emphasizing passages in the Gospels that show great solicitude for the poor. By the end of the twentieth century, figures such as Daniel Bell, Stanley Hauerwas, and Oliver O'Donovan stress what is variously called a "social ethic" or an "ecclesial ethic." Despite differences among these figures, they unite around a vision in which the Lord's Supper, viewed as a communion of humanity in God, sets a basic frame of economic justice. All the same, other contemporary Christian movements, such as the so-called prosperity gospel, allow for considerable inequality in wealth, income, and property holdings.

Judaism and Islam illustrate the roles of canonical texts in responding to economic inequality. Lifshitz uses passages in the Hebrew Bible and rabbinic writings to give a picture of Jewish responses to economic inequality. Judaism, he says, requires judging all persons equally. Charitable giving to the poor is not an act of justice but an act of personal mercy and communal obligation. Interestingly, the situation of the always poor differs from that of the newly poor; a wealthy man who loses his wealth is entitled—or so a passage in the Babylonian Talmud has it—to receive from the community "a horse to ride on and a slave to lead his way." The line just quoted illustrates the difficulty Lifshitz faces in moving from Jewish principles for a rural economy to Jewish principles for a modern economy, while avoiding anachronism. He believes that Jewish law presupposes a situation in which small-scale communities take care of their own members. He appeals to Michael Walzer's "spheres of justice," in which "poverty is judged differently in every social sphere," but is aware that going down such a path could lead to inequality. Walzer's views might not be well suited to Lifshitz's needs. Walzer's theory of complex equality and spheres of justice, which is broadly communitarian, tries to ensure appropriate equality within each sphere and to prevent one sphere from unduly affecting another.[2] Although his theory has roots in Jewish thought, it is not an exposition of Jewish law on economic inequality.

Mohammad H. Fadel deftly explores the development of Islam over the centuries to give increasing attention to substantive equality. A bit like Locke, Islam allows for a state of nature in which everyone has an equal right to what is on or in the earth, and later for a polity in which some persons accumulate more wealth and property than other persons. Unlike some forms of Christianity, classical Islamic law does not have a "just price" theory, but rather insists on a supposed equal capacity of all adult persons to contract in the marketplace. Although classical Islamic law recognizes market exchange as a just means for gaining wealth, it also articulates an ethic of generosity to counteract the acquisitiveness underlying the market. Even at this early point of development, however, Islamic law has an incipient substantive conception of equality that requires traders to bear their fair share of risks. By the twentieth century, Islamic thinkers such as Sayyid Qutb and Muhammad Bāqir al-Ṣadr strengthened the idea of substantive equality to preclude unjust agreements. Here one sees an effort to hold down economic inequality that can issue from market forces. Nonetheless, over the course of the twentieth century, we can espy countercurrents in predominantly Muslim countries. Egypt once favored an

Islamic socialism, Pakistan a market capitalism, and the Gulf Arab states an Islamic neo-liberalism.

The natural-law tradition draws on philosophical sources but also enriches, and has been enriched by, the Jewish, Christian, and Islamic traditions. From natural law, Joseph Boyle suggests, one can extract two fundamental principles of economic justice. First, all human beings have a rational nature on which bonds of social unity and cooperation rest. Second, all human beings have an equal membership in the human community. One, therefore, ought not arbitrarily privilege or disfavor some human beings over others. A central problem for natural-law theory is to move from these Olympian principles to practical realities in a modern economy. Saint Thomas Aquinas holds that although the goods of the earth must, in some sense, be available for the benefit of all, natural law nevertheless justifies private property rights to things, or at least some authority or discretion over who can use which things, for otherwise a society would be economically chaotic. The purpose of the conventions and laws governing property is the fair, efficient, and peaceful use of external things to serve human benefit generally, and each adult person should have at least a minimum level of property. But beyond that, little justification exists to narrow the gap between those who are best-off and those who are less well-off, even if the latter are not poor. Contemporary natural-law theorists, such as Germain Grisez and John Finnis, are perhaps more inclined to narrow the gap. Yet we still see in natural-law theory, when push comes to shove, a good deal of indeterminacy on the particulars of economic justice. Some research after the turn of the millennium might reduce this indeterminacy.[3]

At this stage, it makes sense to turn to traditions, such as liberalism and feminism, which are considerably less ancient and often unmoored from religious perspectives on economic inequality. William Galston separates liberalism into three rough categories: classical, social, and distributive. Each advocates liberty but sets different limits on the extent to which society and the state may interfere with individual choice. Classical liberalism, associated especially with Locke, insists on emancipation from unjustified authority. Social liberalism, championed by L. T. Hobhouse in the early twentieth century, stresses that social life is fundamental to the arrangements that promote human flourishing and to the dimensions of liberty that need securing. Distributive liberalism, characteristic of John Rawls, seeks to limit inequalities of opportunity, income, and wealth.

No form of liberalism demands equal wealth, income, or property. But nearly all forms of liberalism demand equal political and religious freedoms. As to economic goods, one can see F. A. Hayek and Robert Nozick as followers of Lockean classical liberalism. Hayek, for example, emphasizes equal needs for food, clothing, and health care. Nozick, who follows Locke more closely than does Hayek, argues that things justly obtained through original acquisition belong to the acquirer. The government may not, in Nozick's view, interfere with property gained by just initial acquisition. Redistribution of justly held property, wealth, or income by the state is not permitted, and any state effort to do so smacks of forced labor or even slavery. By contrast, Hobhouse was much more concerned with redistributing these material goods to promote each individual's personal flourishing.

Rawls's difference principle holds that social and economic inequalities are to be arranged so that they are "to the greatest benefit of the least advantaged."[4] Exactly how the difference principle is to be understood is open to interpretation. One view is that the difference principle, put generally, distributes lifetime expectations with respect to social and economic advantages. Another view is that it aims to enlarge the distributive share of primary goods going to the least well-off. Other views are possible. In any case, the life prospects of the least well-off link up, to some degree, with economic goods such as wealth, income, and property. Unlike natural-law theorists, who usually have positions on what is good for rational beings, Rawls endorses the choice of each individual as to his or her conception of what is good.

One might debate the differences between Rawls and Hobhouse, but the heart of the matter is that Hobhouse has a more value-laden understanding of what promotes the good of each individual in society. Hobhouse, in his emphasis on personal flourishing, has ties to Aristotelian views about what it takes for human beings to have flourishing lives in society. Rawls, writing mainly in the late twentieth century, is keenly interested in economics. Some of his intellectual heirs who are trained as professional economists try to make Rawls's contribution more determinate than is often the case with rival traditions.

Feminism has a markedly shorter history than other traditions represented in this collection, and perhaps has less thoroughly developed views on economic inequality. Christine Di Stefano points out that feminism reflects some liberal and Marxist influences but distinguishes itself by emphasizing the equality of women and girls to men and boys. This emphasis requires some redistribution of wealth, income, and property so that equality of these economic goods becomes a practical reality rather than a mere aspiration. Liberal democratic feminism tends, however, to give pride of place to equal rights and opportunities for women. As these become available to women, a greater amount of economic equality is likely to follow. Di Stefano draws attention to need-based claims, which ought to aim for proportional equality. In turn, proportional equality rests on an idea, she says, of "what is due to specific individuals and members of groups." Fundamental to her discussion are an ethic of care and a "capabilities" approach to securing a decent quality of life for women.[5] Somewhat like Martha Nussbaum, Di Stefano believes that property systems should not discriminate against women, for the right to hold property is a central human capability.

The term *Marxist* applies both to the thought of Karl Marx and the assorted positions, typically both theoretical and political, of those who see themselves as belonging to a tradition that stems from Marx. The concerns of Marx himself do not really respond to the questions that most traditions represented in this collection try to answer, because Marx seeks mainly to criticize morality and justice rather than to assess social problems from the standpoint of morality and justice. As Andrew Levine's chapter points out, "History, in Marx's view, is comprised of discrete 'modes of production' or economic structures; each structure possesses its own characteristic views on justice and equality." Levine looks at Marxism as an ideology within a broader socialist tradition and as a Rawlsian ideology that has dominated Marxist literature by analytic philosophers such as Allen Buchanan. Buchanan, unlike Levine, considers it possible to identify a distinctively Marxian justice-based critique of capitalism.[6]

Levine has a more abstemious view of Marx's thought, which is one version of analytic Marxism, but it is not a common view among analytic philosophers. Levine does not say whether he is talking about wealth, income, or property, or whether he would prefer to talk—as Marx does in his most important work—of capital. Levine does suggest that property, in the sense of rights to benefit from and control resources, is permissible in the case of personal items that ordinary citizens typically possess. Productive property must usually be collectively owned, with state ownership being one form of collective ownership. Any limited property rights that remain to individuals are revocable, non-inheritable, and hence insecure. A common Marxist position is that under prevailing political systems it is not generally possible to reduce inequality in property holdings or, for that matter, in wealth or income. There needs to be a socialist revolution in order to "expropriate the expropriators." If both Marx and Levine find it difficult to take on board concerns about reducing inequalities of these economic goods, that may be largely because the mature Marx was centrally concerned with capital and capitalism. For Marx, capital is not something that can be distributed or redistributed in the ways that income and wealth can be.

The traditions surveyed divide: some take the position that economic inequality is just a fact of human life in society, whereas others attempt to show how economic inequality can be reduced or its deleterious effects eliminated. Not all of them, however, mark out their views on what to do about it by distinguishing between wealth, income, and property. Certainly they do not all define them exactly, as the beginning of this chapter does. It is productive to think about differences between wealth, income, and property and the roles that these economic goods sometimes independently play in society and in efforts for reform. Let us take them in order.

Inequality of wealth has become a prominent theme on the Left in the United States. It was visible in the Occupy Wall Street movement and the presidential candidacy of Bernie Sanders. The currency of this theme does not automatically mean that there is new, insightful thinking about the ethics of wealth inequality. In fact, though, the 2013 publication of Thomas Piketty's book *Capital for the Twenty-First Century* contains not only new thinking of this sort but a large amount of data on inequality of wealth.[7]

In terms of traditions mentioned so far, Piketty's position most resembles a strand in liberalism—namely, the distributive liberalism of, for example, Rawls. Piketty cites Rawls's difference principle as "similar in intent" to his own investigation.[8] He also invokes the "capabilities" approach, which he considers "not very different in its basic logic" from his ethical principle that "social inequalities are acceptable only if they are in the interest of all and in particular of the most disadvantaged social groups."[9] Feminist ethical theory, as Di Stefano shows, can also develop and apply the capabilities approach. The moral foundations of Piketty's position are visible in those strands of utilitarianism that hold one can maximize utility—whether understood as preference-satisfaction, happiness, or in some other way—by setting limits on wealth inequality. Jeremy Bentham, John Stuart Mill, and Arthur Sidgwick belong, to a greater or lesser degree, to this strand. Some other utilitarians do not. Piketty's moral foundations are consonant with ethically and politically "Left" versions of Christianity and Islam, though it is not his intent to embrace faith-based ideologies. Insofar as Piketty addresses capitalism, his book obviously has something in common with Marx's *Das Kapital*. The point of these remarks is that even though Piketty is an economist by profession, the ethical underpinnings of his book result in positions that target wealth inequalities.

The heart of Piketty's analysis relates the rate of return on capital to economic growth. Returns to capital include interest, dividends, rents, and profits. Economic growth is national income. If returns to capital are equal to returns to economic growth, then capital and economic growth increase, or decrease, at the same rate. But if returns to capital are greater than economic growth, then the accumulation of wealth occurs more quickly from returns to capital rather than returns to labor. As a result, wealth increases for those who are in the highest 10 percent, and increases even more for the highest 1 percent, of the wealth distribution. The main cause of wealth inequality is the tendency of returns to capital to outstrip returns to labor, for in that case wealth inequality rises. Piketty sometimes treats this tendency as a sort of economic law or principle. Taken as a law or principle, it predicts that wealth inequality will continue to rise. At other times, he treats it as an empirical generalization from data on wealth inequality in France, Britain, and the United States during the period from 1800 to 2000. Here the inequality relationship functions as an explanation of past variations in wealth inequality over time. Piketty is particularly concerned about increases in wealth inequality that stem from intergenerational transfers of wealth—in short, from inheritance.

Make no mistake, Piketty has his critics. Some question whether inequality of wealth matters; this objection is not a common position among most of the traditions treated in this book, but some utilitarians and some

non-utilitarian moral philosophers do make this objection. Some thinkers believe that Piketty does better with explanations of past variations in
wealth inequality than with predicting the future. Some doubt the explan-
atory account and take issue with Piketty's analysis of the data. Some point
out that many persons with great wealth obtained it not from capital, but
from their labor as, say, investment bankers or hedge-fund managers. And
some take issue with Piketty's equating wealth with capital, which raises
issues about similarities and differences between Marx and Piketty regarding the analysis of the concept of capital. For instance, if capital is a factor
of production, then your rich uncle's Picasso counts as wealth, because it
has a monetary value, but it is not capital unless it is used to produce something. None of these important issues can be tackled here, but Piketty has
replied to many of the points raised by critics.

Piketty also discusses inequality of income. Some work on the inequality of income suggests that the inequality of these two economic goods—
wealth and income—need not march in step or be of equal significance in
all contexts. Matthew Drennan contends that the financial crisis and the
Great Recession of 2008–2009 cannot be fully understood without attending to the rising inequality of income in the period 1984–2005.[10] If one
thinks of wealth, rather crudely, as congealed unspent income, and thus
what is left over from a person's income after consumption, then income
may have a story of its own. Drennan contends that many professional
economists were in the grip of a theory—which he calls the Friedman-
Modigliani-Brumberg paradigm—that hindered them from grasping the
specific importance of income inequality.

So far as property is concerned, works by philosophers and some academic lawyers often seem to convey the opinion that property holdings
are more or less identical with wealth. This opinion is not unreasonable.
To the extent that it is true, there might not seem much that is distinctive
about property that needs saying. Academic property lawyers in the law
and economics movement usually focus on the efficiency of resource allocations and seek determinate solutions to problems that courts and legis-
latures confront, and simultaneously slight philosophical foundations and
issues about just distribution, work, and the state. Determinate solutions
are not helpful if they are simplistic or wrongheaded. Those who approach
property more broadly throw light on distributive economic justice, property and freedom, and the limits of property.[11] Recent work in the natural-

law tradition by Gary Chartier, trained as both a theologian and a lawyer, explores economic justice in relation to property, work, and distribution.[12]

Property looms large, though, in the thinking of many feminists. At one time, in most common-law countries, upon marriage women had few rights to property. And often property they held before marriage fell under the control of their husbands. Nowadays, that is no longer true in Western liberal democracies. Still, property is controversial among feminists. They endorse the idea that "women should have property rights on an equal basis" with men, but see it as troubling that "equal rights to property do not necessarily translate into egalitarian patterns of property ownership." Feminists are also concerned with property rights in women's bodies and who controls any such rights. This matter receives attention in the section on employment, which briefly considers prostitution.

This book covers many traditions. But it is not exhaustive. It does not consider stoicism or republicanism, or every strand within the traditions included here. Neither does it tackle indigeneity and race as factors in economic inequality. Among thinkers who write about race, some complain that liberalism and perhaps other traditions effectively ignore race. Some of these thinkers, such as Charles Mills, claim that contractarian forms of liberalism only *seem* to ignore race, and that they are, in fact, organized around conceptions of racial differences.[13] Other thinkers contend that disparities in wealth, income, and homeownership point to a widening economic gap between blacks and whites in the United States.[14]

Natural Resources and Products

Natural resources are material things supplied by nature. Examples include oil, gas, water, minerals, and air. Products are things generated by physical labor or intellectual effort. Tangible products include harvested crops, cut timber, compressed air, and synthetic chemical compounds. Intangible products include songs, poems, inventions, and mathematical proofs. Connections exist between some natural resources and some tangible products. Oil in the ground can be extracted and then fractionally distilled into various petroleum products, such as gasoline and diesel fuel, or made into plastics. Water in a river can be diverted to irrigate crops planted by a farmer in a neighboring field. Two diamonds can be qualitatively identical, even though one is formed in the ground by geological processes and hence is a natural resource, and the other is formed in the laboratory by putting pure carbon under immense pressure and thus is a product.

Some of the traditions discussed in this volume have no definite position on natural resources and products. Other traditions do. Natural-law theory, for example, regards natural resources as open, in principle, to being owned so long as the person or other entity designated as the owner makes fair and effective use of them. This theory does not usually see air, or large bodies of water such as oceans, as fit for private ownership, and maybe not even fit for ownership by nation-states. Lakes of modest size, however, might be suited to community or government ownership. What lawyers call "fugitive resources"—oil, natural gas, underground aquifers—are often seen by the natural-law tradition as privatizable to some extent, but subject to regulation so that no one extracts too much of them. This tradition is more likely to see fundamentally stationary resources such as forests, land suitable for grazing, and fertile soil as open to private ownership. Natural law also supports safety and conservation in the extraction of natural resources. Products, in contrast, square nicely with private ownership because they are, in Boyle's words, "improved by human initiative for human purposes."

The various categories of liberalism make similar points about natural resources and products. In state-of-nature original acquisition, no single individual may, through labor or otherwise, gain too large a share of natural resources. In Locke's language, there must be "enough and as good" for those who come later. Often the state lays down rules concerning natural resources. The beneficial side of these rules is evident in national parks, good wildlife management, and protection of the environment—for both present and future generations. Sometimes, though, the state does not manage natural resources well. It might allow original acquirers to gain too large a share of water, oil, or gas. It might issue grazing permits to ranchers at unwarrantedly low prices. Also, government policy for patenting biological resources is sometimes debatable. The *Myriad Genetics* case, for instance, prevented a company from patenting the *genomic* DNA of genes that increase the risk of breast and ovarian tumors. Nonetheless, the United States Supreme Court allowed the company to patent the *complementary* DNA (cDNA) for the same genes, because cDNA, in which noncoding DNA is spliced out, does not occur in nature.[15] It is easy to convert genomic DNA to cDNA, and owing to this ease it might be unwise public policy to allow patents on genes in cDNA form.

Products that issue from labor have a visible role in Locke's classical liberalism. By mixing one's labor with natural resources, the story goes, one gains a share—sometimes a large share—of the product, or of the value of the product. If a cobbler takes an animal hide and makes twenty pairs of shoes out of it, the shoes are likely to be worth much more than the hide. Some, however, take issue with Locke on products. Often the most valuable labor is not sweat-of-the-brow work. Coming up with a new invention might take the inventor only thirty minutes; patent law rewards inspiration rather than perspiration. Distributive and social liberalism do not take Lockean natural rights as a starting point. These last two forms of liberalism typically start from the premise that, in modern economies, there is joint production of most goods.

One might think that the first step in a Marxist perspective would say that natural resources are owned and controlled by the state. But this step heads down an unhelpful path, for under Marxism the state will wither away, and it is not clear what "collective ownership" would mean once the state ceases to exist. So at least Marxists who hew to Marx's own views would have comparatively little to say about natural resources or the environment. Current Marxist literature on the environment is "more or less explicitly anti-capitalist," but that is not a specifically Marxist position.

Christian responses to natural resources and products are not, taken as a whole, seamless or even particularly coherent. All of nature, from a Christian point of view, is divinely created, but only animate objects like trees, fish, animals, and human beings are creatures. If early thinkers read Genesis 1:28 to mean that God gave Adam and Eve dominion over all living things, then after the fall, God had to renew human sovereignty over all animals in Genesis 9:2–3. Long suggests that owning natural resources is a post-lapsarian practical reality, but he stresses that Christianity has long supported the commons. The plight of the environment and the relation of human beings to other creatures, according to the historian Keith Thomas, go back at least five hundred years, even if these concerns have accelerated in the last three decades.[16] Pope Francis underscores concern for the environment and the threat of climate change.[17]

Islam takes a position similar to that of Locke with respect to nature by identifying the origin of property in original acts of appropriation in the state of nature. Islamic law, for example, recognizes the right of each person to extract from the commons, through her own labor, what she reasonably requires for her own needs, provided that by doing so she does not undermine the rights of others to do the same. However, Islamic law takes a differentiated approach to the ownership of natural resources, depending on the nature of the resource, its location, and the amount of labor required to extract it. A resource such as water located on privately owned land, which is extracted by the owner's digging a well, vests in him a private right to the water so found. In contrast, digging a well on unowned property outside of settled regions gives only a right of first-use. Islamic law does not generally permit the private ownership of minerals, whether visible or underground, if they are located on state property. Yet it authorizes the state to grant concessions to private individuals to exploit such mineral resources for limited periods of time.

One of the most ancient traditions—Buddhism—says a great deal that resonates with contemporary preoccupation with the environment. Early Buddhism favored harmony in the relation between human beings and nature. Memorably, the Buddha experienced enlightenment under the *bodhi* ("awakening") tree. As Queen points out, the Vinaya monastic code asks monks not to cut trees and not to contaminate water with human waste. Over a long history, various strands in Buddhism practice the periodic liberation of animals to guide humans in developing compassion for all creatures. Moderation in the use of natural resources is a common theme in Buddhist sources. In the twentieth and twenty-first centuries, "green Buddhism," "eco-Buddhism," and related movements not only reiterate Buddhist teachings about humility, mindfulness, and compassion in relation to all living things. They also encourage social action to oppose the testing of nuclear weapons and to fight environmental destruction.

Perhaps unexpectedly, Buddhism has a lot to say about products. Relics, monuments, amulets, robes, rings, statuettes, and milled grain are tangible products often sold by monks and merchants. There are also quite a few intangible products, which can be thought of as cultural or intellectual property: teachings and monastic ordination certificates are examples. And then, as if between tangible and intangible products, there is a wide range of services: blessings, money lending, mutual financing associations, and quite a few financial products (e.g., monastic certificates for use as tax exemptions). It might strike some readers as remarkable that so much commercialization coexists with the lofty concerns of many Buddhists.

Di Stefano suggests that the distribution of natural resources, if it is to be just, must be alive to context-specific environments, needs, and practices. In the global North, women do not depend on forests for subsistence. In rural South Asia, women do. Eco-feminists are interested in promoting a different attitude toward nature: that it deserves respect, and is not merely an exploitable resource. Like eco-Buddhists, eco-feminists seek concern and non-domination in regard to nature. As to products, Di Stefano thinks that women and men, girls and boys, should have equal access to needed tools, food, household goods, and books and newspapers.

Employment and Taxation

Even in undeveloped economies, relatively few people are individual proprietors. Many people work for someone else, which is to say that they have jobs. As employees, they receive money from others for the work they do. In a modern economy, the employer is often a partnership, a company of some kind, a corporation, a school board, or a unit of government, such as a city, county, province, or nation. This list should awaken the thought that one way of taxing people is to tax them on their incomes. It hardly follows that one should leave unexplored other modes of taxation.

Marx's *Economic and Philosophic Manuscripts of 1844* offers a penetrating analysis of work, alienation, capitalism, and private property. This somewhat dense work investigates the "alienation" that arises from work carried out under certain conditions, and above all under capitalism. Alienation is the separation of persons from the natural world, from the products of their labor, from themselves, and from other human beings. Worker and capitalist alike suffer from alienation, though in different ways. Workers suffer more under capitalism, for they receive only subsistence wages, while capitalists take away the "surplus value" generated by the workers, and thereby exploit workers.

By the time of *Das Kapital*, Marx is more interested in the dialectic of capitalism than in the details of alienation and exploitation. He can, of course, still muster biting passages:

> [Original acquisition] plays in Political Economy about the same part as original sin in theology. . . . [There] were two sorts of people; one, the diligent, intelligent, and, above all, frugal élite; the other, lazy rascals, spending their substance, and more, in riotous living.

. . . Thus it came to pass that the former sort accumulated wealth, and the latter sort had at last nothing to sell except their own skins. And from this original sin dates the poverty of the great majority that, despite all its labour, has up to now nothing to sell but itself, and the wealth of the few that increases constantly although they have long since ceased to work.[18]

Das Kapital appeals especially to analytic Marxists and scientific socialists. But even when a communist society emerges, labor in it is sometimes as dismal as it was in many places across Europe in the nineteenth century. Marx's masterpiece is nevertheless flush with insights into the workings of capitalism. He is, for example, among the first to have a prescient analysis of joint stock companies and cooperatives.[19] He identifies what today we call the separation of ownership and control in the modern corporation, in which shareholders ordinarily have no managerial role. As one might expect, Marxists today consider work—at least interesting work—to be a good thing. They are also likely to think that workers should have higher wages and shorter hours, and that executive compensation in the United States is grossly out of proportion to the compensation received by workers. All of these are reasonable positions, but they are not peculiar to Marxism.

Earlier there was a brief reference to the Buddhist concept of right livelihood, which refers to work that avoids harm, does good, and supports social harmony. Buddhists should not do jobs that involve raising or trading in livestock, meat, fish, alcohol, or street drugs. They should not make weapons, conduct experiments on animals, or work in advertising (insofar as it promotes greed). Above all, they should not traffic in human beings for slavery, indentured servitude, or prostitution. So what should they do? They should, as employees, work hard, repay trust, and support their employer's merited reputation. In return, employers should assign tasks to workers according to their strengths, pay them decent wages, and honor quitting-time rules. By the twentieth century, new forms of work sprang up, and contemporary Buddhism had to adjust. Perhaps the most visible adjustment was cooperative work across wider socioeconomic and geographic areas. In Sri Lanka, for example, people who might not otherwise be in much contact with each other—monks, students, townspeople, and government officials—would work together on infrastructure projects.

Islamic law permits employment contracts, albeit with some reluctance, owing to the formal contractual requirement that the consideration be physically present at the time of contracting. This condition is impossible to satisfy in the context of a sale of the worker's labor power, which comes into existence only during the course of performance of the contract. This technical objection to employment contracts overlaps with a substantive concern that binding employment contracts would result in the exploitation and subordination of laborers to owners of capital. Because legal doctrine makes it difficult, from a formal perspective at least, to enter into binding bilateral employment contracts, employers are not entitled to compel performance, and laborers work at their own option.

Di Stefano, in her chapter on feminism, pays careful attention to sexual divisions of labor. These divisions, which operate differently in varying cultural contexts, have the effect that some jobs—nanny, nurse, secretary, K-12 teacher, house and office cleaner, and more—are disproportionately done by women. Usually these jobs are the least highly compensated. Two correctives, I think, stand out for this predicament: first, make all jobs open to and encouraged for women and men; and second, give equal pay for equal and comparable work.

These correctives receive more than lip service in Western liberal democracies, especially in the Nordic countries. A higher percentage of women than ever before are now lawyers, physicians, soldiers, college professors, and business executives. Women still lag in fields such as dentistry, engineering, and computer science. Comparable-worth laws and policies, together with changes in the labor market, have benefited many women, especially educated women. These laws have been less successful for women who have a high school diploma or less, and for women who do a lot of uncompensated work in the home. A minimum or a living wage, mandated for each individual adult person capable of work, would reduce income inequality. It would also treat women as individuals in their own right and thereby reduce dependency.

It bears mention that women more frequently than men end up in a sometimes underground and often illegal economy of prostitution. The matter of prostitution is complicated and not susceptible to satisfactory treatment here. Some, perhaps, think of prostitution in terms of property: whether women do, or should be able to, "sell" their bodies. Though the English language has property-related words and phrases that describe providing sex for money, it is more accurate to think of prostitution as sex work: providing sexual services in return for money. Granted, men as well as women can be prostitutes, but usually demand for the former is much lower than for the latter. As a practical matter, providing sex for money raises more acute questions about the use and control of women's bodies than of men's bodies, especially in societies in which men control much more money than women and have more control over their bodies than women. Prostitution can be a dangerous and demeaning occupation. It typically lacks respectability even in countries that allow it by law, which can inflict psychological harm on women who engage in it. Forcing and enticing girls to become prostitutes should be crimes for all of the obvious reasons.

Lastly, there is taxation, one of the two great inevitabilities. Some traditions say little more about taxation than that it funds government programs and operations, and sometimes redistributes wealth, income, or property to those who have little. Feminists, in the eyes of Di Stefano, usually favor both progressive and redistributive taxation. If need be, there should be taxes that remunerate those who do unpaid labor in the home or for family members. According to Lifshitz, Jewish law defines taxes as a means for paying for government services, but only recently has begun to support progressive taxation (which need not be redistributive). Marxists typically see no way to raise funds in capitalist societies other than by taxation. In post-capitalist societies, Marxists usually prefer to fund the state in ways other than levying taxes. But according to Levine, Marxists have no objection, in principle, to taxation if needed to fund government projects in a post-capitalist society. What there might not be in a post-capitalist society are taxes for redistributive purposes, at least to the extent there are now, because equality or something close to it would be achievable by other distributive mechanisms. Beyond that, writes Levine, there are no distinctively Marxist positions on taxes.

Islam has a fuller approach to taxation. Classical Islamic law allows only those taxes approved by revelation. Otherwise, taxes would infringe on the right to private property. The *zakat* is a redistributive tax mandated by the Quran. Its receipt is a right of the poor, and hence its payment is a duty the state owes to the poor. It is, therefore, enforceable against those Muslims who are wealthy enough to pay it but fail to do so. Basically, the *zakat* functions as a tool to guarantee a minimum subsistence income for all Muslims. Muslims today, writes Fadel, largely accept the legitimacy of taxes to raise revenue for government services, but the historical rules pertaining to the *zakat* have not been updated. Non-Muslims living in predominantly Islamic societies are not, technically, eligible to receive the proceeds of the *zakat*. Nevertheless, they are beneficiaries of other redistributive institutions established by Muslim states.

The role of taxation is typically embedded in particular societies or cultures. One can perceive as much in Jewish and Islamic law. In Buddhism, embedded as it is in predominantly Asian cultures, there are interactions—sometimes complementary and sometimes conflictual—between the ordained *sanghas* (monastic religious orders) and the state. Often the *sangha* was untaxed; bankers and large landowners paid most of the taxes. For many years, the *sangha* and the state created a safety net for less fortunate members of society. King Aśoka Maurya, for example, provided food, drink, and sometimes shelter for the poor. This complementary arrangement worked tolerably well until the state began to lose needed tax revenue because many persons were becoming monks, and expensive festivals consumed *sangha* financial resources. By the modern period, relations between Buddhists and the state changed. The lay *sanghas* (i.e., lay religious orders) to some extent watered down the authority of the ordained *sanghas*, and the lay *sanghas* were insufficiently numerous to threaten the state. Nowadays, taxation plays a negligible role in the central Buddhist mission: to relieve suffering and to thwart materialism and violence.

In the Gospels, the most visible target is tax collectors rather than taxation. The Jewish populace sees tax collectors as suspect, sneaky, and extortionate. But in Matthew 22:21, Jesus, in responding to a trick question about the lawfulness of paying taxes to the emperor, says to give imperial things to the emperor and divine things to God. This cryptic answer leads, in later centuries, to ecclesiastical approval of paying taxes to legitimate political authorities. In light of *Rerum novarum*, the Roman Catholic Church supports some redistributive taxation. Yet there remains tension, in the case of some Christian denominations, between ecclesiastical and secular authorities on some issues, in particular whether it is appropriate to use taxes to pay for wars and abortions. Relatedly, natural-law theory endorses taxes to pay for government operations and services. According to Boyle, it also endorses redistributive taxation under the doctrine of subsidiarity, at least among contemporary Catholic natural-law theorists.

It is liberalism that has the most distinctive views on taxation. These views differ sharply, depending on whether one is looking at classical, social, or distributive liberalism. Classical liberalism is divided within itself. Nozick contends that income taxes amount to forced labor. This contention commits him to supporting even a night-watchman state by charitable donations. Hayek, in a blow for common sense, holds that taxes are a legitimate way to finance limited state activities. He strongly opposes anything other than a flat tax. Social liberalism, as discussed by such figures as Hobhouse, maintains that the varieties and levels of taxation turn on what a particular society needs. These needs include a productive economy and social requirements—the latter, in Hobhouse's case, rest on what best promotes human flourishing. Hobhouse's position, though earnest, is indeterminate on the best tax system for achieving the goal of human flourishing.

Galston believes that distributive liberals such as Rawls occupy a middle position. For Rawls, taxes should raise revenue for public goods and redistribute individual economic goods in accordance with the difference principle. As one might expect, Rawls has no problem with redistributive taxes on gifts and bequests. Unexpectedly, he says that a flat tax on consumption rather than any sort of income tax might be best in well-ordered societies. In societies that are not well-ordered, progressive taxation might be a superior alternative. He says, cautiously, that the details regarding taxation lie outside the theory of justice.

Liam Murphy and Thomas Nagel, who count as distributive liberals and are sympathetic to Rawls, parachute themselves into what is for them a new area in a fine study of justice and tax policy.[20] Though Rawls is keenly interested in the economics of taxation, he is wary of overcommitting himself on what justice requires. Murphy and Nagel are not wary and they have done their homework. They look at old chestnuts such as vertical equity, ability to pay, the functions of taxation, and the tax base. They bestow particular attention on progressivity, inheritance, and discriminatory taxation (e.g., the so-called marriage penalty). At a practical level,[21] they believe that while a capitalist market economy does well in many ways (e.g., creating employment and generating wealth), it is essential to limit the damage done to those who fare poorly in market competition. They survey various ways to redistribute wealth and income: minimum basic income, cash transfers, and earned-income tax credits. And they approve of inheritance taxes and progressivity.

While Murphy and Nagel bring philosophical skills and good sense to the matter of taxation, they do not hold themselves out as economists. There is, however, a vast literature on the economics of optimal taxation. This literature rests in part on various ethical perspectives and busies itself mainly with the taxation of income rather than wealth. Deep disagreements exist on the optimal taxation of income. Limits on space permit mention of only two divergent articles. Mankiw, Weinzerl, and Yagan suggest that a flat tax could be close to optimal, and that ordinarily it is not a good idea to tax income from capital assets.[22] Diamond and Saez fundamentally disagree, on the basis of data and economic theory, with another suggestion.[23] They support high and rising marginal rates on earnings, subsidizing the earnings of low-income families, and taxing *income* from capital, including income from realized capital gains. The two articles agree that the optimal extent of redistribution rises with wage inequality, and that optimal marginal tax rate schedules depend on the distribution of income.

At this point, one can usefully revisit Piketty's work. Many U.S. economists spend little time on the taxation of *capital* itself, either because they oppose it or because they consider it politically unrealistic. Piketty says that taxes on capital can take two forms: taxes on identifiable capital assets and taxes on inheritance. Land is the prime example of an identifiable capital asset. Unlike cash, jewelry, and stock in certificate form, land cannot be hidden in a safe-deposit box in a bank in another country. Whether capital assets insusceptible to being squirreled away should be taxed requires careful analysis. Deferring for the moment defining exactly what counts as an "inheritance," one might think that taxing large inheritances would be a better target. It is usually easy for the government to learn of the death of a wealthy person and to identify his or her heirs, and it is not clear why heirs morally deserve to receive a large inheritance tax-free. Piketty favors an international banking system that is quite transparent, along the lines of the U.S. Foreign Account Tax Compliance Act of 2010. He hesitates on tax rates: from 1 percent on inherited capital between one and five million euros, and of 2 percent on inherited capital above five million euros, to 10 percent on assets above 1 billion euros.[24]

Two final points: first, some moral and political theorists support taxes on wealth not because they are huge sources of revenue but because they tend to break down large concentrations of wealth. If one's aim is to raise revenue or dismantle large concentrations of wealth, it is doubtful that Piketty's tax rates are high enough to achieve either aim.[25] Second, lawyers are frequently more specific than political theorists on which wealth should be taxed: the wealth of the decedent (an "estate" tax) or the wealth received by a particular heir (an "inheritance" tax strictly understood).

Concluding Thoughts

Looking back over the essays that inform this chapter, one can see that there are areas of moral agreement and disagreement, as well as some lacunae. Almost every tradition agrees that poverty should be eliminated or at least reduced or allayed. Perhaps one cannot eliminate poverty forever, if only because poverty, once wiped out, could arise again through calamities like famine or war or through misguided choices by individuals. If that is correct, then it makes sense to isolate two different things marked out by the word "poverty." The first is the *circumstance* of not having enough material goods or the money to buy them. This circumstance is largely objective, or at least objective within a given society. It is possible, with some effort, to reduce poverty in this sense. The second thing is the *felt experience* of being poor. This experience is, primarily and obviously, subjective. Examples of this felt experience include worry about losing one's job, anxiety about providing for the material needs of one's children, and fretting over the need to both pay the rent and buy enough food for the month. With some effort, it may be possible to allay poverty in this sense, but not wholly so, if only because some poverty-stricken individuals are less resilient than others.

Ethical disagreement is evident on the issue of whether the government should redistribute wealth. Some traditions seem unenthusiastic on this issue. Jewish economic justice, as expounded by Lifshitz, reveals little appetite for having the government shift wealth from one person to another or from one group to another, or to achieve a similar result through redistributive taxation. Nozick has no appetite at all for such interference. To him it would be a form of forced labor or even slavery to redistribute justly acquired property in this way. By contrast, feminism and distributive liberalism are much more sympathetic to redistributing wealth.

Some opportunities are not pursued in this collection. One opportunity is the chance to figure out what, if anything, is so attractive about economic equality. Plainly, it makes moral sense to eliminate or reduce the harmful effects of economic inequality. It is, though, far from plain that economic equality is an indefeasible obligation on everyone, or an intrinsic moral ideal. Another opportunity is that the perspectives of indigenous peoples and racial minorities are barely touched on in this book. One should not assume that the interests of these groups are satisfactorily, albeit implicitly, covered by some or all of the traditions represented in this collection.[26]

Notes

1. Christopher S. Queen, citing Russell F. Sizemore and Donald K. Swearer, "Introduction" to part II of Russell F. Sizemore and Donald K. Swearer, eds., *Ethics, Wealth, and Salvation: A Study in Buddhist Social Ethics* (Columbia, South Carolina: University of South Carolina Press, 1990), 58 (referring to an argument by David Little).

2. Michael Walzer, *Spheres of Justice: A Defense of Pluralism and Equality* (New York, New York: Basic Books, 1983).

3. See especially Gary Chartier, *Economic Justice and Natural Law* (Cambridge, Great Britain: Cambridge University Press, 2009).

4. John Rawls, *A Theory of Justice* (Cambridge, Massachusetts: Harvard University Press, 1971), 302.

5. On the latter, see Martha C. Nussbaum, *Creating Capabilities: The Human Development Approach* (Cambridge, Massachusetts: Harvard University Press, 2011).

6. Allen E. Buchanan, *Marx and Justice: The Radical Critique of Liberalism* (Totowa, New Jersey: Rowman & Littlefield, 1982).

7. Thomas Piketty, *Capital for the Twenty-First Century*, trans. by Arthur Goldhammer (Cambridge, Massachusetts: Belknap Press of Harvard University Press, 2014; French original, 2013). Those unwilling to tackle the nearly seven hundred pages of Piketty's book might read the exposition and mild critique by Branko Milanovic, "The Return of 'Patrimonial Capitalism': A Review of Thomas Piketty's *Capitalism in the Twenty-First Century*," *Journal of Economic Literature*, 52 (2014): 519–534.

8. Piketty, *Capital for the Twenty-First Century*, 480.

9. Piketty, *Capital for the Twenty-First Century*, 480. Piketty credits Amartya Sen for the capabilities approach, whereas Di Stefano credits Martha Nussbaum for it. In my view, Nussbaum and Sen can share the credit.

10. Matthew P. Drennan, *Income Inequality: Why It Matters and Why Most Economists Didn't Notice* (New Haven, Connecticut, and London, Great Britain: Yale University Press, 2015).

11. E.g., J. W. Harris, *Property and Justice* (Oxford, Great Britain: Clarendon

Press, 1996); Ross Zucker, *Democratic Distributive Justice* (New York, New York: Cambridge University Press, 2001).

12. Chartier, *Economic Justice and Natural Law*.

13. Charles W. Mills, *The Racial Contract* (Ithaca, New York: Cornell University Press, 1999); Charles W. Mills, "Racial Liberalism," *PMLA,* 123 (2008): 1380–1397.

14. Thomas Shapiro, Tatjana Meschede, and Sam Osoro, "The Roots of the Widening Racial Wealth Gap: Explaining the Black-White Economic Divide," Institute on Assets and Social Policy, Research and Policy Brief (Brandeis University, February 2013).

15. Association for Molecular Pathology v. Myriad Genetics, Inc., 569 U.S. 576 (2013).

16. Keith Thomas, *Man and the Natural World: A History of the Modern Sensibility* (New York, New York: Pantheon, 1983).

17. Pope Francis, *Laudato Si': On Care for Our Common Home* (Vatican City: Libreria Editrice Vaticana, 2015).

18. Karl Marx, *Capital,* Frederick Engels, ed., trans. by Samuel Moore and Edward Aveling (New York, New York: International Publishers, 1967), vol. 1, 713–714.

19. Marx, *Capital,* vol. 3, 435–441.

20. Liam Murphy and Thomas Nagel, *The Myth of Ownership: Taxes and Justice* (New York, New York: Oxford University Press, 2002).

21. Murphy and Nagel, *Myth of Ownership,* 181–188.

22. N. Gregory Mankiw, Matthew Charles Weinzerl, and Danny Ferris Yagan, "Optimal Taxation in Theory and Practice," *Journal of Economic Perspectives,* 23(4) (2009), 147–174.

23. Peter Diamond and Emmanual Saez, "The Case for a Progressive Tax: From Basic Research to Policy Recommendations," *Journal of Economic Perspectives,* 25(4) (2011), 165–190.

24. Piketty, *Capital in the Twenty-First Century,* 517.

25. Josiah Wedgwood, *The Economics of Inheritance* (Port Washington, New York, and London, Great Britain: Kennikat Press, 1971 [1929, 1939]), in some ways anticipated Piketty by nearly eighty-five years, and expressed his attack on untaxed and lightly taxed inheritances with moral urgency.

26. Jeremy Peretz contributed immeasurably to improving this chapter and I am most grateful for his help.

Selected Annotated Bibliography

Liberalism

Berlin, Isaiah. *Four Essays on Liberty.* London, Great Britain: Oxford University Press, 1969. His essay on "Two Concepts of Liberty" is the best-known modern defense of negative liberty as the core of liberal politics. Unlike many classical liberals, Berlin sees no incompatibility between non-interference and the welfare state.

Boaz, David. *Libertarianism: A Primer.* New York, New York: Free Press, 1997. A clear, comprehensive introduction to the strand of classical liberalism that minimizes government's legitimate role in the economic sphere as well as individual lives.

Fawcett, Edmund. *Liberalism: The Life of an Idea.* Princeton, New Jersey: Princeton University Press, 2014. An erudite, lively historical account of liberalism's development during the past two centuries, with an emphasis on the relationship between ideas and practical politics.

Goodin, Robert E. *Reasons for Welfare: The Political Theory of the Welfare State.* Princeton, New Jersey: Princeton University Press, 1988. A broadly liberal defense of the modern welfare state. Chapter 11, which addresses the tension between individual freedom and activist government, will be of particular interest for readers of this essay.

Miller, David. *Principles of Social Justice*. Cambridge, Massachusetts: Harvard University Press, 1999. This book weaves together political philosophy and empirical social science to generate a broadly liberal account of justice in the economic sphere. Unlike Rawls, Miller sees a role for conceptions of need, desert, and merit in this account.

Wolfe, Alan. *The Future of Liberalism*. New York, New York: Knopf, 2009. Chapters 1 and 9 offer a broad defense of contemporary liberalism against its major philosophical and political competitors.

Readers who want a deeper understanding of the philosophical foundations of social liberalism should consult *The Stanford Encyclopedia of Philosophy*, especially Colin Tyler, "Thomas Hill Green," http://plato.stanford.edu/entries/green/, and Gerald Gaus and Shane D. Courtland's "Liberalism," http://plato.stanford.edu/archives/spr2011/entries/liberalism/. The latter is an excellent, brief introduction to the philosophical foundations of liberalism and the debates within the liberal tradition.

Marxism

Anderson, Perry. *Considerations on Western Marxism*. New York, New York, and London, Great Britain: Verso, 1976.

Cohen, G. A. *Karl Marx's Theory of History: A Defense*. Princeton, New Jersey: Princeton University Press, 2000. Expanded edition. A seminal text in the emergence of "analytical Marxism."

Elster, Jan. *Making Sense of Marx*. Cambridge, Great Britain: Cambridge University Press, 1985. A comprehensive account of the state of play in the analytical Marxist movement in the mid-1980s.

Kolakowski, Leszek. *Main Currents of Marxism: The Founders—The Golden Age—The Breakdown*. New York, New York: W. W. Norton, 2008. A magisterial and not altogether sympathetic account of Marx and orthodox Marxism.

Lukes, F. Steven. *Marxism and Morality*. Oxford, Great Britain: Oxford University Press, 1987. An insightful and accessible account of Marx's views on ethics and moral theory.

The best way to acquire familiarity with the breadth and depth of Marx's thinking is, of course, by reading Marx himself. There are many serviceable anthologies of his writings, though some of the best are currently out of print. Still readily available is Robert Tucker (ed.), *The Marx Engels Reader.* Second edition. New York, New York: W. W. Norton, 1978.

Feminism

Ehrenreich, Barbara and Arlie Russell Hochschild, eds. *Global Woman: Nannies Maids, and Sex Workers in the New Economy.* New York, New York: Henry Holt and Company, 2002. This anthology offers illuminating accounts of the mass migration of women workers from Third World to First World countries, documenting the global transfer of feminized caring labor and its implications for the lives of workers and their societies.

Folbre, Nancy. *Who Pays for the Kids? Gender and the Structures of Constraint.* Oxford, Great Britain, and New York, New York: Routledge, 1994. Widely regarded as a classic in the field of feminist economics, this book offers a compelling explanation for social distributions of the "costs of caring" that situates individual choices within various "structures of constraint." The concept of "social reproduction" figures prominently in the theoretical section of this book (part I). Part II explores histories of social reproduction in Northwestern Europe, the United States, and Latin America and the Caribbean.

Held, Virginia. *The Ethics of Care: Personal, Political, and Global.* Oxford, Great Britain, and New York, New York: Oxford University Press, 2006. For over twenty years, this feminist philosopher has been crafting an account of the ethics of care as an alternative moral theory to theories of justice. This book offers a systematic account of the ethics of care and its implications for political and social issues, including the question of whether "the market" should be the ultimate arbiter of value.

Nussbaum, Martha C. *Creating Capabilities: The Human Development Approach.* Cambridge, Massachusetts, and London, Great Britain: Harvard University Press, 2011. Martha Nussbaum is best known for the capabilities approach to questions of social justice, much of which has been worked out in relation to the life circumstances of women in economically underdeveloped regions of the world. See also *Women and Human Development: The Capabilities Approach* (Cambridge, Great Britain: University of Cambridge, 2000). According to Nussbaum's version of this approach, the quality of life for humans (as well as non-human animals) should be assessed in relation to their capabilities (what they are able to be and do). In the context of international development policy, the capabilities approach is invoked and utilized as an alternative to the gross domestic product approach.

Seager, Joni. *The Penguin Atlas of Women in the World.* New York, New York: Penguin, 2009. This atlas, compiled by a feminist geographer, is an indispensable resource for those who would like to learn about the life circumstances of women throughout the world.

Natural Law

Finnis, John. *Natural Law and Natural Rights. Second edition.* Oxford, Great Britain: Oxford University Press, 2011. Classic study of natural-law theory, a rigorous philosophical analysis of natural-law claims and a robust defense of "the new natural law theory."

Finnis, John. *Aquinas: Moral, Political and Legal Theory.* Oxford, Great Britain: Oxford University Press, 1998. Exhaustive textual treatment of Aquinas's political theory, including key texts concerning Aquinas's treatment of economic issues.

MacLeod, Adam J. *Property and Practical Reason.* Cambridge, Great Britain: Cambridge University Press, 2015. Useful and up-to-date survey of natural-law theory that shows the connections between common law and property law.

Journal of Markets and Morality. Years 1998–2015. Volumes 1–18. Useful source of writing on natural law, classical liberalism, and traditional Christian sources.

Christianity

Bandow, Doug and David Schindler. *Wealth, Poverty and Human Destiny.* Wilmington, Delaware: Intercollegiate Studies Institute, 2003. A collection of essays divided between those Christian theologians and economists who find Christianity and capitalism allied and those who find them opposed. It examines basic elements of markets as well as Christian anthropology by juxtaposing authors from the two schools on similar themes.

Bell, Daniel. *Economy and Desire: Christianity and Capitalism in a Postmodern World*. Grand Rapids, Michigan: Baker Academic, 2012. Bell argues that every economy presupposes a theology because theology and economics share in common the production, distribution, and communication of desire. His work is theological, but he also draws on the philosophers Gilles Deleuze and Michel Foucault to diagnose the formation of capitalist desire. He then compares the formation of desire in capitalism to the formation of desire by the Christian church. He finds the formed desires to be at odds with each other.

Cavanaugh, William. *Being Consumed*. Grand Rapids, Michigan: Wm. B. Eerdmans Publishing Company, 2008. Rather than arguing for or against free markets, Cavanaugh asks the penetrating question: when are markets free? To answer the question, he attends to diverse accounts of human freedom. This work shows real insight into everyday economic practices, especially as they bear on our attachment and detachment to persons, places, and things, to the relation between the local and the global, and the difference between scarcity and abundance. Cavanaugh draws on a Roman Catholic doctrine of the Eucharist to evaluate economic exchanges.

Gutiérrez, Gustavo, *A Theology of Liberation: History, Politics, and Salvation*. Maryknoll, New York: Orbis Books, 1988. A classic introduction to Latin American Liberation theology, Gutiérrez's work launched a movement both in the academy and the church to reconsider Roman Catholic social teaching. Rather than emphasizing "development," he suggested "liberation" was the order of the day. The church must make a preferential option for the poor, and in so doing it will be inclined toward socialist forms of economics. He makes his case with both theological and sociological skill.

Novak, Michael. *The Spirit of Democratic Capitalism*. New York, New York: Simon & Schuster, 1982.

Novak, Michael. *The Catholic Ethic and the Spirit of Capitalism*. New York, New York: Free Press, 1993. Novak's Christian economics opposes Weber's thesis suggesting that Catholicism rather than Protestantism gave rise to the spirit of capitalism. For Novak, this is positive, because he is convinced that capitalism and Catholicism together work best to alleviate poverty. It is an apology for capitalism that gives insight into neo-conservative Catholic approaches.

Stackhouse, Max L., Dennis P. McCann, Shirley J. Roels, and Preston N. Williams, eds. *On Moral Business: Classical and Contemporary Resources for Ethics in Economic Life.* Grand Rapids, Michigan: Wm. B. Eerdmans Publishing Company, 1995. This large edited volume accomplishes exactly what the title suggests. It provides a breadth of resources, ancient and modern, investigating the relationship between Christianity and economics. It is a good basic introduction to the central issues.

Tanner, Catherine. *Economy of Grace.* Minneapolis, Minnesota: Fortress Press, 2005. *Economy of Grace* is a solid introduction to a Reformed theological economics. It has three sections. The first section develops a methodological analysis for bringing theology and economics into conversation. The second section develops two basic theological principles, which are to be applied to the economy: unconditional giving and mutual benefit. These two principles could set too high a bar for economics, so the third part, "Putting a Theological Economy to Work," avoids any hint of utopianism by taking the social study of economics seriously.

Judaism

Kahaner, Larry. *Values, Prosperity and the Talmud: Business Lessons from the Ancient Rabbis.* Hoboken, New Jersey: John Wiley & Sons, 2003.

Levine, Aaron. *Economics and Jewish Law.* New York, New York: Yeshiva University Press, 1987.

Levine, Aaron. *The Oxford Handbook of Judaism and Economics.* Oxford, Great Britain: Oxford University Press, 2010.

Levine, Aaron. *Economic Morality and Jewish Law.* Oxford, Great Britain: Oxford University Press, 2012.

Neusner, Jacob. *The Economics of the Mishnah.* Chicago, Illinois: University of Chicago Press, 1990.

Tamari, Meir. *The Challenge of Wealth: A Jewish Perspective on Earning and Spending Money,* Northvale, New Jersey: J. Aronson, 1995.

Tamari, Meir. *With All Your Possessions: Jewish Ethics and Economic Life.* Jerusalem, Israel: Koren Publishers, 2014.

Islam

Abu-Saud, Mahmoud. *Contemporary Zakat.* Cincinnati, Ohio: Zakat and Research Foundation, 1988. The author of this work was an Egyptian economist who attempted to lay out a unified theory of *zakat* in light of contemporary economic principles. Although not well-known, it is a good exemplar of modernist attempts to recast the pre-modern Islamic tradition to make it suitable to modern conditions.

Al-Qaraḍāwī, Yūsuf and Fiqh al-Zakāt. *A Comparative Study of Zakah, Regulations and Philosophy in Light of the Qur'an and Sunnah,* vols. 1 and 2. Trans. by Dr. Monzer Kahf. Jeddah, Saudi Arabia: Scientific Publishing Centre, King Abdulaziz University, n.d. Both volumes are available online. This is an influential work by a leading reformist jurist. In addition to giving an overview of the classical law of *zakat,* Qaraḍāwī in this book attempts to adopt synthetic positions in an attempt to rationalize and systematize the rules of *zakat.*

Al-Ṣadr, Muḥammad Bāqir. *The Islamic Economic Doctrine: A Comparative Study.* Trans. by Dr. Kadom Jawad Shubber. London, Great Britain: MECI Ltd., 2010. A translation of the seminal Arabic text *Iqtiṣādunā* by one of the leading Shī'ī clerics of Iraq. His career and this work were part of the fundamental transformation of Shī'ī Islam from a politically quietist faith into one that aspired to govern society. The Ba'thist regime of Iraq under Saddam Hussein executed Ṣadr in 1980.

El-Gamal, Mahmoud. *Islamic Finance: Law, Economics and Practice.* New York, New York: Cambridge University Press, 2008. This work provides a very readable introduction to classical Islamic commercial law and how it has been transformed in the last fifty years to promote the rise of an Islamic financial economy. Professor Gamal, as far as I know, coined the term *shari'a*—an arbitrage to describe the operations of the Islamic financial sector.

Shepard, William E. *Sayyid Quṭb and Islamic Activism: A Translation and Critical Analysis of Social Justice in Islam.* New York, New York: Brill Publishers, 1996. A translation and study of the influential Egyptian Islamist Sayyid Quṭb's *Social Justice in Islam.* Quṭb's economic ideas reflect an important strand of twentieth-century Sunnī Muslim thought on questions related to economics, capitalism, socialism, equality, and religion. He was executed by the Egyptian state in 1966.

Confucianism

Angle, Stephen C. *Contemporary Confucian Political Philosophy: Toward Progressive Confucianism.* Cambridge, Great Britain: Polity Press, 2012. An overview of contemporary Confucianism, together with an argument that Confucianism can and should play a progressive role in the modern world; chapter 7 focuses on problems of inequality and oppression.

Chan, Joseph. *Confucian Perfectionism: A Political Philosophy for Modern Times.* Princeton, New Jersey: Princeton University Press, 2014. A major statement of modern Confucian political philosophy; chapters 7 and 8 focus on social justice issues.

Kim, Sungmoon. *Confucian Democracy in East Asia: Theory and Practice.* Cambridge, Great Britain, and New York, New York: Cambridge University Press, 2014. Argues that a fully democratic interpretation of Confucianism makes sense in modern East Asia; chapter 6 focuses on economic issues and opposes unbridled inequality.

Li, Chenyang. *The Confucian Philosophy of Harmony.* New York, New York: Routledge, 2013. A general treatment of the central Confucian idea of harmony.

Munro, Donald. *The Concept of Man in Ancient China.* Stanford, California: Stanford University Press, 1969. An influential explanation of the way that early Confucianism seeks to combine "natural equality" with social and political meritocracy.

Buddhism

Chakravarti, Uma. *The Social Dimensions of Early Buddhism.* New Delhi, India: Munchiram Manoharlal Publishers, 1996. Based on a close reading of ancient Pali records, the author details the political, economic, social, and religious setting of the movement, with particular reference to the role of new wealth in Lower Ganges Valley societies. Buddhism is seen as a response to the breakdown of traditional society and the rise of urban professions and values.

Harvey, Peter. *Introduction to Buddhist Ethics.* Cambridge, Great Britain: Cambridge University Press, 2000. A comprehensive survey of ancient and modern teachings in their Asian and Western manifestations. The volume is organized thematically, with chapters on founding principles, attitudes toward the natural world, economics, war and peace, sexuality, and medical ethics. The author cites most of the relevant literature available at the time of publication.

Ornatowski, Gregory K. "Continuity and Change in the Economic Ethics of Buddhism: Evidence From the History of Buddhism in India, China and Japan." *Journal of Buddhist Ethics*, vol. 3, 1996. A detailed exposition of economic teachings and institutional expressions in South and East Asia. Particularly useful is the distinction between relatively stable principles of economic behavior and the changing cultural variables with which they interact over time.

Queen, Christopher S., ed. *Engaged Buddhism in the West.* Boston, Massachusetts: Wisdom Publications, 2000. Twenty studies of the rise of social service and activism as organizing principles in a globalizing, modern Buddhism. The economic and political implications of the shift from personal discipline, virtue, and altruism to collective responses to social suffering are evident throughout, as is the influence of the Western notions of liberty, equality, and community.

Sizemore, Russell F. and Donald K. Swearer, eds. *Ethics, Wealth, and Salvation: A Study in Buddhist Social Ethics.* Columbia, South Carolina: University of South Carolina Press, 1990. Twelve scholars of Buddhism and comparative religious ethics consider the roles of material and spiritual values in the Theravada Buddhist societies of South Asia. The authors bring empirical and theoretical considerations to bear in a broad consensus on the distinctiveness of this tradition.

Overview

Frankfurt, Harry G. *On Inequality.* Princeton, New Jersey and Oxford, Great Britain: Princeton University Press, 2015. This slim volume by a distinguished moral philosopher argues that economic equality is not in itself a moral ideal and does not have any intrinsic or inherent moral importance. He is, however, in favor of eliminating poverty and the harmful effects of economic inequality.

Munzer, Stephen R. *A Theory of Property.* New York, New York: Cambridge University Press, 1990. This work of moral, political, and legal philosophy offers a three-principle justification of property and limits on it. One principle supports not only the elimination of poverty but also narrowing the gap between those who are best off and those who, even if they are not poor, are rather less well off than the rich. The book also discusses taxes on estates and inheritances.

Pateman, Carole and Charles W. Mills. *Contract and Domination.* Cambridge, Great Britain: Polity Press, 2007. This collaborative work by a political theorist and a philosopher—the authors write separate chapters—challenges contemporary contract theories of justice and the state. They claim that such theories neglect gender justice and all but ignore racial justice.

Rawls, John. *A Theory of Justice.* Cambridge, Massachusetts: Harvard University Press, 1971; rev. ed. 1999.

Rawls, John. *Political Liberalism.* New York, New York: Columbia University Press, 1993; 2nd ed. 2005. Together these books are not merely the leading statement of distributive liberalism. They are probably the most influential works of political philosophy of the twentieth century.

Smith, Adam. *An Inquiry Into the Nature and Causes of the Wealth of Nations.* Edwin Cannan, ed. George J. Stigler, pref. Chicago, Illinois: Chicago University Press, 1976. This classic text argues that the best economic structure is a decentralized market system that creates more and more wealth. Smith's laissez-faire capitalism also generates economic inequality.

Waldron, Jeremy. *The Right to Private Property.* Oxford, Great Britain: Clarendon Press, 1988. This modern classic is skeptical of Locke, Nozick, and historical entitlement theories generally. The author moves gracefully from Marx and Proudhon to an insightful discussion of Hegel's theory that property is important for the development of individual freedom.

Contributors

STEPHEN C. ANGLE is Director of the Fries Center for Global Studies, a professor of philosophy, and Mansfield Freeman Professor of East Asian Studies at Wesleyan University. A specialist in Chinese philosophy, Confucianism, neo-Confucianism, and comparative philosophy, he is a past president of the International Society for the Comparative Study of Chinese and Western Philosophy. His books include *Neo-Confucianism: A Philosophical Introduction* (with Justin Tiwald); *Virtue Ethics and Confucianism* (with Michael Slote); *Contemporary Confucian Political Philosophy: Towards Progressive Confucianism; Sagehood: The Contemporary Significance of Neo-Confucian Philosophy;* and *Human Rights and Chinese Thought.* His blog on Chinese and comparative philosophy is warpweftandway.com.

JOSEPH BOYLE was Professor Emeritus of Philosophy at the University of Toronto, Retired Fellow and Principal Emeritus at Saint Michael's College, and a member of the university's Joint Centre for Bioethics. His research was in the area of moral philosophy, particularly in the Thomist moral tradition. He collaborated with Germain Grisez and John Finnis in developing and applying a distinctive version of natural law theory.

His recent work was focused on just war theory, end-of-life issues, and the double-effect rule. He was a visiting fellow in 2010–11 at the Madison Program of Princeton University.

CHRISTINE DI STEFANO is an associate professor of political science at the University of Washington, Seattle, and past president of the Western Political Science Association. She is the author of *Configurations of Masculinity: A Feminist Perspective on Modern Political Theory* and co-editor (with Nancy J. Hirschmann) of *Revisioning the Political: Feminist Reconstructions of Traditional Concepts in Western Political Theory*.

MOHAMMAD H. FADEL is the Canada Research Chair for the Law and Economics of Islamic Law and an associate professor at the University of Toronto Faculty of Law. He wrote his PhD dissertation on legal process in medieval Islamic law while at the University of Chicago. Professor Fadel was admitted to the Bar of New York in 2000 and practiced law with the firm of Sullivan & Cromwell LLP in New York City. He also served as a law clerk to the Hon. Paul V. Niemeyer of the United States Court of Appeals for the 4th Circuit and the Hon. Anthony A. Alaimo of the United States District Court for the Southern District of Georgia. He has published numerous articles on Islamic legal history, as well as on Islam and liberalism.

WILLIAM A. GALSTON is a senior fellow in the Brookings Institution's Governance Studies Program, and formerly deputy assistant to President Clinton for domestic policy. A past acting dean at the School of Public Policy, University of Maryland, College Park, and past director of the Institute for Philosophy and Public Policy, Galston is the author of nine books and more than a hundred articles on political theory, public policy, and American politics. His most recent books are *Liberal Pluralism*, *The Practice of Liberal Pluralism*, and *Anti-Pluralism: The Populist Threat to Liberal Democracy*. A winner of the American Political Science Association's Hubert H. Humphrey Award, he was elected a fellow of the American Academy of Arts and Sciences in 2004. Galston has appeared on all the principal television networks and is frequently interviewed on NPR. He writes a weekly column for the *Wall Street Journal*.

ANDREW LEVINE is a senior scholar, frequent contributor to such publications and media outlets as *Counterpunch* and *The Real News Network*. He is the author of *The American Ideology* and *Political Key Words*, as well as of many other books and articles on political philosophy. His most recent book is *In Bad Faith: What's Wrong with the Opium of the People*. He was a professor of philosophy at the University of Wisconsin, Madison, a research professor of philosophy at the University of Maryland, College Park, and a senior scholar at the Institute for Policy Studies, Washington, DC.

JOSEPH ISAAC LIFSHITZ is a senior lecturer at Shalem College, Jerusalem, and a fellow at the Goldstein-Goren Diaspora Research Center, Tel Aviv University. His publications include the books *R. Meir of Rothenburg and the Foundation of Jewish Political Thought*; *One God; Many Images: The Dialectic Thought of Hasidei Askenaz*; and *Judaism, Law and the Free Market*. He has also published seven articles on Jewish economic theory.

D. STEPHEN LONG is Cary M. Maguire University Professor of Ethics at Southern Methodist University. Previously, he worked at Marquette University, Garrett-Evangelical Theological Seminary, Saint Joseph's University, and Duke Divinity School. An ordained United Methodist minister, he served churches in Honduras and North Carolina. He works in the intersection between theology and ethics, and has published over fifty essays and fourteen books on theology and ethics, including *Divine Economy: Theology and the Market*; *The Goodness of God: Theology, Church and Social Order*; *Calculated Futures*; *Christian Ethics: Very Short Introduction*; and *Augustinian and Ecclesial Christian Ethics: On Loving Enemies*.

RICHARD MADSEN is a Distinguished Research Professor of Sociology and former provost of Eleanor Roosevelt College at the University of California, San Diego. He is a co-author (with Robert Bellah et al.) of *The Good Society* and *Habits of the Heart*, which received the *Los Angeles Times* Book Award and was jury-nominated for the Pulitzer Prize. He has authored and co-authored eight books on China, including *Morality and Power in a Chinese Village*, for which he received the C. Wright Mills Award; *China's Catholics: Tragedy and Hope in an Emerging Civil Society*; and *China and the American Dream*. He also co-edited (with Tracy B. Strong) *The Many and the One: Religious and Secular Perspectives on Ethical Pluralism in the Modern World*.

STEPHEN R. MUNZER is a Distinguished Research Professor of Law at the University of California, Los Angeles. He holds degrees in philosophy from Oxford University and in law from Yale. He practiced law briefly with Covington & Burling. His work ranges broadly to include moral, political, and legal philosophy; law and biotechnology; indigenous peoples; and the philosophy of religion. He is the author of *A Theory of Property*, and the editor of *New Essays in the Legal and Political Theory of Property*. He has published over sixty articles in a wide spectrum of academic journals. He is a recipient of the Berger Prize and the Baumgardt Fellowship from the American Philosophical Association. Since 2012, he has chaired the board of directors of the Ethikon Institute.

CHRISTOPHER S. QUEEN, a leading scholar on socially engaged Buddhism in Asia and the West, has authored and edited many works in the field, including *Engaged Buddhism: Buddhist Liberation Movements in Asia* (with S. B. King); *American Buddhism: Methods and Findings in Recent Scholarship* (with D. R. Williams); *Engaged Buddhism in the West;* and *Action Dharma: New Studies in Engaged Buddhism* (with C. S. Prebish and D. Keown). He has taught Buddhism and World Religions and served as dean of students for continuing education at Harvard University (1989–2018). He also served as a president of the Barre Center for Buddhist Studies, a convener and honorary chairman of the *Journal of Buddhist Ethics* online conference on Socially Engaged Buddhism, and a co-founder of the Dharma Chakra Mission and Academy in Bodhgaya, India.

WILLIAM M. SULLIVAN is a senior scholar at the New American Colleges and Universities. He is formerly a senior scholar at the Carnegie Foundation for the Advancement of Teaching. He is a co-author (with Robert N. Bellah et al.) of *The Good Society* and *Habits of the Heart,* which received the *Los Angeles Times* Book Award and was jury-nominated for the Pulitzer Prize. He is also a co-editor (with Will Kymlicka) of the Ethikon volume *The Globalization of Ethics.* His most recent book is *Liberal Learning as a Quest for Purpose.*

Index

Names starting with "al-" are alphabetized by the subsequent part of the name.

Idolatry, 143, 162

Ikeda, Daisaku, 250

Income: Buddhism on, 251–252, 262, 267; from capital gains, 29, 285; for care work, 83–84; Christianity on, 130, 142–144; Confucianism on, 219, 227–229; defined, 265; and discrimination, 111; family-based wage, 82, 83; feminism on, 78, 80–84, 263; guaranteed basic, 35, 57–58, 80–82; inequality of, 1–2, 70, 78, 227, 235, 262–263, 274; Islam on, 201–05; Judaism on, 170–171; liberalism on, 15, 29, 35–36, 262–263; Marxism on, 49–50, 57–60, 280; minimum wage, 36, 110–111, 159, 171–173; natural-law theory on, 107–09; racial differences in, 275; redistribution of, 13, 35–36, 61; regulation of, 170–171. *See also* Employment; Taxation; Wealth

Income gap, 70, 81, 82, 140, 171

Inheritances: Christian views on, 142; family endowments, 196–198; feminism on, 80; inter vivos gifts, 197; Islamic views on, 196–198; liberalism on, 29, 34–35; Marxism on, 48, 57; natural-law theory on, 106–07; taxation of, 29, 34–35, 80, 227, 284–286; women's rights to, 72, 197

Inheritance tax, 29, 34–35, 80, 227, 284–286

Intergenerational wealth. *See* Inheritances

International Council of Mining and Materials (ICMM), 137

International Network of Engaged Buddhists, 251, 257

Intersectionality, 64

Inter vivos gifts, 197

Irenaeus (bishop of Lyons), 141

Islam, 181–208; contract law in, 185–187, 199, 203–04; economic inequality as viewed in, 187, 268; economic justice in, 17, 183, 188; on employment, 203–05, 280–281; equality in, 184–189; on income, 201–05; and natural-law theory, 92; natural resources in, 192–194; on poverty, 187, 196; on products, 194–195; property in, 17, 182, 189–192, 205–07, 277–278; revealed sources of, 17, 182; on taxation, 205–07, 282–283; theoretical influences in, 181; on wealth, 17, 182, 187, 195–201. *See also* Quran

Islamic banking and finance, 188–189, 198–200

Islamic neo-liberalism, 188, 199, 269

Islamic socialism, 187–188, 190, 269

Jesus Christ: on almsgiving, 132, 141; crucifixion of, 147; disciples of, 144; kingdom of God proclaimed by, 122, 127, 147; on love, 123, 126, 141; on property,

itances, 29, 34–35, 80, 227, 284–286; Islam on, 205–07, 282–283; Judaism on, 173–175, 263, 282; of land, 206, 285; liberalism on, 13, 29, 34–35, 37, 283–284; Marxism on, 45, 49, 60–61, 282; natural-law theory on, 109, 111–115, 283; proportional, 37; super-tax, 29. *See also* Progressive taxation; Redistributive taxation

Technologies: agricultural, 75, 239; criticisms of, 3, 4; and Darwinian competition, 12; fossil fuel, 7–11, 224; and modes of production, 22; patenting of, 30–31, 276; progress as measured by, 6; social media, 252; traditional moral paradigms undermined by, 9

Teleiosis, 126

Tertullian, 143

Theft, 17, 133–134, 156, 162, 182, 252

A Theory of Justice (Rawls), 46

Theravada Buddhism, 239, 249, 254, 255

Thomas, Keith, 277

Thomas Aquinas: on basic human goods, 92–93; justice, definition of, 97; and natural-law theory, 16, 92; on property, 99–101, 103, 112, 165, 269; on self-evident principles of morality, 95; on stealing, 133–134

Torah: as basis of Jewish law, 262; on communal life, 167; on creation of model human society, 156–157; on property, 162–163; in reasoning about economic life, 153; on slavery, 172. *See also* Judaism

Tragedy of the commons, 136

Troeltsch, Ernst, 122, 123, 267

Trotskyists, 42

Two Treatises of Government (Locke), 262

Unconscionability doctrine, 185

Unions, 51, 111

Universal Basic Income. *See* Guaranteed basic income

Universal destination of goods, 133, 134, 137, 147, 148

Untouchables, 242, 256

Use values, 55

Usury prohibition, 130, 138

Utilitarianism, 23, 47, 123, 143, 273

Utopian socialism, 44, 46–48, 61

Vatican II (1962–1965), 121, 124, 143

Vessantara (king of Sivirattha), 237–238, 243

Voltaire, 10

Von Humboldt, Wilhelm, 23

Voting rights of women, 85

Wages. *See* Income

Wages for Housework campaign, 74

Waldron, Jeremy, 170

Walzer, Michael, 160, 268